For Jo

A good and
"faithful" Friend

Joan Sherwood

INFECTION OF THE INNOCENTS

MCGILL-QUEEN'S/ASSOCIATED MEDICAL SERVICES STUDIES
IN THE HISTORY OF MEDICINE, HEALTH AND SOCIETY

SERIES EDITORS: S.O. FREEDMAN AND J.T.H. CONNOR

Volumes in this series have financial support from Associated Medical Services, Inc. (AMS). Associated Medical Services Inc. was established in 1936 by Dr Jason Hannah as a pioneer prepaid not-for-profit health-care organization in Ontario. With the advent of medicare, AMS became a charitable organization supporting innovations in academic medicine and health services, specifically the history of medicine and health care, as well as innovations in health professional education and bioethics.

Infection of the Innocents

Wet Nurses, Infants, and Syphilis
in France, 1780–1900

JOAN SHERWOOD

McGill-Queen's University Press
Montreal & Kingston • London • Ithaca

© McGill-Queen's University Press 2010
ISBN 978-0-7735-3741-5

Legal deposit third quarter 2010
Bibliothèque nationale du Québec

Printed in Canada on acid-free paper that is 100% ancient forest free
(100% post-consumer recycled), processed chlorine free

This book has been published with the help of a grant from the
Canadian Federation for the Humanities and Social Sciences, through
the Aid to Scholarly Publications Programme, using funds provided
by the Social Sciences and Humanities Research Council of Canada.

McGill-Queen's University Press acknowledges the support of the Canada
Council for the Arts for our publishing program. We also acknowledge the
financial support of the Government of Canada through the Canada Book
Fund for our publishing activities.

Library and Archives Canada Cataloguing in Publication

Sherwood, Joan, 1929–
Infection of the innocents : wet nurses, infants, and syphilis in France,
1780–1900 / Joan Sherwood.

(McGill-Queen's/Associated Medical Services studies in the history
of medicine, health and society; 37)

Includes bibliographical references and index.
ISBN 978-0-7735-3741-5

1. Hospice de Vaugirard – History. 2. Syphilis, Congenital, hereditary,
and infantile – Treatment – Social aspects – France – History. 3. Syphilis –
Patients – Legal status, laws, etc. – France – History. 4. Wet nurses – Legal
status, laws, etc. – France – History. 5. Medical personnel – Malpractice
– France – History. I. Title. II. Series: McGill-Queen's/Associated Medical
Services studies in the history of medicine, health, and society; 37.

RC201.6.F8S54 2010   614.5'4720944   C2010-901944-X

This book was typeset by Interscript in 10.5/13 Sabon.

Contents

Illustrations

Preface

Vaugirard hospital had a short tenure from 1780–90 but it has had an impact on the medical history of France. It witnessed what was, for the time, an innovative belief that the precarious lives of new-borns, even those of abandoned and illegitimate origin, could be saved. The avowed aim of Vaugirard was to find a cure for congenital syphilis, by passing on mercury to syphilitic infants in a "mild" form in women's milk. The use of mercurialized milk as a source of medication had important implications for medico-legal practice.

Records concerning lawsuits brought by wet nurses against families and doctors are not to be found (with one notable exception) in the formal legal compilations of the period. This means that references to incidents that caused considerable disquiet among medical professionals of the time have left almost no trace in the historiography of the period. Therefore, I have relied primarily on articles in the journal *Annales de l'hygiène publique et de médecine légale*. There were also discussions (sometimes heated) in the Academy of Medicine of Paris and in medical treatises about contagion and congenital syphilis. They document how wet nurses in nineteenth-century France who had been infected by syphilitic infants took their claims to court and successfully challenged the medical power structure. This was no small accomplishment on the part of poor women given the political, social, and economic climate of the day.

This book has a long history. When in Spain, preparing my doctoral thesis, subsequently published as *Poverty in Eighteenth-Century Spain: The Women and Children of the Inclusa* (Toronto: University of Toronto Press, 1988), I ran across numerous references to the Vaugirard hospital in Paris. In particular, a five-volume manuscript by

Ignacio Ruiz de Luzuriaga contained an excerpt written by François
Doublet, the chief physician at Vaugirard, describing the hospital.
There was much interest in Vaugirard among contemporaries and
there have been many other references and articles but no history
exclusively devoted to the institution. I decided to take up the project. It involved looking at much more than the ten-year period of
Vaugirard's existence. No historian will find that surprising.

The Archives of the Assistance Publique-hôpitaux in Paris contain
the original documents of the hospital. These consist of the admissions of infected women who were brought in to nurse infants with
congenital syphilis: their symptoms, treatment, place of origin, the
names and numbers of the individual infants they cared for, when
and why they were discharged, including occasionally comments
about their character, temperament, and personality. Other records
dealt with the infants themselves: their birth dates, parentage, when
available, and the accounts of their stay in the hospital including
their symptoms and ultimate fate – whether they were cured and
discharged, or whether (more usually) they died. I am grateful for a
grant from the Social Sciences and Humanities Research Council of
Canada for research and publication, and for travel assistance from
the Hannah Institute for the History of Medicine, which also supported my research in France.

I would like to thank the archivists of the Assistance Publique-
hôpitaux and the staff of the Bibliothèque Nationale and the
Bibliothèque Interuniversitaire de Médecine in Paris. The Osler
Library of the History of Medicine at McGill University and the
Drake Collection of pediatric treatises at the Thomas Fisher Rare
Books Library, University of Toronto, were valuable for their ear-
ly medical treatises on congenital syphilis. I am grateful to Lily
Szczygiel of the Osler Library for her patience and help in accessing
their rich collection on pediatric medicine. The staff at the Bracken
Health Sciences Library at Queen's University have also been of as-
sistance. I am particularly indebted to Bonnie Brooks of the Stauffer
Library interlibrary loan system at Queen's University for retrieving
material from many sources. The Nahum-Gelber Library at McGill
University and the law library at Queen's University were also help-
ful, as was Dominique Lapierre, Conseillère à la documentation en
Droit at the library of the University of Laval. The University of
Pennsylvania Law School provided microfilm copies for select years
of the *Gazette des Tribunaux*.

The bibliographic essay for the period by Dora B. Weiner in *The Citizen-Patient in Revolutionary and Imperial Paris* (Baltimore and London: Johns Hopkins University Press, 1993) was invaluable. Alex Dracobly's doctoral thesis filled in much of the background on nineteenth-century medico-legal malpractice. I am deeply indebted to Michael Pacey of the Department of Geography at Queen's University who prepared the charts and tables in chapters 3 and 4.

Michael Carley, Departmental Chair and Professor of History at the University of Quebec at Montreal, read the manuscript. His editorial advice and generosity in sharing his time and expertise are much appreciated. Two anonymous readers have made a significant contribution to this work. Their detailed and comprehensive reports have been very helpful.

I want to thank Professor Don Akenson of the Department of History at McGill for his support as senior editor of McGill-Queen's University Press. I owe a huge debt of gratitude to Kyla Madden, editor at McGill-Queen's University Press, for her help and encouragement. With good humour and patience she has dealt with the many details on which I needed advice and contributed many useful suggestions concerning the presentation of the manuscript.

On a personal as well as professional level I want to thank Professor Jacalyn Duffin, Hannah Chair of the History of Medicine at Queen's University. Her encouragement, enthusiasm, and intellectual astuteness have been an inspiration. Jacalyn Duffin is a model of collegiality as well as scholarship. She commented in detail on one of the early chapters (which on her suggestion became two chapters). I am grateful for her suggestions on many aspects of this work. Her friendship has meant a great deal to me.

This book is dedicated to my three daughters, Michelle Sherwood, Barbara Sherwood Lollar, and Jacqueline Sherwood di Marchi. Their father, John, if he were still alive, would have been as proud of them as I am.

INFECTION OF THE INNOCENTS

Introduction

In August 1855, Sieur B. and his physician arrived at the Bureau des Nourrices on rue Pagevin where they examined four wet nurses for an infant born in July. They mentioned in passing that the child was suffering from excoriated gums and a slight fever, which they believed could be relieved with baths and herbal teas. The chosen wet nurse accompanied the parents to their country home.

In October the family physician informed the parents that the child was in fact suffering from congenital syphilis and prescribed a strong mercurial treatment to be given through the milk of the nurse. Mercury had long been considered the specific for treating syphilis and the practice continued well into the twentieth century, despite its harsh and painful side effects. The doctor's intention was that the nurse should transmit the mercury to the infant through her breast milk in a concentration that the child could tolerate. The nurse refused to cooperate, however, and left her situation. Soon after, she was replaced by a twenty-four-year-old married woman with three healthy children of her own. Neither the family nor the doctor informed the new nurse of the true nature of the infant's ailment. As part of her terms of employment, the nurse agreed to undergo what was termed a "depurative" treatment and was given strong doses of a mercurial formula called Van Swieten's liquid, as well as mercury in pill form. Yet the infant remained sickly and, within two months, mucous plaques and whitish outbreaks were found on the nurse's breast. Although she was assured by the family doctor that these were simple ulcers, he doubled her dose of mercury. Despite the higher dosage her health deteriorated. The worried physician called in a colleague, who diagnosed that the wet nurse had syphilis and insisted that she stop nursing.[1]

Syphilis was recognized as a sexually transmitted disease, with a large and complex set of symptoms. The disease in adults was only gradually understood by medical practitioners to have three distinct stages. The first was the highly contagious primary, or hard chancre (sore), stage, which would disappear after some days or weeks. It was usually followed by a secondary stage characterized by a multiplicity of outbreaks on the skin, the scalp, etc. The contagious nature of these so-called secondary symptoms remained the subject of debate among experts well into the nineteenth century. The disease could advance into a crippling third stage, in which sufferers would experience severe joint pain and ostosis and neurological symptoms in the form of tremors, palpitations, and convulsions. Complete debilitation, insanity, and death could ensue. Until the mid-nineteenth century, this third stage of the disease was diagnosed as a separate illness called "tabes."[2] Congenital syphilis raised a different set of issues in newborn infants. Its etiology was dramatic. It evolved rapidly, displaying a variety of symptoms that could be confused with other childhood illnesses such as thrush (a mouth infection that made it difficult or impossible to nurse) or common fevers and numerous skin outbreaks. The illness was obviously inherited, but questions remained as to how and by which parent it was transmitted to newborns.[3]

When, in the case described above, the infected wet nurse's husband demanded reparation from her employer, Sieur B. balked: "I paid her wages, I will only pay her medical bills and 300 sous on top of this." In response the nurse brought a suit before the Tribunal of the Seine in August 1856. The lawyer for the prosecution claimed that the incident was not the result of error but of deliberate deception on the part of the family and their doctor. "They had conspired to use the body of the nurse as an alembic to pass on mercury to the infant in the nurse's milk," he argued, "but realized after their experience with the first nurse they must deceive the woman to do so."[4] The woman's health had been profoundly compromised as a result. The lawyer for the family, countering that Sieur B. was a respected businessman from an honorable family, added, "But before all that, have you not been a young man yourself?"[5] This was an allusion to the high rates of syphilis in urban France, where the disease was regarded almost as a rite of passage. Prudent doctors advised infected young men to observe a waiting period of months to years before they married – even for those who had undergone the so-called "cure" of mercury treatment.[6]

The tribunal awarded the wet nurse damages of five thousand francs (half of what was asked), to be paid by the family. The doctor was acquitted of any wrongdoing since it was "not certain that the nurse, even if warned, would have escaped contagion, and therefore her condition was not necessarily the result of the doctor's reticence."[7]

The incident draws together the main themes of this book: the long-standing use of mercury in the treatment of syphilis and congenital syphilis, the highly contagious nature of congenital syphilis, the fate of healthy wet nurses who were hired to nurse infants with the disease, the social and ethical implications of this practice, and the legal consequences for families and doctors when infected women sued for damages. Although the case described above took place in 1855–56, its roots can be traced back to the eighteenth century and the growing confidence of physicians that advancements in science would uncover new treatments and cures for infectious diseases – particularly in children.

Until the mid-eighteenth century, there was little expectation that society could do anything but endure the high rates of mortality among children – especially newborn infants, of whom approximately one-quarter died in their first year. But by 1750 many French doctors were envisaging great possibilities for medical progress and had begun to question the inevitability of high mortality levels among newborns. They were encouraged by the French government, which was alarmed by reports that the population was in decline and was anxious to ensure the future vitality of the nation.

In 1795 the Marquis de Condorcet articulated the optimism of physicians about recent advancements in scientific research. "It is manifest that the improvement of the practice of medicine … must eventually put a period to the transmission of contagious disorders, as well as those general maladies resulting from climate, ailments in general, and the hazards of certain occupations … Would it even be absurd to suppose this betterment of the human species as susceptible of indefinite progress?"[8] Condorcet premised a future where the evils associated with sickness, disease, and even death could be mitigated by medicine, if not eradicated completely. The heavenly city of the eighteenth-century philosophers was to take place here and soon.

In this new "enlightened" age doctors began to see themselves as empowered proponents of reason and science, increasingly confident in their function. This allowed them to expand their sphere

of operation to implement an agenda that included even the newborn as a patient, one who could be cured. Inoculation for smallpox, the development of milder formulas for drugs such as mercury,
the importance of maternal breast-feeding and attempts to develop
"artificial feeding" for newborns who were unable to nurse – all
were addressed in the medical literature of the day. Yet bringing the
agenda to fulfillment would require rectifying the appalling loss of
life in the foundling hospitals, where many deaths, even the majority,
were attributed to congenital syphilis.[9]

It has been estimated that the number of abandoned infants in
France rose from 372 in 1670 to an annual average of 4,000 by the
end of the eighteenth century, reaching a peak of 7,676 in 1772.[10]
Over the century admissions to the foundling hospital of Enfants
trouvés in Paris increased twenty-five times.[11] In all, between one-
quarter and one-third of all newborns in Paris, and perhaps one-half
of all illegitimate births, ended up in the care of Enfants trouvés.
These were augmented by infants from the provinces whose over-
whelmed administrators prevailed upon the Paris facilities.[12]

The pattern of abandonments to foundling hospitals in the Old
Regime followed the rhythm of periodic distress endemic to a pre-
industrial economy. Increases in the cost of living, associated with a
rise in food prices after a crop failure or a particularly severe winter,
were reflected in admissions to the foundling hospitals. Not all such
infants were illegitimate, although an increase in illegitimacy has
been linked to the growth of urban centres.[13] In Paris, abandoned
infants were often a by-product of the desperate situation of young
women from the countryside who had immigrated to the city in
search of work as servants, dressmakers, or milliners. These women
were employed in conditions that left them open to sexual exploitation, and meagre wages often forced them to resort to "part-time"
prostitution in order to survive.[14] The relationship between poverty,
illegitimacy, and abandonment was well established by the first half
of the nineteenth century when illegitimate births accounted for approximately one-third of all births in Paris.[15]

At Enfants trouvés, a staff of between fifteen and twenty-two Sisters
of Charity and about the same number of wet nurses struggled to cope
with as many as 180 abandoned infants at a given time. The children,
both healthy and sick, were bundled together in cots on crowded
wards, leading to an inevitable increase in the spread of contagion
and death. Studies of infant mortality in foundling hospitals showed

that infants were dying at a rate of 420 per 1,000 live births well into the 1800s.[16] It has been estimated that sixty percent perished in their first year. Of those who survived, a further thirty percent died before the age of five.

Infants admitted to Enfant trouvés with evident signs of congenital syphilis were assigned to a single room, with a melancholy motto emblazoned above the door: "Abandoned by father and mother, God cares for me." The care consisted of bathing the infants, feeding them goat's milk, and applying ointments (usually mercurial). The results of this treatment were not encouraging. One of the Sisters of Charity, who served as director of the hospital for thirty-five years, stated in a 1790 report that the numbers of such newborns had increased considerably in the period of her internship, and that syphilitic infants rarely survived more than ten weeks.[17]

The loss of life in foundling hospitals was especially tragic since the purpose of these institutions was to *prevent* deaths from infanticide or abandonment in fields, on church steps, or in doorways. In the vast majority of cases baptism in preparation for the next world was all that could be done for the infants. A failure of this magnitude was not lost on the medical and political establishment. Infant mortality in France, and congenital syphilis in particular, became matters of public policy.

In 1780 the French government established the hospital of Vaugirard in Paris, dedicated to the experimental treatment of infants afflicted with congenital syphilis.[18] Vaugirard represented an early attempt to deal with a public health issue in a clinical setting and it may have been the first specialized pediatric hospital in history.[19] The hospital's avowed purpose was to bring together syphilitic pregnant women and their infants and to treat both with mercury. In accordance with the humoural theory of the time, mercury was believed to expel "corruption" or debilitating humours by means of purging, sweating, and salivation. Abundant expectoration, as much as four pints daily, was considered a sign of its efficacy. Despite attempts to mitigate its harsh effects, mercury ingestion could cause inflammation of the tongue, stomach, and bowels and bring on constant diarrhea. Other side effects were softened gum tissue, loosened teeth, and bone structure that was weakened to the point where noses collapsed and jaws disintegrated.[20] Although mercurial treatments were dangerous, particularly for vulnerable patients, confidence in their curative properties remained high.

This dilemma inspired the experiments at Vaugirard in the 1780s. Innovative in its approach, the technique employed at Vaugirard was to determine the best way to administer mercury to newborns, who were otherwise unable to tolerate its fierce impact on their delicate systems. The technique involved preparing the milk of a syphilitic woman with mercury in order to have her pass on the medication in a milder form to her own infant and to another syphilitic child, usually from the foundling hospital. This medicalized use of milk was not original to Vaugirard, but it was to be tested under "scientific" conditions and the impact of the milk on the infant evaluated and modified as required. Vaugirard provided a clinical setting where physicians could initiate a cure for congenital syphilis under a rationalized and controlled set of circumstances.

The first part of this book (chapters 1 through 4) explores the history of the Vaugirard hospital and its experimental treatment of congenital syphilis. Chapter 1 describes the etiology and symptoms of adult and congenital syphilis and discusses the reasons for the persistence of mercury in the treatment of the disease. Chapter 2 details the operation of Vaugirard hospital as a clinic focusing on treatment of congenital syphilis. Chapter 3 deals with the infants, their symptoms, their treatment, mortality rates, and other factors that influenced the experiments with mercurialized milk. Chapter 4 considers the wet nurses in the hospital setting. Hospital records and an account written by the supervising physician, François Doublet (1751–1795), provide intimate details concerning the social and economic backgrounds of these women, as well as opinions on their personalities, characters, and temperaments.

After a decade of experimental treatments, the Vaugirard hospital closed in 1790. It was deemed a failure because the small number of syphilitic infants who had been cured could not justify its high operating expense. Despite the closing of the hospital, the practice of administering mercurial treatments for congenital syphilis continued. When the new Venereal Disease hospital opened on the rue St Jacques in 1802 it employed the Vaugirard technique of mercurializing women's milk for infants.[21] Beyond this, the Vaugirard experiments played a role in the treatment of congenital syphilis in the public and private spheres of medical practice in France, often with disastrous consequences for healthy wet nurses. The second part of the book turns to the nineteenth century and addresses the medical, social, ethical, and legal consequences of the experiments that had begun at Vaugirard.

The etiology of congenital syphilis was not well understood in the nineteenth century. Congenital syphilis evidently passed from the parents to the fetus, although exactly how it was transmitted and by which parent remained problematic. Also uncertain was the possibility of transmission to others through so-called "secondary symptoms" (the many outbreaks associated with the second stage of syphilis), rather than by direct, usually sexual, contact with a primary symptom (the indurated chancre). Some families argued that an infected wet nurse could be the source of the illness in a nursling. Others, including Vaugirard's Dr François Doublet, were convinced that a wet nurse could contract syphilis from an infected infant. In Doublet's opinion, the disease was usually passed on from a syphilitic outbreak on the mouth of the nursling coming in contact with the nipple of the nurse. Nevertheless, some nineteenth-century doctors, including the prominent physician Philippe Ricord, remained sceptical about the possibility of contagion from secondary symptoms. The controversy led to a series of heated debates at the prestigious Academy of Medicine in Paris in the mid-nineteenth century where Ricord defended his case with his usual rhetorical flair.[22]

It was not until 1858–59 that Ricord was forced to recant his position on the contagiousness of secondary syphilis as a result of a series of controversial experiments on human subjects by Joseph-Alexandre Auzias-Turenne and Camille Gibert. The subjects were injected with pus from a patient with secondary symptoms of syphilis and subsequently they contracted the disease.[23] The Academy of Medicine then commissioned Joseph Rollet, a prominent student of the disease at the hospital of Antiquaille in Lyon, to conduct an enquiry in order to clarify the contagion issue.[24] Rollet put together a comprehensive guide for physicians on the transmission of congenital syphilis between infant and nurse and reiterated the numerous sources for infection by secondary symptoms.[25] Rollet's analysis became the basic manual for doctors who were called as experts or witnesses in court cases. More detailed studies by Etienne Lancereaux, and the later work of Charles Vibert, owe much to his account.[26]

Even before these debates and experiments concerning the contagiousness of congenital syphilis, wet nurses were often apprehensive about contracting the disease. If a nurse was apprised that the infant for whom she was being hired had syphilis, she might well refuse to take on the charge. Consequently many families, with the compliance of their doctors, conspired to keep wet nurses in ignorance of syphilitic infants' conditions. In some instances (such as in the case that begins this book), nurses were given mercury to ingest so that they could pass it on in their milk, although the actual nature of the medicine was kept from them. In most cases, healthy women who nursed syphilitic infants contracted the disease themselves and then passed it on to their husbands and families. Some took the bold step of suing for damages and a series of court cases in the nineteenth century raised the question who gave syphilis to whom in the wet nurse-nursling encounter.

The situation of unsuspecting women who contracted syphilis while nursing infants and the legal measures they brought against their employers, and sometimes against family doctors, to rectify the wrongs they had suffered are examined in chapters 5 and 6. Using a wide range of sources, I have documented more than thirty cases in which wet nurses claimed that they had contracted syphilis from an infant they had been hired to nurse. Not all of those claims ended in court. As the legal confrontations played out, there were numerous examples of wet nurses successfully proving their claims and winning financial compensation. The cases and their outcomes are described in chapter 5 and the cases are summarized in appendix 1.

The response of the medical profession to the legal issues raised by infected nurses is dealt with in chapter 6. The professional standards regulating the doctor-patient relationship dictated that the physician should keep the nature of his patient's ailments strictly private. However, the medical "secret," as the issue of doctor-patient confidentiality was termed, left many doctors in a situation of ethical and legal uncertainty when the illness was venereal disease. In his defence the doctor usually stressed his role as confidant of the family to whom he owed his principal loyalty. But after a landmark case in 1868 this defence was judged inadequate. The result was that ultimately limitations were imposed on medical confidentiality in order to protect the hired woman from exploitation. At that point French jurisprudence explicitly recognized that in such circumstances the doctor was responsible for the well-being of the wet nurse as well as for the family that hired her.

Doctors remained vulnerable to the threat of lawsuits from wet nurses throughout most of the nineteenth century. As chair of legal medicine at the University of Paris, Professor Ambroise Tardieu had had to warn colleagues as early as 1864 about the potential problems posed by wet nurses and congenital syphilis.[27] Into the 1880s

Paul Diday, an expert on congenital syphilis, and Alfred Fournier, the most respected syphilologist of the late nineteenth century, were explicit in their advice to doctors and their patients about how to avoid or, if necessary, deal with situations where wet nurses had been infected by syphilitic infants.

The history of congenital syphilis in the period 1780–1900 illustrates the growing professionalism and politicization of physicians in France. The prominence of physicians in the field of public health conferred both authority and prestige.[28] Welcoming students to the Faculty of Medicine in Paris in the fall of 1863, Professor Tardieu addressed "the Public duties of the Doctor." Tardieu foresaw unlimited opportunities for these young medical initiates: "The virtues and duties of doctor are not confined to home, bedside, family or hospital. His public role is growing and the practitioner who understands this will gain for society and his profession the high rank it deserves."[29] The physician was to derive his public status not from his membership in a corporation, as formerly, but from his connection to the state and his commitment to the integrity and advancement of medical science. Medical practice came to be defined not as an art but as a science.[30] A claim to expertise in public health, which in the nineteenth century was often focused on the treatment and prevention of syphilis, fostered this process.[31]

Surprisingly, despite intense debate over congenital syphilis in nineteenth-century France, and despite many articles on the subject in the influential journal *Annales de l'hygiène publique et de médecine légale* and in medical treatises, little attention has been paid to the subject in the historiography of medical practice. Even in the legal compilations of the time it is difficult to find references to malpractice suits, and specifically those cases concerning the accountability of doctors as they interacted with wet nurses.[32]

My aim in this study is to address that neglect by documenting the history of a group of vulnerable and often disadvantaged women who helped to shape legal, ethical, and medical practice in nineteenth-century France. I place these events in their wider historical context, beginning with the foundation of the Vaugirard hospital and its pioneering experiments with mercurialized milk in the effort to cure congenital syphilis.

I

Mercury and Syphilis:
A Dysfunctional Relationship

Vaugirard hospital marked the attempt to tackle an old problem with new technology, but the basic element of treatment remained what it had been for centuries – mercury.

From its first appearance in the fifteenth century there had been hospitals to treat syphilitic adults with mercury. As early as 1497, it had been decreed by Order of Parlement that strangers with *grande vérole* were to be sent back to their own country, while citizens who were wealthy enough to remain in their homes could be visited by surgeons until certified cured. Those without homes were dispatched to the Faubourg St Germain des Près where there was a hospital to treat them, though in the tradition of the time it was as much a prison as a hospital. Anyone disregarding these terms was to be punished by execution or, after June of 1498, simply thrown into the Seine. In 1557 this *maladrerie*, or lazaretto, of Saint-Germain became the Hôpital des Petites Maisons (hospice of small houses), a name that aptly conjures the variety of "sick poor" who were treated there. In 1790 there were still eighteen beds at Petites Maisons where the afflicted could pay for treatment.[1]

Women had long been considered the source of venereal disease, and prostitutes were sent to Salpêtrière to contain the spread of the illness, not only on the streets but in other hospitals. Bicêtre, however, was the principal institution for treatment. The deliberations of the administration of Hôtel-Dieu in 1700 read: "The commissioners have found several (women) infected with venereal disease among the other sick and enjoin surgeons and sisters to be more exact in their visits and more severe in admissions. In cases where the malady is detected they are to be sent to the Grand Bureau des Pauvres (Bicêtre) with a certificate stating their condition, but before being sent off they will be punished and whipped."[2] This decree was either ignored or contradicted; I have found no evidence that it was enforced for a room in Hôtel-Dieu was set aside for pregnant syphilitics, and Bicêtre admitted such women without the whipping.

Both genders soon outstripped the resources available for their care. In June 1701 there were nineteen admissions to Bicêtre's male wing, St Eustache; by December the numbers had tripled. In 1726 there were 190 admissions overall, and 250 four years later. In 1781 362 individuals were being treated for syphilis at Bicêtre, of which 138 were males and 224 females.

By all accounts, conditions at Bicêtre were horrendous. In 1737 George Mareschal, first surgeon to King Louis XV, claimed that *vénériens* would be better off on straw in a stable or a barn than in such a pestilential place. One observer described it as a "hell-hole." Nevertheless it was a hell-hole with a waiting list. According to a report made to the Comité de Mendicité (poverty committee) in 1790, would-be patients could wait years.[3] It is not surprising that two-thirds of the deaths among *vénériens* at Bicêtre occurred in the *salle d'attente* (waiting room). Mareschal had recommended a new building and construction began in 1743, but funds ran out and it was never completed. In 1789 a similar account of Bicêtre, brimming with indignation, was prepared by the baron de Breteuil. The result of his report was that years' worth of accumulated garbage was cleaned up, walls were painted, and new coverings were provided so that "although still hideous, it became less unhealthy."[4]

The need for improved facilities was compelling. It was not until 1792, however, that a new facility, the Hôpital des Vénériens in the Faubourg St Jacques, was opened. After 1836 women, once again segregated, were sent to the Hôpital de Lourcine. Eventually all venereal disease services were amalgamated in the Hôpital de Midi, renamed the Hôpital Ricord in 1892. Then in 1904, venereal services were located at Cochin hospital. Specialized treatment of syphilitic infants was incorporated in these institutions, but congenital syphilis had its earliest and its own specialized hospital at Vaugirard.

The prevalence of congenital syphilis among the general population in Paris had led to the creation of an "out-patient" service. A notice from the lieutenant general of police dated 3 May 1770 called attention to free treatment for infants with venereal diseases on application to M. Gardanne of the Faculty of Medicine of Paris.[5] Much of the support for Vaugirard hospital came in response to the desperate need to find adequate facilities in which infants with congenital syphilis could be treated with mercury.

THE TREATMENT

Whatever the institution, the traditional therapy for syphilis was the *grandes remèdes* (major cures), which consisted of the ingestion of mercury either orally, or by massages with ointment (frictions), or by inhalation (fumigations). Originally, mercury was commonly prescribed for leprosy and ailments afflicting the skin. Many crusaders had returned to Europe in the thirteenth century allegedly with leprosy, and the liquid metallic element mercury had been beneficial,[6] but the remedy could be almost as debilitating as the disease. It is generally believed that syphilis, spread by the armies of Charles V in Italy and thence through the rest of Europe, was a new disease coinciding with the return of Columbus's sailors. It is possible, however, that the outbreak at the end of the fifteenth century was a particularly virulent recurrence of an older disease with a long history.

The reputation of mercury as *the* specific treatment had equal longevity. As noted in the introduction, mercury was thought to expel "corruption," or debilitating humours, by means of purging, sweating, and salivation. Abundant expectoration, as much as four pints daily, was considered a sign of its efficacy. Regardless of attempts to mitigate its harsh effects, mercury lacerated the tongue and irritated the stomach and bowels, often bringing on constant diarrhea. Mercury treatment could soften gum tissue, loosen teeth, and, as we have seen, weaken bone structure to the point where noses collapsed and jaws disintegrated.[7] Until the recognition of tertiary syphilis in the mid-nineteenth century, the neurological symptoms associated with the final stages of the disease – damage to the nervous system typically resulting in tremors, palpitations, convulsions, and insanity – were sometimes attributed to mercury.[8]

Dr François Rabelais (1504–1553), more famous for his writing than for medicine, provided one of the earliest descriptions of iatrogenic mercury intoxication, associated with the metal. "But what shall I say of those poor men that are plagued with the pox and the gout? ... anointed and thoroughly greased till their faces glister like the key-hole of a powdering tub ... Their teeth dance like the jacks when someone plays upon organs or virginals and they foam from their throats like a boar the mongrel hounds have driven in."[9] Mercury poisoning could call forth symptoms now associated with Minimata disease or a heroic course of cancer chemotherapy.

Among mercury's first proponents were Konrad Schellig (1448–1508), Joseph Grünpeck (1470–1531), and Hieronymus Fracastorius (1478–1553). The latter was a physician and a poet who gave the name "Syphilis" to one of his literary characters, whereupon it took on a life of its own. Another contemporary, Paracelsus (1493–1531), brought his skills as chemist and polemicist to the promotion of mercury.

Problems associated with its side effects led to a search for alternatives from the earliest days. Guaiac wood, which had the cachet of coming from South America, was vaunted by Ulrich von Hütten(1488–1523), a colleague of Martin Luther's and poet laureate of Emperor Maximilian I of the Holy Roman Empire. He had himself attained remission through the sudorific (sweat-producing) effects of the guaiacum bark. Unfortunately for Von Hütten, it did not bring about a permanent cure, and he died in 1523. Some practitioners proposed plant alternatives such as sarsaparilla, extracted from the vine of the lily, quinine (cinchona bark), cubeb (a plant with a bitter berry), and copaiba (resin of the senna tree). Other resins, in particular turpentine, were popular, as were concoctions through which minerals such as lead, zinc, copper, gold, and alum could be ingested. The ubiquitous beetle, popularly known as the "Spanish fly," was administered as a counterirritant to raise blisters on the skin or sometimes given internally as a diuretic. There is some irony in the use of this particular potion, which had a long history as an aphrodisiac.

Although these substitutes had their advocates, mercury retained its primacy. There was a brisk and profitable trade in substances designed to make mercury more palatable, such as Keyser's Blue Pills or Van Swieten's brandy-based liquid. One entrepreneur developed a recipe for putting mercury in chocolates. To ensure that treatments interfered as little as possible with everyday life, patients sometimes squished along in ointment-impregnated socks or shoes or wore anti-venereal underpants that applied these ointments directly to the genitals.[10]

Attempts to modify mercury's side effects and facilitate its absorption into the body led to the development of numerous compounds,

among them calomel, sublimate, iodide, perchlorate, cyanate, albu-
minate, peptonate, formamide oxide, carbolate, salicylate, benzoate
thymolate, iodo-tannate, succinamide, thymol-acetate, and cinnabar.[11] In the late 1880s a scientist as respectable as Robert Koch
(1843–1910) thought he could demonstrate the anti-sporicidal activity of mercurous chloride. More convincingly, Adolf Jarisch in
Vienna, with later contributions by Karl Herxheimer, studied the effects of administering mercury treatments while keeping the patient
in an extremely hot room close to a fire for five to thirty days, in
order to induce a feverish condition and copious sweating. If begun
early, this procedure, called hyperpyrexia, could sometimes prevent
and always delay the development of secondary or tertiary symptoms.[12] In an early application of the procedure, several hardy souls
had inserted themselves in heat boxes in order to ingest fumes directly thereby inducing sweating to expel the venereal virus.[13] But as
the nineteenth century progressed, many physicians were becoming
sceptical that it could produce a fundamental cure. Owsei Temkin,
originally from Germany and head of the first Institute for the
History of Medicine in the US at Johns Hopkins University, is considered one of the founding fathers of medical history. In the 1950s
he conceded that the technique of hyperpyrexia could conceivably
have a beneficial impact on the patient.[14] It is also possible that mercury could have a mild antiseptic effect on the spirochete. In other
words, mercury could have some effect on the disease. Historians
of medicine agree, however, that any positive benefits of mercury
therapy, questionable to begin with, were nullified by its negative
consequences for the human system.

Although quicksilver seemed to make symptoms disappear, the
French royal physician Jean Fernel (1497–1558) observed that it
did not root out the disease, which could still be passed on to a
partner and to infants.[15] Increasingly physicians expressed reservations about mercury's efficacy, but overall it retained its reputation
as the specific therapy for syphilis. That is, it remained for most
physicians the best available agent. This was the case not only for
general practitioners but also experts in the field as renowned as
Philippe Ricord.[16] Paul Diday of the hospital of Antiquaille in Lyon
wrote in 1854, concerning the employment of a wet nurse willing to
take mercury, "One can be happy for the family." Moreover, "with a
healthy nurse mercurialized for the sole purpose of treating the child,
the aggregate of the elements favorable to this mode of treatment will

be realized."[17] By 1861, however, though still dedicated, he was less enthusiastic. "Mercury [therapy] cannot ensure a cure, but only slow down the spread and hasten the disappearance of primary symptoms." In a sample of fifty-seven cases he found that, when given immediately, mercury could generate a positive outcome: "After two to three bouts of symptoms they decrease [in virulence]." He acknowledged, however, the debilitating side effects that could accompany its use: phagedisme (rapid spread of the primitive ulcer), stomatitis and gastroenteritis, (digestive upsets), trembling in the extremities, and, in rare cases, apoplexy and mental alienation. On the other hand, he believed that mercury, given along with potassium iodide, or occasionally the latter given alone, cured patients, though it might take from four to fourteen years.[18]

Military hospitals had a strong incentive and viable subjects on which to experiment. At Val-de Grâce the director of the Department of Venereal Diseases, H.M.J. Desruelles, carried out trials on nearly fifteen hundred cases between April 1825 and July 1827. He had encouraging results treating external symptoms with vegetable and emollient remedies, antiphlogistics, and simple cleanliness. In another experiment involving 1,312 cases, he found that those given mercury for primitive and secondary symptoms required fifty days' recovery time and those without mercury only thirty-two.[19] Richond de Brus had similar results in a sample of three thousand subjects with primitive symptoms. These findings influenced military and naval hospitals in Sweden, Germany, and America.[20]

As time went on evidence became more persuasive and sceptics more numerous. By 1893 Alfred Fournier (1832– 1914), the most renowned syphilologist of his day, was less optimistic. "There is neither a dose nor a pharmaceutical form, nor any length of treatment which confers immunity with certainty, [and] carries the guarantee of complete, absolute and radical extinction of the pox."[21] Experiments on four hundred patients in the 1920s, carried out by Alfred Sézary of the Paris hospitals of Broca and La Charité, indicated that the element made no difference at all in effecting a cure.[22]

Conclusive as this might appear to the lay person, it did not end the debate. In 1930 a medical textbook illustrated the technique for injecting mercury into the jugular vein of an infant.[23] As late as 1941, J.E. Moore's standard text, *The Modern Treatment of Syphilis* (second edition), states, "The administration of mercury by inunction (ointment) is the best method of use of the drug."[24]

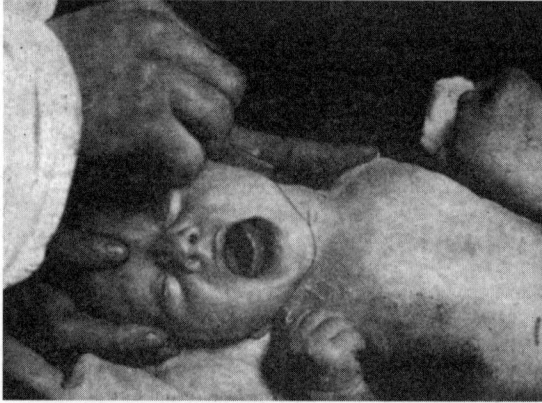

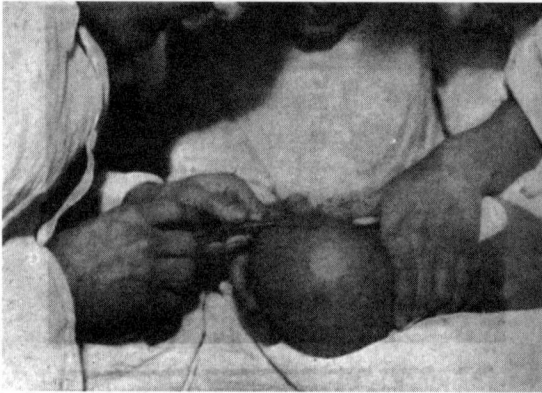

Injection of infant with mercury from a 1930 textbook
by A.B. Marfan and H. Le Maire, *Précis d'hygiene
et des maladies du nourrisson* (Paris: Baillière et fils,
1930).

Modern research tends to support the critics of quicksilver therapy. Given the long controversy over its efficacy, extending from the
fifteenth to the twentieth century, how can we account for the stay-
ing power of mercury in the medical pharmacopoeia? One viable
explanation is that symptoms of first stage syphilis always disappear,
under any treatment or no treatment, sometimes to recur, sometimes
not. This meant that mercury ingestion could be coincidental with
a dissipation of symptoms and therefore tenable. And, as demonstrated in the Jarisch-Herxheimer experiments, on occasion mercury
could have an impact on early signs. In the nature of the disease
sometimes these symptoms did not recur.

A second factor in the persistent use of mercury was its accom-modation to whatever current scientific hypothesis was in vogue at any given time. As we have seen, mercury treatment was embedded in the theory of humours, which, although superseded by a series of other paradigms by the 1830s, nevertheless continued to reson-ate with remarkable tenacity. Advocates of both the iatromechan-ical and the iatrochemical schools credited mercury with expelling diseased humours. The pox, as syphilis was termed until the end of the eighteenth century, was understood by the "chemical" devotees to be the result of an active and penetrating poisonous fluid (virus), which could be modified or neutralized by its affinity with mercury. Similarly, for those positing a "mechanical" interpretation of physi-ology, mercury was considered capable of penetrating the physical tissue of the patient, atomizing the diseased particles, thus releas-ing them into the bloodstream, after which they would be expelled through the saliva. The temporary success of François Joseph Victor Broussais's inflammatory explanation of disease as "irritation of the tissues" discredited mercury's hold only briefly. Theoretical con-structs that replaced humoural explanations at the end of the eight-eenth century did little to undermine its long-standing credibility.[25]

Not until the initiation of a pathology, which situated diseases in organs, tissues, and cells, did syphilis come to be treated as a local-ized disease whose spread through the whole body might be pre-empted if the primary local symptom was extirpated early enough. For instance, the nineteenth-century syphilologist Philippe Ricord believed that cauterization or excision of the indurated chancre, if done within five days of its appearance, could prevent the develop-ment of syphilis into a full-scale disease.[26]

Most doctors at mid-century considered syphilis a virus caused by a material agent. Finally, with the evolution of a bacterial frame-work, based on evidence of the microscope, it became possible in 1905 for the team of Schaudinn and Hoffmann in Germany to iden-tify the spirochete *tripomena pallidum* as the microbe organism causing syphilis. Then in 1909 Paul Ehrlich, on his six hundred and sixth experiment with arsenical compounds, produced the "magic bullet." Salvarsan, literally "I save" (a trademark name for arsphena-mene) was welcomed as having the potential to destroy quickly the scourge of two thousand years.[27] Arsenical therapy, in conjunction with bismuth, was able to make some inroads, but even so recov-ery could not be guaranteed. Ultimately, and at last successfully, the development of sulfa drugs and penicillin during the Second World War meant that mercury permanently lost its cachet.

Mercury's long hold on both the popular and medical mind could also be explained in social terms. Ludwig Fleck's "carnal scourge" thesis has become part of the medical-historiographical tradition. He argued that mercury therapy was considered an appropriate punishment for concupiscence. As later extrapolated in the work of Thomas Khun, Fleck pointed out that neither scientists nor physicians are isolated from their culture. As a result, numerous extraneous influences – cultural, economic, religious, and ethical – can have an impact on both medical practitioners and their patients.[28] That is, the suffering mercury inflicted on the body could be interpreted as a fitting price to be paid for sins of the flesh.

Mercury and syphilis were inextricably interwoven throughout the ages in a cycle of sin/pain/punishment. In an elaboration of this, Owsei Temkin, a forthright exponent of social construction in history, suggested that mercury therapy, with its distressing concomitants, continued to be endured by the average patient, who had bought into the punishment aspect. However, those who were scientifically aware and better educated were more likely to demand, and receive, less-debilitating treatment.[29]

Medical professionals were only gradually swayed by scientific developments that undermined a reliance on mercury as a treatment of choice.

CONGENITAL SYPHILIS

Experiments on mercury treatment in a clinical setting were an important aspect of the work at Vaugirard. Throughout its long tenure as the favoured medication, mercury, even in its mildest form as calomel, or *mercure doux* (gentle mercury), remained too harsh for the fragile system of a newborn. Attempting to administer the chemical to a pregnant syphilitic woman and thus treat the infant in vitro was equally controversial because abortion could result. But its long-standing reputation as a specific for syphilis inspired physicians to continue to search for some viable method to treat infants.

Finding a successful technique for applying the medication of choice to the newborn was the ostensible object behind the establishment of Vaugirard hospital, but treating congenital syphilis offered other challenges. There were a number of complicating factors to be addressed in a specialized hospital. First, as we have noted, symptoms did not always appear at birth but might take anywhere from ten days to ten months, and allegedly to ten years. One physician describes a classic case.

> It may be clean and healthy ... and at the time of birth or soon afterwards [usually within the first month], the infant acquires a wrinkled countenance, having the appearance of old age in miniature ... [with] scarcely any hair on the head ... [it]cries continually in a low murmuring tone ... Other symptoms presently appear, the earliest and most frequent being inflammation of eyes, spreading to the lids ... copper-coloured blotches ending in ulceration of skin surface, or numerous livid, flat, suppurating pustules ... sometimes attended by the eruption of pale shining pimples on the face which enlarge, become red and run together ... genitals and anus become inflamed ... Foul sores with retorted edges and a pale and lard-like centre cover the inside of the mouth and chancrous ulceration takes place on the lips, especially about the angles of the mouth ... The gums are red and raw, the nostrils stuffed ... The child's voice is hoarse, and the glands of neck and those below the jaw are swollen.[30]

The multiplicity of characteristics presented serious problems for the physician attempting a diagnosis. Symptoms of syphilis could be mistaken for other diseases, or vice versa. P.A.O. Mahon, a French venerologist writing at the end of the eighteenth century, noted that "syphilis may appear to be other eruptions common to children, such as crusta lactea [a scalp outbreak], herpes, psoriasis [skin irritations], or it may mistakenly be diagnosed [as syphilis] when in fact [it] was only thrush [muguet], or apthes [both mouth infections that were endemic in foundling hospitals]."[31] It could even be confounded with eczema or diaper rash. As a result almost any genital infections or mucous discharge, even in infants with healthy parents, might be attributed to syphilis. The symptoms of diseases as diverse as rickets, hydropsy (edema), or tuberculosis were also sometimes taken as signs of congenital syphilis. All of this was complicated by outbreaks brought on by the mercury itself.

The result was to lead researchers into blind alleys. A hospital setting allowing for careful observation in order to clarify and classify the symptoms of congenital syphilis offered an opportunity to resolve some of these questions. Not that physicians were always successful. In 1799, for instance, René Bertin, appointed physician in charge of the Venereal Diseases hospital in the Faubourg St Jacques, was frustrated in his attempts to inoculate ophthalmia (eye inflammation, a symptom of gonorrhea) in syphilitic infants. "How can this be reconciled," he fumed, "with examples of *sage-femmes* [mid-wives] and *accoucheurs* [obstetricians] who contract the virus through a cut on the hand or finger after contact with an infected vagina?"[32] Later, it was determined by J.F. Hernandez and Philippe Ricord that gonhorrea and syphilis were two separate venereal diseases.[33]

Understanding the sources of contagion by heredity remained a matter of conjecture. Clearly the disease could be passed on by progenitors, but which progenitor? According to Mahon, many were convinced that women must be the source of contamination.[34] This influenced legislation aimed at controlling prostitution throughout the nineteenth century and remained a major theme in the publicity dedicated to keeping troops healthy during the First and Second World Wars. Or was the germ present in the semen of the father and absorbed in the mother's womb, or perhaps simply contracted in a treacherous birth passage through an infected vagina? John Hunter (1728–1793), a British surgeon who carried out some of the earliest experiments on syphilis, argued that the newborn could only be infected by direct contact with a primary symptom in the birth canal. Anything else could only produce an illness "*resembling* syphilis."[35]

Then there was the problem of contagion after birth. Bodily fluids of all types were associated with the spread of syphilis; it was feared that using the same utensils could pass on the virus in the saliva of a caregiver. Even more disturbing were claims that the disease could be contracted from sheets or clothing or pillows, or a chaste kiss between brother and sister.

Anxiety concerning contagion through the medium of fluids was exacerbated by the practice of sending out newborns to wet nurses. Could the virus come from the milk of a syphilitic wet nurse? Nils Rosen von Rosenstein, the prestigious Swedish author who studied children's diseases, discussed the case of a respectable merchant in Stockholm whose wife, three children, a servant woman, and two apprentices were infected by an imprudently chosen nurse.[36]

Physicians had long recommended that a mother nurse her own infant, rather than risk contagion through the milk of a problematic wet nurse. Diseased mothers could nurse their own infants with impunity, according to Colles's definitive "law" of 1837. But less attention was paid to his corollary, which warned that the life of an innocent woman and her family could be in jeopardy if, as a nurse, she was hired to care for an infected charge. Many foundlings had been admitted from Hôtel-Dieu without warning that their syphilitic mothers had died in childbirth. When such infants left with an unsuspecting wet nurse the illness was often passed on to the woman's family, or to other nurslings. Long before this, moreover, William Buchan had gone so far as to recommend that the nurse should be the one to require a certificate from a skillful physician, vouching that the child was clean. In his experience, "some children have two or three nurses and give syphilis to them all. They [the nurses] in their turn pass it on to others, and sometimes to their own family, so there is no saying where the malady may end."[37]

All these questions were to be addressed in a hospital dedicated to newborns with congenital syphilis, although they were not resolved until the nineteenth-century debate over the contagion of secondary symptoms. Given the unknowns in terms of treatment, diagnosis, and etiology, an institution specializing in infants with congenital syphilis was an innovation whose day had come. Milk, in itself, was credited as a health-giving fluid. The possibility of passing on mercury in nurses' milk was to be tested at Vaugirard. A hospital that could treat both a syphilitic woman and child seemed humanely and medically opportune in this early example of public health policy. In the tradition of the eighteenth-century Enlightenment, a process of rationalization would combine the expertise of bureaucrat and physician. It was not coincidental that administrators, physicians, and surgeons associated with the principal institutions of the city, Hôtel-Dieu, Bicêtre, Salpêtrière, and the hospice for foundlings (Enfants trouvés), found themselves cooperating on the project. An ideology of progress, encompassing even the weakest constituents of the body politic, was to be implemented by an enlightened government in the hospital of Vaugirard. Moreover, as we shall see, the technology developed at Vaugirard continued to have consequences throughout the nineteenth century.

The Making of a Modern Hospital in Eighteenth-Century Paris

Vaugirard hospital, with its mandate to deal with infants with congenital syphilis, was a prototype of the innovative and specialized institutions that were coming into existence in the eighteenth century. Government-sponsored by officials with a specifically secular orientation, its administrators conceived of the hospital as free of the strictures that limited their opportunities for teaching and practising in traditional establishments administered by religious orders. "The new hospital aimed at the patients' recovery rather than their salvation."[1] Its proponents envisioned small establishments where they could function within an innovative set of scientific paradigms.

The principal forces behind the "new hospitals" were Jean Charles Pierre Lenoir, lieutenant general of police and chief administrator of the Hôpital Général of Paris, and his inspector general of hospitals, Jean Colombier. A document published in 1781 under the auspices of Lenoir described Vaugirard's physical characteristics and mode of operation.[2] The document was based on Colombier's proposals for the organization and functioning of the hospital, which drew on his experience as a former administrator of military hospitals, institutions renowned for the training of surgeons. The report can be read as an exercise in public relations, promoting Lenoir's role as a proponent of the enlightened ideals of the day.

Vaugirard was conceived as a project that would give physical expression to the innovative ideas of the two men. In the words of a contemporary, Colombier had established "an institution – the first of its type in Europe [to treat infants with venereal disease] – bringing honour equally to those who conceived its plan, those who executed it and to the government which adopted and encouraged it."[3]

Congenital syphilis, a disease that was seen as a threat to the demographic potential of a progressive state, was to be brought under control at Vaugirard.

PHYSICAL STRUCTURE AND STATUTES OF OPERATION

It requires some effort of imagination to envisage the chateau at 345–371 rue Vaugirard, between rue Dombasle and rue de l'Abbé, as it looked when it was built. An incessant rush of traffic and cars parked bumper to bumper on the street hinder the view of this gracious example of eighteenth-century design. A functional late-twentieth-century hospital built of glass and concrete now forms the backdrop for the older building. Though the modern hospital is by no means an unpleasing example of the genre, it stands in marked contrast to its predecessor. Of Vaugirard's outbuildings only the gatekeeper's quarters remain – the grounds are now a park. A restoration of the main structure as part of the University of the Sorbonne makes it somewhat easier to appreciate the aesthetic design of the original hospital of Vaugirard.

The building had not been intended as a hospital at all. It was the seigneury of the Mareschal family and through marriage came into the estate of Louis Angran, Conseiller du Roi [royal councillor]. At this point the government had claims to it for nine years, perhaps as a form of compensation for back taxes. Eventually, the state obtained a clear title when Denis-François Angran d'Alleray, Procureur général, Lieutenant civil de la Prévôte, and Vicomte de Paris, was guillotined on 27 April 1794 (8 Floreal, Year 2 of the first Republic of France].[4] Meanwhile Vaugirard had completed its tenure as a vehicle for the latest trends in eighteenth-century hospitals and been incorporated into the new venereal diseases hospital in the Faubourg St Jacques.

Vaugirard's suburban setting was considered optimum by hospital planners. Throughout the period medical practitioners, inspired by "anti-contagionist" theories, emphasized the importance of improved ventilation, small-scale buildings with fewer beds in more spacious wards, and the practice of disinfection and fumigation. Miasma, the theory that associated disease with vapours from marshland or decomposing matter, promoted the healthful importance of fresh air

Main entrance of Vaugirard hospital from rue
Vaugirard, Paris. (Author photo)

Rear view of Vaugirard hospital, Paris. (Author photo)

in a building open to prevailing winds, with green space so that patients could walk outside when their condition permitted.

These considerations were addressed at Vaugirard, with its collection of separate, for the most part small, buildings in an open, spacious setting. The *quadrillage* (pattern or layout) ensured that the walls and windows of sickrooms were exposed to currents of air on all sides for the continual dispersal of "corruption." Pierre Cabanis had pointed out the problems of collecting the healthy and sick indiscriminately in large institutions, where contact and contagion were inevitable.[5] Vaugirard allowed for the separation of the sick, not only from each other but from residents of the area whose dwellings were often crowded up against the hospital walls, or who relied on the same water supply as patients for drinking, cooking, and laundry; such was the case with the Hôtel-Dieu, which to this day lies at the geographic centre of Paris.

Spacial isolation remained the cornerstone of progressive hospital design until the early twentieth century. This can be seen in the expansive accommodation provided in sanatoriums for the treatment of tuberculosis patients in northern New York State. It is only in relatively recent times, in highly populated urban centres, that the expense of such buildings has required their replacement by high-rises. Today's multistoried, crowded, centralized hospitals call for new strategies, not always successful, for germ control.[6] The setting of Vaugirard was an important feature in reformers' plans for a healthy environment.

The main building housed the essentials. On the ground floor were an admissions office, a pharmacy, and a laboratory. Here too were the quarters of the director, a kitchen, a meeting room, and a parlour where visitors were received. On the second floor, medical services with baths and a maternal delivery room adjoined the resident surgeon's quarters. There were four nurses with eight infants in each of three large rooms. On the third floor, four smaller rooms with tiny round windows accommodated twelve women and twenty infants, the matron, and servants.

Nearby were the outbuildings. A porter's lodge, with rooms a few steps above ground level, had space for women who were no longer able to nurse, whether because their milk had dried up or because they were deemed too ill. Additional sleeping quarters for servants were also in this building.

Facing the street, a stable with its own small courtyard sheltered two asses, two goats, three cows, and a milking room where the animals were milked and also perhaps where the milk was stored. Next to it were two dining rooms: one for men and another for serving girls, as well as two large storerooms. Above this were sleeping quarters for sixteen pregnant women and a segregated area for those who had been cured and were now weaning their infants. Other small buildings included a chapel, gardener's quarters, a shelter for infants waiting to be sent out to nurse, more storehouses, and, near the main water supply, a laundry and ironing room. Under all these structures were cellars for provisions.

A well on the property and a drainage ditch to carry off waste contributed to the salubrious environment at Vaugirard. There was plenty of room for a vegetable garden and pasture for livestock. The whole compound encompassed the essentials that reformers had envisaged as ideal for a hospital.

Traces remained, however, of the traditional function of the hospital as *maison de force* – a quasi-prison – in the substantial walls and the bars at the courtyard to the left of the porter's lodge. To the right of the entryway was a promenade where nurses could enjoy fresh air with their infants, but access to, and especially exit from, this area were strictly controlled.

The internal appointments of the hospital provided for cleanliness and comfort. Each sick person was assigned an individual bed in quarters separate from the staff; each infant had its own cradle. The beds were of wood, with straw mattresses, a pillow, and two covers for winter. Close attention was paid to hygiene in linens and supplies. A pump carried water to a reservoir and from there into the washroom in the main building. Both upper floors had separate sets of lavatories for nurses and employees off the main corridor. Milkrooms and stables were well ventilated, and there were stoves in the nurses' rooms to keep infants warm. Personnel consisted of the director of the hospital and refers to three health officers: a doctor, a chief surgeon, and a resident surgeon, who also supervised the pharmacy. The matron, a Sister of Charity of St Vincent de Paul,[7] was in charge of housekeeping. Her duties encompassed everything except the medical: laundry, kitchen, the servants (three male employees and six serving women, later six menservants and five serving girls), the nurses and their nurslings, all came under her watchful eye. If the hospital was well run, and there is no evidence to the contrary, it was largely due to the matron.

The duties of each staff person were clearly designated. The director was in charge of administration, expenses, assigning duties, and overseeing general policy. He kept track of the women and the infants in separate sets of registers: admissions, personal effects of patients, deaths, and discharges. The latter set included medical reports vouching for the state of health of anyone leaving. In practice the signature on these records was usually that of the chief surgeon. These records, along with financial accounts, were submitted monthly to the lieutenant general of police or the inspector general of hospitals.

Health officers carried out daily visits. The chief surgeon attended childbirths, performed operations, and saw that treatments were followed up. In practice the duties of chief surgeon and resident surgeon seem to have been combined in the office of the chief surgeon. The clinical aspects were explicit: name and assigned number, symptoms, medication and food allotted to each sick patient. Under the supervision of the physician and chief surgeon, medicine was prepared and distributed from the pharmacy. Prescriptions for purges or laxatives usually took the form of suppositories given by a maidservant assigned to a particular dormitory.

The hospital focused on the wet nurses and their infants. For each woman and child admissions records noted the date and place from which they came to Vaugirard – usually Hôtel-Dieu, Bicêtre, or an address in one of the local parishes. In return for decent quarters, food, and medical treatment, the wet nurse had an obligation to breast-feed her own newborn and, when her health allowed it, at least one other infant. The nurses were paid seventy-two livres per infant and forty sols monthly for the second child, as well as an allowance of fifty-two sols per month for small extra expenses for two infants, or eighteen sols for those able to nurse only one infant. When the newborn was not her own, the pay was seventy-two livres for one and forty sols per month for the second. An important aspect of recompense may have been the meals. The nurses' daily rations consisted of one and a half pounds of bread, some of it in soup; one pound of beef (two-thirds of that in soup), and the remainder either roast lamb or veal and vegetables, presumably also in the stew or soup. They also received a litre and a quarter of wine with meals, and a cup of milk or bouillon in the morning. These portions could be adjusted on the advice of the doctor. Servants' rations approximated those of the women, except that they received only half a pound of meat, which came from the nurses' leftovers. On fast days and during Lent everyone's meat portion was cut back.

On average there were fifty nurses at the hospital (a few more in winter), most of whom stayed for approximately four months. Infants numbered around ninety, but not all women had two charges, and indeed some were incapable of nursing. Those infants who lived long enough to be weaned were cared for at a reduced rate of pay and then either sent back to Enfants trouvés or given directly to a rural nurse at the going rate, with a twenty-four-livres supplement for children who reached the age of four.

There was some flexibility for the sick, but in general nurses were kept to a tight schedule. A bell marked the hours of rising, retiring, recreation, prayer, and work. Movements were rigidly controlled and women were expressly forbidden to enter the courtyard or kitchen, or to approach the outside walls. Time outdoors was closely supervised to see that "they do not run after one another or play games which could affect their health" (this, because many of the nurses were no more than girls). Visitors were carefully screened and only admitted with a voucher signed by a magistrate, and another from the health officer or director. When Vaugirard came under the administration of Enfants trouvés the required documentation was enough to daunt any but the most persistent: permission was required from the lieutenant general of police, the inspector general of hospitals, and the chief surgeon and director of Vaugirard.[8]

The precise attention to detail reflected Colombier's background in military hospitals. Pregnant women were expected to be up by 5:30 A.M. in summer and 7:00 A.M. in winter. After prayers and washing, the beds were made, the dormitory was swept and aired, and then breakfast was eaten at 6:30 in summer and 7:30 in winter. Dinner was at 11:00 A.M., with a snack at 4:00 P.M. and supper at 7:00 P.M., after which the rooms were swept and aired again. An hour of recreation followed each meal. The remaining time was devoted to the infants, or to sewing and knitting, unless the nurse was too ill. To encourage industry, the women were recompensed at one-fifth the value of any handiwork they produced. There were evening prayers at 8:30 and then bed fifteen minutes later. Lights were kept burning in each dormitory.

This routine could be described as monastic as much as militaristic but for one factor: there were few references to religion in Colombier's statutes. Sundays were the exception: wet nurses and staff were expected to attend two services in the chapel and listen to at least one hour of devotional reading by a chaplain. Registers of admissions included a baptismal certificate for the infants (pro forma for the time) as well as for the *sage-femmes* (midwives) or *accoucheurs* (obstetricians). But the hospital did not keep its own record of baptisms for those who were born there. Doubtless such documentation existed in one of the local churches, but the lack of direct parochial affiliation is surprising. An annual sum was allocated to a chaplain for masses on Sundays and feast days, and for burials. Given the high mortality rate, it was hard-earned. There were no details in the records of where the infants were buried, but it is likely that formal interments, such as they were, took place at the nearby parish church.

As noted earlier, the *soeur officière*, or nun in charge, was a Sister of Charity of St Vincent de Paul, but there was no indication that any particular religious order had an administrative role in Colombier's statutes. Such an omission was unlikely to be an oversight in a document that regulated everything from the duties of the director to the daily number of diaper changes (eight) for the infants. Tenon's account of Paris hospitals in 1788 states that Vaugirard was in the charge of officers of the Augustinian sisters of the general hospital; this referred, however, to the period when, despite Colombier's protests, Vaugirard came under the aegis of Enfants trouvés. [9]

Hospitals of the day, run by religious orders, were concerned to save the souls as much as the bodies of their patients. One of the priorities of the foundling hospital was to prevent the crime of infanticide. In effect, however, conditions at the foundling hospital consigned most of its infant charges to the same fate. In contrast, saving their lives was the explicit mandate of Vaugirard. This change in focus sheds light on Colombier's reluctance to see Vaugirard controlled by an outside institution run by the Augustinian sisters. At Hôtel-Dieu a power struggle had emerged between the nuns and first surgeon Pierre Desault (1744–1795), whose concerns were strictly medical. [10] The root of the conflict was the clash between the nun's traditional approach to caring for the sick poor and implementation of the new code of fifty-two articles regulating the full gamut of medical services and patient care that had been outlined comprehensively by Colombier in July 1787. [11] In the words of one historian, the outcome of the dispute in Desault's favour "marked a turning point in the concept of the hospital ... as a refuge providing Christian care, food and shelter to the sick poor ... and the beginning of a new kind of medicine ... for the study of diseases and the training of students."[12] In this revised format, the ill were to be treated according to scientific rather than religious principles. Colombier, given the experience at Hôtel-Dieu, was understandably adamant that Vaugirard should operate as far as possible as a secular institution. It is only in Lenoir's version of the statutes that religious duties are given some emphasis. In what was otherwise a close transcription from his primary source, Lenoir may have considered it prudent to interpolate the following: "There is to be strict attention to morals, hours of prayer, and divine office; before childbirth all women must take the sacraments."[13]

Jacques Necker (1732–1804), finance minister under Louis XVI, was much concerned with the laicization of welfare and with centralizing administrative mechanisms for all hospitals of the kingdom. Louis Greenbaum notes that Necker's policy was itself largely shaped by Colombier, who, along with his colleague Antoine Louis Chaumont de la Millière, "did more for the practical reform of health institutions in France during the 1780s than any other individuals."[14] Vaugirard was to be an example of the implementation of those objectives.

FINANCES

The principal expenses at Vaugirard were salaries and sustenance. At least on paper, rations were generous, especially for administrators, who were given almost twice as much food as anyone else. It is unclear, however, just how substantial the food portions actually were. Colombier had boasted that the average cost of food was twenty-two sols per day, including the taxes (entrées) on wine and wood. When Doublet presented his report to La Rochefoucauld-Liancourt's Comité de Mendicité (poverty committee) in 1790, he admitted that the nurses received considerably less food than the amounts prescribed in Colombier's recommendations, which, at that, had allowed for vegetables in "equivalent amounts" to be substituted on occasion for meat. [15]

Between August 1780 and October 1781 the source of funding for the hospital was the archbishop of Paris.[16] This was revised under Lenoir's plans for the hospital's incorporation into Enfants trouvés (about which Colombier was informed after the fact) by placing

Vaugirard under the governance of two administrators from Hôtel-Dieu and two from l'Hôpital Général, over whom Lenoir would preside. Hôtel-Dieu was to be responsible for one-third of the expenses and Hôpital Général the remainder.

This joint management became an issue for Colombier, who feared interference with his plans for the new hospital. He documented his conflict with Lenoir over the general direction of Vaugirard and the choice of supervisor.[17] He argued that "to place this house [Vaugirard] on the same footing as Hôpital Général and Hôtel-Dieu will bring about the same wastefulness and carelessness [as in those hospitals]."[18]

Doubtless Colombier's reluctance to report back to other administrators pertained to more than finances. It meant that the inspector general would not be in a position to appoint the director or the physician or surgeon of Vaugirard. Understandably, Colombier also resented being kept from directly implementing the statutes he had so carefully drawn up. "There is no reason I should not be a member of the administration, while at the same time doing the work [as Inspector-general of hospitals] I presently do," he insisted querulously.[19]

Indeed he had been pre-empted. In May 1781, perhaps as an economy measure, perhaps as a form of rationalization, Vaugirard formally became an adjunct to Enfants trouvés. In compensation for the added expense, Enfants trouvés was given the income of the defunct hospital St Jacques des Pélérins. Nonetheless the senior hospital still experienced a shortfall. Over an eight-year period the income of Vaugirard came to 165,536 livres, twenty sols, (sous) and six denier, but the expenses came to 500,000 livres.[20]

Though Vaugirard was a drain on the finances of Enfants trouvés it retained its reputation for being carefully managed. In his discussion of the advantages of small over large hospitals, Cabanis contrasted Vaugirard with Hôtel-Dieu in order to bolster his contention that small hospitals operated more efficiently and economically. He claimed that the cost per patient at Hôtel-Dieu was twenty-seven sous per day compared to only eighteen at Vaugirard.[21]

Finances had to be a major consideration if the high expectations for Vaugirard were to be realized. The actual costs of running the hospital are supplied in the 1790 response to the questions of La Rochefoucauld-Liancourt's committee. It lists internal yearly expenses at 27,948 livres, one sol, and eight denier. In fact, over an eight-year period (1781–89) yearly expenses averaged 49,763 livres, thirteen

Dépense

Table showing expenses for hospital Enfants trouvés, including Vaugirard, 1781–88. (Archives nationals, Paris, France)

Table showing income for hospital Enfants trouvés, including Vaugirard, 1781–88. (Archives nationals, Paris, France) sols, and eight denier. This put the cost per individual at one livre and three denier, admittedly a rough estimate since it made no distinction between officials, servants, and infants. Moreover, the staples of bread, wine, candles, wood, coal, salt, cheese, and drugs came from suppliers for the Hôpital Général who billed Enfants trouvés directly every three months. (See illustrations 5 and 6, income and expense for Vaugirard encompassed in the tables of Enfants trouvés for 1781–88.)[22]

At that, Vaugirard lived up to the claims of its founders: financially, a small hospital could operate more efficiently than larger institutions.

THE HOSPITAL AS CLINIC AND THE CONFLICT OVER ADMINISTRATION

Politicians and ideologues, as well as doctors, considered Vaugirard a model of enlightened practice. Under his management Colombier expected Vaugirard to become a flagship for a new approach, implementing clinical methods in an institution where building, administration, and medical practitioners could function free of the trammels of traditional ways. As a new institution there would be no obstruction from a pre-existing administration dedicated to past principles of operation.

With an emphasis on practical training under both surgeons and physicians, institutions like Vaugirard were becoming workshops for the medicine we have come to call "clinical." Vaugirard offered an opportunity to observe, regulate, chart, and modify the treatment of a single disease and allow medical personnel to experiment with methodologies. The hospital lacked one important characteristic: it did not explicitly train students, though there were often observers. It qualified, however, in all other aspects of clinical practice, which included autopsies, experiments, and careful recording of symptoms in order to understand and treat congenital syphilis in an independent setting. Doctors saw this as a chance to put into effect a new agenda, bringing science and technology to the relief of society's ills – a course of action that would also enhance their prestige.

Colombier had a dedicated disciple in François Doublet (1751–1795) who wrote in 1785, "If there is one place where everything favors medical observation, it is in the hospitals. In these refuges, built by charity for the care of unfortunates, the physician can study the history of diseases as they really are, and the value of remedies." In a statement prefiguring Foucault's famous reference to the medical gaze, Doublet went on, "The hospital will always be the physician's school, as a picture gallery is the painter's school."[23] Doublet would seem to be articulating the insights that have become associated with the work of the French historian Michel Foucault. Foucault claimed that the medical profession made its appearance as a clinical science at the end of the eighteenth century in France when the "gaze" of the physician became a tool of scientific objectivity as it passed over, around, and gradually into the concrete nature of things (symptoms). This meant the doctor examined the patient in pragmatic terms rather than in relation to a set of theories or a philosophical system as in the past. Medical practice at the bed of the patient in the clinic, he stated, "was constantly praised for its empiricism, for the modesty of its attention, and the care with which it silently let things surface to the observing gaze without disturbing them with discourse ... The clinic owes its real importance to the fact that it is a reorganization in depth, not only of medical discourse but of the very possibility of a discourse about disease."[24]

In other hospitals of the time doctors could encounter obstruction from an administration run by religious who held that the hospital existed for the patient, not for the physician. At Hôtel-Dieu nuns of the Augustinian order both controlled and interfered with medical staff. The sisters objected to the disruption of their patients' routine as unruly students, accompanying the physician on his rounds, surrounded (even climbed on) the beds, crowded into the operating room, and interrupted the sleep and meals of the sick.[25] Doctors, on the other hand, prioritized the cure of patients, not their comfort.

Colombier envisioned a hospital that resembled the clinic of the future, free from impediments to surgeon's and physician's agendas. For him it was an ideal worth fighting for. But Lenoir was probably less single-minded. He was willing to make compromises even if they might interfere with his colleague's medical priorities for Vaugirard. For bureaucrats like Lenoir, Vaugirard was only one, and a small one at that, among a number of hospitals that made up an elaborate system of health care. In the interests of overall strategy, Lenoir may have felt obliged to take economic and political considerations into account. For this he was willing to sacrifice Colombier's, and perhaps even his own, ideals.

In the late eighteenth century what we would now call public health policy fell within the mandate of the "police." When Lenoir, as lieutenant general of police and chief administrator of the Hôpital-Général of Paris, proudly announced the opening of Vaugirard, there was no hint of future difficulties. In 1780 Colombier was asked by Lenoir to look into setting up a new hospital. Whether there was some misunderstanding on the part of one or both men, or whether the inspector merely assumed that he had been given carte blanche, he took his charge seriously. The project required – and found in Colombier – a strong hand to transform the country home of a noble family into a hospital. At the point where he was called in, a master locksmith was in charge of renovations and had already spent more than forty thousand livres on additions and furnishings, most of which Colombier deemed unnecessary and inappropriate. Five officials and thirty servants had been installed, though there were as yet no patients, nor had any arrangements been made for their treatment.

The new broom wasted no time in putting Vaugirard in working order. This required drawing up the terms of governance, listing anticipated expenses for food and medicine, and organizing the program of treatment. So large an undertaking called for daily visits by Colombier from July 1780 to January 1781.[26] At the end of this period, Colombier seemed content to hand over the medical administration to Doublet, though he clearly expected to oversee the hospital in a controlling capacity.

There followed, however, a period of confusion and misunderstanding over who actually was to be the main administrator. From the first, this had been a matter of some uncertainty. Most accounts name René Adrien Faguer-Despérrières (1740–1785) as head of Vaugirard and resident (chief) surgeon, and François Doublet as chief physician. Both were well qualified. Faguer had originated the idea of establishing a hospital in which syphilitic women could treat syphilitic newborns. As *gagnant-maîtrise* at Bicêtre (the senior surgeon in charge of students) he was well situated to appreciate the urgent need for such a facility. His aim was to rationalize the treatment of syphilitic pregnant women and their newborns. Faguer subsequently wrote his thesis on the subject of venereal diseases in newborns, and he accompanied Colombier once a week on his supervisory visits to Vaugirard.

For his part, François Doublet was Regent doctor on the Faculty of Medicine at Paris. He practised at the hospital of La Charité and had also worked at Enfants trouvés. Doublet had a history of collaboration with Colombier and was in fact Colombier's son-in-law. As part of his duties as inspector, Colombier had employed Doublet on a tour of the institutions under his governance, and in 1785 they jointly published a series entitled "Observations Concerning the Department of Civilian Hospitals" in the *Journal de médecine, de chirurgie, et de pharmacie*. One of these papers was about "L'Institution des hospices des Enfants trouvés atteints de la Maladie vénérienne fait à Paris en 1780."[27] Clearly, Doublet would have no difficulty in accommodating the expectations envisaged by his father-in-law.

In the end it was Faguer who was given credit, and this publicly, for the hospital's plan of operation and then appointed to implement the very proposals that Colombier had initiated. Indignant, Colombier was convinced that this humiliation could not have been a simple oversight but involved a deliberate scheme on the part of Lenoir. He protested that he was perfectly capable of supervising Vaugirard while carrying out his normal duties – which at that point included drawing up a new set of regulations for Hôtel-Dieu.[28] The inspector general retained more than a casual interest in what he considered to be his special project.

Colombier suspected that the agenda underlying this insult was directly related to a plan to amalgamate Vaugirard with Enfants trouvés. Such a move, he feared, could only weaken the independence of doctors and surgeons and interfere with Vaugirard's ability to function as a self-sustaining entity in the fullest sense of the word. Presumably, a junior surgeon like Faguer who lacked the authority and credentials of Colombier would be in no position to contest Lenoir's efforts to make Vaugirard a subsidiary of Enfants trouvés.

Evidently, Colombier identified himself with the hospital to such an extent that he believed he was the key to its operation as a modern clinic.

Success of the treatment ... will depend on skilled practitioners, who must be able to modify and change the distribution of medication, take into account the circumstances of different parties, who themselves change positions constantly, and there is a vital need to inspire cooperation among these disparate interests. I have taken the responsibility of overseeing daily the order, discipline and dedication of both administration and staff – a task which calls for a complex combination of gentleness, co-operation, energy and firmness on the part of all those associated with the establishment.[29]

This, of course, could only be read as a criticism of Faguer who had just completed his training as surgeon at Bicêtre. Colombier believed that only someone of his own stature could ensure the promise of Vaugirard.

Consumed with zeal, Colombier was willing to extend himself beyond what could normally be expected from the inspector of the hospital system. This may indicate his enthusiasm for a new institution where innovative medical techniques could be brought into play, unencumbered by an administration, staff, or practices harnessed to traditional ways. Colombier's fears were given substance by the conflicts with the religious authorities taking place at Hôtel-Dieu. For him, it was an opportunity to expand and implement methods he had already instituted in the military hospitals, and to silence sceptics who might claim that purveyors of enlightened medicine had overstated their role.

Although his position was outlined in forthright terms, Colombier's motivation for embroiling himself in the politics of Vaugirard remains ambiguous. It could be read as altruism on the part of someone who believed he was the best, and in fact the only, person capable of bringing the potential of the hospital to fulfillment. Alternatively, it could be seen as simply wounded pride on the part of a senior official bypassed by a junior surgeon of lesser qualifications and experience. As in most such contretemps there was probably a mixture of the two.

Colombier had wasted no time in building a case for the work being undertaken at Vaugirard. In August 1781 he and Faguer collaborated on a paper on the treatment of children and nurses for a public meeting of the Royal Society of Medicine. It included tables of symptoms based on observations of infants admitted to Vaugirard. This was followed in November 1781 by a memoir by Doublet and the inspector general on the occasion of the formal opening of the hospital, depicting in detail the insights and approach being taken to deal with the its special function. This was subsequently published in the *Journal de Médecine de Département des hôpitaux civils*.[30] One could speculate that much of the credit for these "joint" presentations was owed to the junior colleagues. But there is no denying Colombier's dedication and concern for Vaugirard and his commitment to its successful operation.

For Colombier, Vaugirard was to be a model for the clinical approach; for Doublet and Faguer it was an opportunity to carry on research; for bureaucrats like Lenoir, Vaugirard was just one hospital in the elaborate collection of hospitals and hospices that made up the conglomerate. It seems likely that Lenoir may have deemed it judicious to curb the enthusiasm of the inspector general by limiting his input, especially since Lenoir had evidently determined to operate Vaugirard as an adjunct and subsidiary to Enfants trouvés.

Despite Colombier's strong objections, the assimilation of Vaugirard into Enfants trouvés came into effect in September 1781. But once faced with a *fait accompli*, Colombier changed his tack. The physician had not managed his remarkable career without developing political resourcefulness. In 1782 he proposed a new project that would combine under one roof all the *vénériens* of Bicêtre and the syphilitic infants of Vaugirard. Was this a roundabout way of reasserting control of the hospital on a greater scale? In any event, this time his recommendations fit into the plans of the government. In August 1785 an edict created a new hospital for sixteen hundred venereal patients – and it was to be under the direction of Colombier. The plan was to convert the Convent of Capuchins in the Faubourg St Jacques into the new hospital, which was to be endowed with 62,000 livres annually. The architect of *hôpitaux*, Eustache Saint-Far, drafted the design, although funds gave out before completion of the project. By the time the new hospital was ready in 1792 Colombier had been dead for three years; the cause, in the words of one contemporary, was "overwork."[31] He may indeed have been a typical case of what today we would describe as an overstressed workaholic, fixated on control and unwilling or unable to delegate responsibility to subordinates.

Lenoir's role in all this is unclear. He pushed through his amalgamation plans over Colombier's objections but then placed his former adversary in charge of the new venereal diseases hospital. Perhaps it was simply a conflict between an administrator whose principal aim was efficiency and a physician whose principal concern was to promote his view of medical progress. Ultimately, Colombier was vindicated on two counts: first, the venereal hospital for all patients, males, females, and infants, fulfilled his ambitions for a clinical institution in its fullest sense; secondly, Vaugirard itself was able to function as a specialized hospital under Doublet, Faguer Despérrières, and another surgeon, M. Challupt, who succeeded Faguer on his death. Their approach was carried on later by P.A.O. Mahon, René Bertin, and their successors at the new venereal hospital. For a short period, Vaugirard had given physicians and surgeons practical experience in the treatment of congenital syphilis and provided insight into the complex aspects of an illness that had for so long perplexed practitioners.

Vaugirard operated as a research centre for congenital syphilis. Both Faguer Despérrières and Doublet published findings on congenital syphilis in newborns. Vaugirard was monitored with interest by various well-known men of science, including Félix Vicq d'Azyr (1748–1794). As permanent secretary of the Royal Society of Medicine, Vicq d'Azyr was primarily responsible for the "New Plan for the Reform of French Medicine." The health committee of the National Assembly in 1790 presented a "clinical ideal ... in a new medical system or 'constitution' for France." His committee heard proposals from a number of contributors, including Doublet.[32] The reformer also initiated a series of prizes from the royal society, among which were several works on children's illnesses.[33] Doublet was among the judges for the essays submitted in 1788 and 1790.[34]

Vicq d'Azir's interest in the work initiated at Vaugirard was reflected in a competition on the subject of congenital syphilis, slated to take place on 31 August 1790. There was to be an award of six hundred livres for the best paper on the symptoms and treatment of the disease and the circumstances of its transmission. The contents of the paper were to follow these guidelines: "1) To determine if certain recognizable symptoms indicate the newborn is infected with venereal disease. 2) How does an infected mother give illness to infants? 3) How is illness transmitted to wet nurses and vice-versa? 4) How does the disease compare to venereal disease in adults? And finally 5) What should the treatment be?"[35] The outcome of the adjudication was to be announced at the Feast of St Louis in 1792 in recognition of the importance the king himself assigned to the subject.

The Revolution interfered with the project's completion, but the issues raised and addressed at the hospital of Vaugirard were only interrupted. Many of the questions raised by the proposed *concours* of 1792 had been considered, if not fully answered, in the work carried out at Vaugirard. These same questions, however, raised medical and legal issues that were not definitively resolved until the last half of the nineteenth century – and then, only after a period of conflict about the nature of congenital syphilis and its transmission, its symptoms and its treatment, that had repercussions for the prestige of the medical profession in general.

Vaugirard hospital had its building, its mandate, its set of institutes, its finances, and its staff in place. The operation had the imprimatur of one of the most influential and powerful medical personalities of the day. It set out to find a cure for an illness that affected, in disproportionate numbers, the least powerful and most pathetic group of the day – the abandoned infants of Paris. We turn now to look at the infants and the treatment they received for congenital syphilis.

3

The Infants of Vaugirard

Vaugirard can claim to be the first pediatric hospital in Europe, perhaps in the world.[1] There were other institutions that accommodated children, but Vaugirard was the first facility specifically devoted
to sick infants, in this case specializing in those with venereal disease. Influenced by Enlightenment philosophy, government officials
and medical men responded to the appalling mortality rate in foundling hospitals such as Enfants trouvés in Paris, where many deaths
were attributed to venereal disease. They embarked on an effort to
save the lives of newborn infants afflicted by congenital syphilis. The
undertaking was all the more remarkable for beng directed at one
of the least valued groups in French society, the infants of the poor.

Though it also treated and studied other infant illnesses in passing,
Vaugirard's main object was to carry out an experiment, employing
observation, dissection, analysis, and categorization, that would lead
to ineluctable conclusions (nosology) about the nature, cause, and
cure of congenital syphilis. The challenge taken up at Vaugirard became an integral part of a significant ongoing medical enterprise,
i.e., the development of clinical medicine.

MEDICAL INFORMATION ON INFANTS
AT VAUGIRARD HOSPITAL

Vaugirard as a Pediatric Clinic

In 1866 Etienne Lancereaux wrote, "The founding of the hospital
of Vaugirard in 1780 for pregnant women with syphilis and their
children, marked a new era in the history of hereditary syphilis. That

era, made famous by the names of René Adrien Faguer Despérièrres, François Doublet, René Bertin, P.A.O. Mahon and Michel Cullerier, has provided us with knowledge of the external manifestations of the disease."[2] The definitive account of the treatment of infant syphilis in this "new era" is available in Doublet's *Observations faites dans le Départment des Hôpitaux civils*, published in 1785.[3]

What little was known about congenital syphilis prior to the establishment of Vaugirard could be summed up by the response of the Paris Faculty of Medicine in 1775 to inquiries received from colleagues at the foundling hospital in Aix-en-Provence. When asked whether there were unmistakable signs by which one could recognize the presence of syphilis in a newborn, the reply was negative. Infants could appear healthy at birth. Sometimes it was only after one to twelve days that the disease became evident, especially if the mother had taken the precaution of using mercury during pregnancy. When asked what method could be used to cure such infants, the response was equally discouraging. All that could be recommended was palliative care. Though convinced of mercury's value, the faculty advised against the use of strong doses. The technique suggested was inhalation of mercury fumes, supplemented by one half grain by mouth of *mercure doux* (mercurous chloride), increasing the amount gradually to three grains and alternating with purges of rhubarb water every second day.[4] Vaugirard was to experiment in finding a solution to these questions, specifically by testing various means of injecting mercury into newborns.

Jacques Richard has discussed a number of eighteenth-century medical practitioners who all placed strong emphasis on the importance of collecting facts. Medical science evolved slowly, however, and it was only gradually that clinical observation was able to impose on a long tradition of rationalization, systematization, and experimental philosophy.[5] As a result experimental medicine in France lagged behind the physical sciences.

In an article published in 1793 in the *Encyclopédie Méthodique de Panckouke* entitled "De l'Expérience," Doublet addresses the characteristics of experimental medicine and the means to practice it. The article is of interest as it sets out the principles and methods on which Doublet's experimental work at Vaugirard was based and the framework within which clinical medicine operated there.

Doublet's contribution outlines how medical experiment at the end of the century differed from the view expounded in numerous articles on the subject in the earlier *Encyclopedia of Diderot and d'Alembert* (1751–77).[6] In particular he focuses on the 1756 article by Jean le Rond d'Alembert entitled "Experimental Philosophy." For Doublet the primary role of medical experiment was based on observation, as in the important descriptive work of Thomas Sydenham.[7] Richard considers that Doublet's argument added little that was new to the discussion. What was innovative was his insistence that experiments in medicine had to be carefully ordered and directed before the results could be considered conclusive. Doublet distinguished between the doctor's "art" of curing, based on what he already knew and practised (i.e., experience based on both observation and erudition), and the "scientific" approach as it operated in the physical sciences, based on trials and experiments aimed at acquiring new insights.

As Doublet saw it, experimental practice presented certain difficulties for the doctor. The subject of medicine – the human body in all its complexity – made it impossible, he argued, to calculate all the factors involved in illness in terms of measuring, weighing, and counting, as one could do for the physical sciences. The challenge facing the doctor was to distinguish those symptoms that were constant and intrinsic from those that were only accidental. With Hippocrates and Rhazes, Doublet believed that "the only school for the doctor to learn to observe is the bedside of the patient."[8] Everything depended on the skill of the observer. For Doublet, employing the scientific method in medicine relied on detailed observation of the patient's symptoms but involved as well a background of knowledge developed by skilled doctors as they attended to their patients. He believed this was essential in order to deal with the variety of factors that could exert an impact on a human being.

Doublet takes as an example twenty patients who are given the same remedy for the same illness. Of these, some get better, some get worse, and some show no difference one way or another. To assume that all those who have not died have been cured would evidently be a false assumption. What was required was a detailed and exact journal in which observations were scrupulously recorded. "The best works of medicine of the century are results of faithful observers working at military and civil hospitals."[9] Such institutions, he claimed, were beginning to attract the most skilled practitioners who not only taught but undertook experiments and, accompanying the latter, depended on repetition for verification. These were the qualities that characterized *véritable* (authentic) experience.

The Vaugirard experiment demonstrates in action the theories and practice of Doublet and his colleagues as they struggled to incorporate the new scientific demands and methods at the end of the eighteenth century into their traditional "art of curing."

Medical Practice at Vaugirard

The pharmacology for preparing mercury was varied, and the results often as unpredictable as the combinations. Highly virulent corrosive sublimates of bichloride and mercuric chloride, found in the popular remedies Bellet's syrup,[10] Keyser's pills, or muriatic mercury, were repudiated as absolutely inappropriate for infants. But even calomel, the so-called "*doux*," or gentle, form that was swallowed in comparatively small doses of six to twelve grains, could prove fatal to newborns. A way had to be found to get mercury into infants without killing them.

The first stage of the experiment at Vaugirard consisted of mercurializing the woman's milk. Wet nurses were prepared by building up their strength. In the ninth month, if healthy enough to endure it without bringing on a miscarriage, the women were given two grains of mercury panacea, a relatively mild formula, and its strength was gradually increased. A week later a series of baths went on for twelve days, beginning at one-half hour, then the immersion time increased by gradual stages up to one hour daily. Sometimes the bath itself was a mercury treatment, sometimes it only served to soften the skin and facilitate the next step, the absorption of mercury ointment by massages. The unguent was a blend of one dram (sixty grains, or one-eighth of an ounce of mercury) increased gradually to three ounces per treatment. When nurses reached the point of salivation, usually three or four days after childbirth, they were given two nurslings: their own when appropriate, and a foundling. Usually, the course of treatments went on for two to three months; doctors were reluctant to interrupt the procedure, even when unfortunate side effects occurred. In some cases both nurse and nursling had to be given an alternative sudorific (a drug causing sweating) such as sarsaparilla in honey, known as the cook's remedy.[11]

In 1785 Doublet asserted that one aspect of mercury's efficacy had been demonstrated at Vaugirard. "Frictions [massages]," he explained, "allow mercury to gradually inform the cellular tissue [of the nurses] and to be distributed to different parts of the body without irritating the alimentary canal, nor the activity of the nervous system ... the tonic action of the fibre is strengthened."[12] Because mercury in their milk was deflected to the nursing infant, the women, he claimed, were less sensitive to side effects. This may have held true for the nurses, but modifying the toxic impact of mercury on newborns remained problematic.

As for the infants, they were to be kept dry and clean in separate cradles in a well-ventilated room. Doublet cautioned that it took only small doses to control symptoms in infants but then went on to prescribe double the quantity recommended by the Paris Faculty of Medicine, that is, one grain of the panacea to a spoonful of liquid, increased gradually to three grains.[13] There was some fear that the mercury in milk might be too diluted, so the infants were also exposed to mercury fumes. Twelve to fifteen grains of powdered cinnabar or vermilion were sprinkled on a container of coals and the infants "smoked" above it in little woven hanging baskets for four to five minutes, the time increasing in accordance with the results. After each session they were taken out into open air or, in bad weather, into a spacious room and immersed in warm water in a specially constructed bath. This allowed the weaker infants who were unable to nurse to absorb the chemical and later, it was hoped, take up the regime followed by their companions. Only reluctantly did Doublet conclude that inhalations were a disappointment.[14] We now know that this was one of the most dangerous ways of ingesting mercury because of its deleterious impact on the lungs of the newborn, often leading to bronchitis and pneumonia. Alternative strategies whereby mercury was applied externally, such as through ointments, were smelly and dirty and destroyed bedding and clothing.

Evidently, mercury treatments required close monitoring. The first six weeks were considered important in that symptoms usually disappeared. Even so, the infant could still appear pale and wan and have colic or other digestive problems requiring gentle purges.[15] Frustrating for the staff were stubborn, or "rebel," symptoms that often reappeared despite treatment. They took the form of various outbreaks such as pustules or flat and livid spots all over the body, and ulcers at the anus. This called for more and stronger mercury treatments, given directly rather than through the nurse's milk.[16] By the third month the infant had either recovered or succumbed. But for the heroic survivors, treatment went on for another three months to prevent a recurrence of skin complications, especially at the time of weaning.

One factor that seems to have worked against mercury absorption was the weather. Extremes of hot or cold could bring on colic, requiring syrups of couch-grass (*chiendent*), marshmallow, or gum arabic (*acacia*), and enemas to calm down their digestive tracts. Sometimes there were months when mercurialized milk had to give way completely to simple beef bouillon or a gruel of rice and bread in goat's or cow's milk. Doublet spoke of one occasion on which, he deemed, a storm caused a veritable epidemic of colic.[17]

Various permutations were tried. Doctors were able to collect evidence concerning results and control cleanliness, temperature, ventilation, and diet before and after treatment, assessing factors that might distort their conclusions. The reports prepared for the Faculty of Medicine of Paris pay scrupulous attention to diet and medicine, functioning by trial and error and cutting back on dosages when outcomes were counterproductive. Though success may have been limited, so were the factors that mitigated against success outside the hospital and made evaluation of various methods difficult. With its attention focused on one specific illness, Vaugirard must have been a venerologist's idea of heaven.

It was noted earlier that the use of mercury was not short-lived. As late as 1930 there was a medical textbook illustrating how to inject mercury into a vein in the neck of a newborn.[18] Choosing the precise form and measuring the amount did not extend to restricting its use. Mercury was the rock on which Vaugirard was founded.

Symptoms of Congenital Syphilis

Despite their confidence in the metal, the sheer complexity of syphilis in general and congenital syphilis in particular, contributed to confusion and frustration among doctors. The ubiquitous nature of its symptoms meant that syphilis could be mistaken for any number of childhood illnesses. Whether in adults or children, syphilis continued to confound experts as to its precise characteristics well into the twentieth century. As the noted physician Sir William Osler wrote in 1897, "Know syphilis in all its manifestations and relations and all other things clinical will be added unto you." Like Joseph Hutchinson before him, he recognized the similarity of its symptoms to those of other diseases: lupus, psoriasis, variola, small-pox, and even the common childhood illnesses of measles, roseola, or scarlet fever.[19] For instance, one author claimed that at puberty syphilitic children could

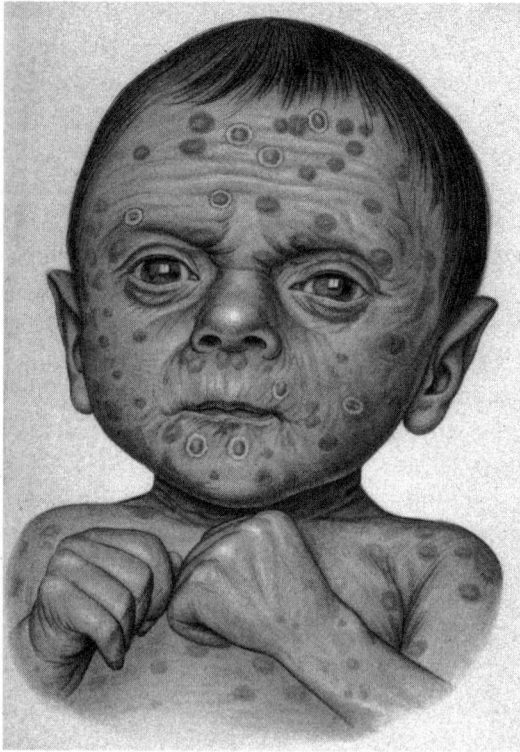

A one-month-old infant suffering from exhaustion, bronchitis, intestinal catarrh, and syphilitic pustules on the skin, who died the day after admission to hospital on 8 July 1897. From Fr. Mracek, *Atlas-Manuel des Maladies Vénériennes* (Paris: J.B. Bailliere et fils, 1904).

be afflicted by worms bringing on epilepsy.[20] Delineating symptoms in a systemic fashion was one of the key forms of research carried out in Vaugirard.

References to the symptoms of congenital syphilis can be found in the earlier writings in France of Ambrose Paré (1510–1590), Jean Astruc (1684–1766), François Mauriceau (1636–1709), and André Levret (1703–1780), among many others. Probably the most detailed, and most quoted, account is that of the Swedish physician Nils Rosen von Rosenstein (1706–1773), to which Doublet refers. It was translated into several languages, including English in 1776. Von Rosenstein pointed out that signs were seldom evident at birth. Early indications were pimples on the mouth, accompanied by lardlike white sores around tonsils, tongue, and cheeks. These could be dangerous if accompanied by hard swollen glands under the lower jaw or neck, and stinking breath. He also called attention to herpetic eruptions (pimples of small white blisters sometimes called *dartres*, or scabs), as well as scurf, or scaly skin, or a discharge from eyes or behind the ears. Such outbreaks should alert the physician to the need to examine the nurse or mother as a source of syphilis. He believed infants could be cured while still nursing, but only with difficulty.[21]

William Buchan was one of the first British physicians to discuss childhood diseases in general, and the symptoms of congenital syphilis in particular, in his 1796 treatise *Observations concerning the Prevention and Cure of the Venereal Disease*. A Fellow of the Royal College of Physicians in Edinburgh, he described graphically the local eruptions of reddish moist outbreaks starting at the seat and adjacent parts and then spreading to cover a good part of the body. These discharged an acrimonious liquid that dried to form scablike excrescences on forehead and eyelids. "The flesh [is] soft, joints feeble, covered with blotches ... as if skin had been flayed and the cuticle taken off with scalding water; occasionally nails of fingers and toes had come off with the skin."[22] A study by the Spanish physician Antonio Nuñez Ribeiro Sanchez elaborated on the characteristic symptoms: "the slow appearance of teeth which were sometimes black and missing, pustules on the upper lip, head and eyes, obstructed glands and general debility of body." In addition, he mentioned one unusual characteristic: "When these children survive they show intelligence and lively spirits."[23]

Despite a literature replete with vivid descriptions, there was still much to be learned about the nature and cause of congenital syphilis. Based on his findings at Vaugirard, Doublet performed his own triage and summarized what he found to be the most common indications of infection. They were first of all ulcers (open sores that were called chancres and were an unmistakable sign of syphilis); secondly, pustules; and thirdly, tumours that principally affected the mouth, eyes, and generative organs.[24] Ulcers could also be simple erosions, usually around the crown of the head, which soon enlarged and discharged greenish liquid – a sign of approaching gangrene. Ulcers around the umbilicus and towards the back were always mortal, and those of the scrotum very difficult to control. Doublet was more optimistic about being able to relieve symptoms of the genital area in girls. Pustules, which suppurated and dried out without opening, were less dangerous than tumours, which could be round and hard or uneven and soft.

An eye condition, "*ophthalmie vénérien*," was common but considered less serious because it was not life-threatening. Doublet was aware of the correlation of eye disorders with gonorrhea. Though a distinction between the two venereal maladies had not been formally made, the standard understanding at the time was that certain categories of gonorrhoetic symptoms were syphilitic in nature and others not. Doublet described the ophthalmia in the humoural context of the day as a positive form resulting from a deflection of the "flux gonorrhea."

Eruptions on heels and hands could be easily cleared up. On the other hand, corrosiveness around the mouth was pernicious because it interfered with the infant's ability to nurse.

No area of the body was immune. Based on Doublet's account, and using his general format, I have prepared an outline that itemizes symptoms he described as they exhibited themselves from head to toe in the infant.

The head. At the scalp and hairline, ulcers, pustules, and tumours on the crown, edges, and base of the head. Ulcers started as simple erosions, then enlarged and discharged a fetid pus. Pustules resembled the pimples of smallpox but usually flattened out and dried up. Tumours at the hairline were either hard and round or soft and irregular, and occasionally became quite large.

The face was pale and clay-coloured, wrinkled with contractions from pain, which gave the appearance of aging. Dry pustules and crusted *dartres* (scabs) could occasionally produce a blackish spot at the end of the nose that became gangrenous. Ears were seldom affected. The eyes had swollen lids and erosions at the cornea, which were whitish and grape-shaped. The nose was either runny with greenish discharge (sometimes bloody), or blocked due to inflammation of the membrane or from dried mucus. On the mouth there were pustules, chancrous ulcers, and apthes (seedlike outbreaks, a sign of millet, or thrush as it is commonly known).

Skin surface. This was pale and sown with either small white pimples or flattened red outbreaks, which later became dry, crusted, and greyish. When older children were infected they often developed a deep red, though usually benign, skin inflammation (erysipelas).[25]

Shoulders. Suppurating tumours along the length of shoulders and spine. Some large tumours of blackish brown colour could be mistaken at first for spina bifida.

Anus, buttocks, and genitals. Erosions, chafing, pustules, and vegetations (outbreaks in the shape of various vegetables or fruits, e.g., cauliflowers or pears; this form of designation for warty execrescences was unfamiliar in English). These were common to both sexes. Among male infants who had not been given mercury at birth, there were symptoms of a serious nature such as chancres, ulcers, and hard swellings. These caused difficulties in urination and tumefaction of the scrotum. In girls it took the form of a burning vaginal pain at urination and a yellowish discharge (not the lymphatic discharge all infants have at birth).

Arms and legs. General skin infections, which developed into suppurating pustules and mucous abscesses. On occasion this was followed by swelling of the cellular tissue, which hardened and was quickly followed by death.

Hands, fingers, feet. Large oozing pustules that sometimes caused the loss of fingernails on hands and feet. Redness at the heel; in severe cases the skin peeled off.

Using a similar format, Doublet categorized the symptoms he considered either curable or hopeless. On the head, ulcers that dried up and disappeared were curable, as opposed to those that continued to discharge putrid humours. On the face, small pustules that disappeared signalled a cure, whereas a senile face meant a fatal outcome. With the eyes, swellings and discharges from opthalmia were more disturbing than dangerous, unless affecting the sinus at the base of the skull, although scars could leave the infant blind. In the nose, blocked nasal passages that constricted breathing could be dangerous but not necessarily fatal, unless the head turned to the back and the face reddened. Chancres and other ulcers on the mouth and lips were serious if the infant could not nurse, and if they spread into the throat and the mouth blackened.

Other conditions that presaged death were *"phlegmons,"* i.e., thick viscous inflammations or ulcers at the navel. Overall swelling or edema (probably a sign of kidney failure) was fatal, especially when the body surface hardened and the infant lost consciousness.

Doublet saw such symptoms in terms of the usual humoural explanation of the time – that the virulent poisons had not been relieved by
the alternative route such as an ophthalmic discharge.[26]

In general, Doublet did not consider symptoms in infants to differ
markedly from those in adults, except for gonorrhea, more common in adult males but rare in infants. He explained that in infants,
syphilis could migrate into a less-serious eye outbreak. As in many
other cases, such as thrush, his explanation displayed an underlying
theoretical assumption based on the humoural theory. While "bad
air" was considered to be a major contributing factor in the prevalence of thrush among the infants,

> it cannot explain all cases ... On occasion it has been surpris-
> ing to have three or four infants of more than three months of
> age suddenly develop a serious case of thrush and die within a
> few days without having caught it from, or spread it to, others.
> However, such infants were in a state of serious debilitation
> [*marasme*] and suffering from a slow fever which indicated an
> internal degeneration [*depravation*] of the humours. This could
> occasionally produce conditions similar to those generally as-
> sociated with "bad air." ... But for whatever reason, even tak-
> ing into account that depraved humours could produce a virus
> when numbers of newborns are kept in close quarters ... one
> cannot presume to have resolved all the mysteries involved in
> causing this illness. It is probable that several other factors may
> be at work; even cold weather could play a role in the origin
> of thrush.[27]

That is, for Doublet, humours remained an underlying factor to be
taken into account along with other explanations of the nature of
syphilis and its signs and symptoms.

Doublet's account varied from many others in that he considered
the signs of syphilis to be visible at birth to the trained eye, and
invariably so within a week. "Some doubt that the symptoms are
evident at birth. This is true of large pustules, ophthalmic ulcers and
apthes [mouth ulcers]. But if one is referring to *marasme* [overall
debilitation], destruction of the epidermis [skin surface], black and
liverish spots and ulcerated outbreaks, such are usually apparent at
birth ... certainly undeniable symptoms are evident by eight days."[28]

Table 3.1
Symptoms of Infants at Vaugirard (Source, Admissions of Infants,
October 1780–December 1781 and January 1789–December 1790)

EYE INFECTIONS	186 total	MOUTH, LIPS, PALATE	59 total
Inflammations	185	Inflammation	55 (thrush)
Blindness	1	Chancre	4
GENITALS	87 total	FACE, HEAD, JAW	25 total
Inflammation	56	Inflammation	19
Virulent discharge	25	Tumour	5
Chancre	4	Flat pimples	1
Pustules	2	ARMPIT	18 total
SKIN	139 total	Inflammation	17
Inflammation	44	Pustules	1
Gangrenous ulcer	2	UMBILICUS	17 total
Apthes (mouth ulcers)	4	Inflammation	17
Boutons (flat pimples)	18	STOMACH	5 total
Pustules	10	THORAX	1 total
Tumour	2	HEELS, LEGS, FEET	43 total
Rash all over body	55	Inflammation	20
Dartres (scabs)	4	Swollen members	22
ANUS	128 total	*Escarre* (gangrenous scabs)	1
Inflammation	96	FINGERS, NAILS	4 total
Bubons(buboes)	2	OTHER SYMPTOMS NOT	
Open tumour	3	NECESSARILY VENEREAL	
Pustules	10	Jaundice	33 total
Crête (flattened excrescence)	1	*Marasme* (exhaustion)	28 total
Excoriation	6	*Millet*, or thrush(mouth outbreaks)	60 total
Boutons (flat pimples)	3	Premature(stillbirth)	1 total
Gangrenous ulcer	6	Unable to nurse	22 total
Scabs	1		

The account gleaned from the registers of Vaugirard is more dispassionate, if less colourful. I have compiled a table of symptoms for 506 infants admitted in two groups: the first, when the hospital opened between October 1780 and December 1781, and the second between January 1789 and December 1790, during its closing years. They are summarized below according to areas of infection. While in many ways the second set resembles the outline given above by Doublet, the purpose of including it is to provide in a concise form a record of all the symptoms observed in infants admitted to Vaugirard. The data are given precisely as noted on the page dedicated to the infant's history. I have retained the original spelling as it appears in the records when a translation is not evident.

The Mortality of Infants at Vaugirard

The Vaugirard medical contingent saw the importance of publicity for the work that was being undertaken. In August 1781 a presentation was made to the Royal Society of Medicine, complete with an overview of the symptoms and a summary of the treatments given to nurses and infants.[29] This was incorporated and expanded upon in November in a more detailed account by Doublet that was published in the *Journal de Médecine, chirurgie et pharmacie*. Part one was devoted to the arrangements for pregnant women, while part two focused on the infants, with a cursory outline of the ulcers, tumours, and pustules affecting mouth, eyes, and genital organs as observed in 156 newborns who had been admitted between August 1780 and 15 October 1781.

As Doublet described:

> In the first eight days after birth many fall into a distressing state with wrinkled faces, sunken eyes, hands that become pale. They take the nipple only momentarily, or not at all, and absolutely reject the sponge imbibed with milk [i.e. other forms of feeding]. If they are not completely exhausted, and their eyes are still lively, the case is not hopeless. What is called for is broths and fortifying formulas as suggested by Rosen. Even those scarcely a few days old can take balm mint [*melisse spiritueuse*], or some drops of lilium [herbs related to the lily plant] in appropriate dilution, which may restore them till they can nurse.[30]

"Artificial feeding" for infants too weak to nurse was no more successful at Vaugirard than anywhere else. Survival for more than four months was unusual for infants fed by means of tampons or sponges soaked with the milk of asses, goats, or cows. It is impossible to know how often death occurred simply from enervation, or as a result of complications due to contaminated milk.[31]

The report of November 1781 concluded with the remarkable claim that one-quarter of the infants born at the hospital or admitted during that first period had survived, and that the recovery of one-third of those survivors could be directly attributed to the mercurialized milk of wet nurses. Doublet's assessment was based on the fact that many of the deaths occurred for reasons other than syphilis. By eliminating such cases from his account he came up with a more positive conclusion than a "strict" reading of the number of deaths at Vaugirard might represent. Understandably, his calculation that twenty-five percent had survived was greeted with much enthusiasm, since previously almost all attempts to save such infants had failed.

The hopes generated by Doublet's statistics remained unfounded. In fact, the data on which the statistics were based could be considered dubious from the start. Admissions records indicate that of the 156 infants listed for the period, only eighteen survived.[32] This might conceivably be explained by deaths that occurred later, but since the majority succumbed within the first three months, and often within the first weeks, it seems possible that Doublet set out a more positive picture than the numbers supported. It is likely that in his enthusiasm to justify the enterprise he simply underestimated the number of deaths that could be directly attributed to syphilis. This might have been done by discounting those who died from exhaustion without evident symptoms, or by imputing many deaths to thrush (eruptions on the mouth that made nursing impossible), a common affliction among the foundlings who made up the majority of admissions. Though his rationale is understandable, the computation of survivors at almost double their actual number, i.e., thirty-nine rather than eighteen of the 156 infants admitted between August 1780 and October 1781, seems excessive. The records show, for example, that of the six infants admitted or born in the house in June 1781, all died, and that of twelve admissions in July 1781, only one lived.

In an expanded account of 1785, Doublet elaborated on his statistics for 1781. Rather than an apology, it is a justification of projections that had not lived up to expectations. In the four and a half years ending in February 1785 there had been 804 admissions and of those 152 were still alive. Sceptics might see in this explanation an example of the assertion that there are "lies, damned lies and statistics." Doublet claimed, and I quote him because the logic escapes me, that

> since 1781 the figures [may] appear less advantageous, but in reality we have had more success. The reason for the discrepancy comes from the numbers who have died from illnesses other than venereal. That is easy to understand as the mortality becomes successively larger when calculated on the basis of one year after another [cumulatively]. This produces considerable difference

in the general outcome. For instance, of the 804 admissions to
this date [admittedly] only 152 remained alive in the month of
February 1785. However, by calculating the mortality rate on the
basis of infants born with syphilis who died between the ages of
six months to two years, one consistently arrives at a figure of
25% survival.

To do otherwise, he argued, was to present a false picture of the
number of deaths directly attributable to syphilis at Vaugirard.[33]
Thus in a general overview of seven hypothetical newborns admitted
to or born at the hospital, two died of either thrush or overall weakness, which prevented them from nursing, two more from congenital syphilis, and three were cured (although one of the three would
later succumb during convalescence before being weaned). This left
two of the original seven, which brought Doublet back to his claim
of 1781 – that approximately one-quarter survived. Since without
treatment it is likely that none would survive at all, Doublet's numbers can be read as a favourable outcome for the Vaugirard experiment. And indeed, in absolute numbers that was true. In 1781 there
were six who left the hospital in perfect health; in 1782 there were
fourteen; in 1783, twenty; and in 1784, forty-four.

Doublet did not feel any need to apologize – in fact his assessment
in 1785 concluded on a note of pride in past accomplishments, and
of optimism for future prospects. He reminded critics of the mitigating factors required to evaluate the relative success or failure of
Vaugirard's experiment. Among these were the quality of the women
who nursed the infants, the fact that almost no infants from the
foundling hospitals with congenital syphilis had survived in the past,
and finally, the high infant mortality in the general population, consistently around twenty-five percent. From this perspective he could
boast legitimately that in overall terms, progress was being made.

Even allowing for this increase in the number of survivors, it took
some ingenuity to describe it as a twenty-five percent rate. Nevertheless
the government continued to support Vaugirard until 1790. Doublet
predicted that in the future, work done at the hospital would not only
justify its existence but lay the groundwork for a larger and more extensive establishment devoted to the treatment of venereal diseases in
general.[34] In this last, at any rate, he was proven right.

Was Doublet being self-serving? We may take him at his word that
in 1785, he remained fully confident that Vaugirard was a worthwhile

undertaking. Undeniably, Vaugirard provided a unique opportunity to explore and understand syphilis and and also to research the causes of women's deaths from puerperal fever. What's more, while syphilis was the main focus at Vaugirard, the hospital also functioned as a pediatric hospital where other childhood illnesses that could affect the health and survival of a newborn were matters of concern and care.

Other Childhood Illnesses Treated at Vaugirard

Mouth infections, especially thrush, were of major interest because they left infants unable to nurse. Thus weakened, they died before they could be treated. Thrush was referred to as millet at Vaugirard because the flourlike pustules on the infant's mouth resembled corn-meal. Sometimes it was called, more poetically, *blanchets* (whites), or *muguet* (lily of the valley). Highly contagious, it first came to the attention of medical practitioners at Enfants trouvés in Paris in 1739. At the time it was attributed to corruption of the air when large numbers of infants were crowded together. Nevertheless, a new building on the Parvis of Nôtre-Dame with larger, well-ventilated rooms, could not halt the spread.[35] Joseph Raulin, a surgeon of the foundling hospital in Rouen, gave an early and definitive description of thrush in 1768. "It begins with a slight redness at the palate and tongue, followed by small pustules spreading through the mouth and thence the body as far as the stomach. Often within three days, the afflicted infant becomes emaciated and dies."[36] Confusion among medical researchers over whether it was caused by abnormalities within the victim, or by an outside source of a contagious nature, or both, delayed a definitive set of criteria for the yeastlike fungi. By the twentieth century, the disease had been assigned the generic term of candida. These eruptions, rather than congenital syphilis, were the main cause of death at the foundling hospitals of the time because the infants were unable to take nourishment.[37]

Thrush merited careful analysis.

The first signs appear within 3–6 days after birth when lips become pale and then take on a deep, almost blackish color ac-companied by redness at the anus. Next, one or two whitish outbreaks can be seen at the root of the tongue or the gums and within six hours these spread to the lips and inside of the cheeks. After 24 hours there are outbreaks all over the tongue, which

soon disappear, but reappear in a few hours deeper, more numerous and expelling a greenish discharge. At this point the infant
becomes agitated, feverish and is unable to nurse, extremely
weak, it soon expires.[38]

Post-mortem dissections revealed an eruption of white pustules from
the esophagus to the anus, often complicated by intestinal gangrene.
On rare occasions it could take less-lethal forms that were curable by
nursing or acidic throat gargles, light cordials or doses of camphor.[39]

It was almost inevitable that infants in close proximity infected
each other. "Children are like sponges who exhale and absorb excre-
tions from fermentations in the pernicious atmosphere around them,
in the same way disease proliferates among adults in armies, hospitals and prisons as contagion moves from one to the next in close
quarters."[40] The ideal solution was to keep infants isolated from one
another with a careful nurse, but that was, in practical terms, impossible. Without the option of prevention, the backups were fresh
air, spraying the room, cribs, and linens with vinegar, and, as a last
resort, moistening their mouths with an acidic disinfectant.

"Bad air" was commonly blamed, in accordance with the miasma
theory of the day. But Doublet recognized other factors with which
the modern reader can readily identify. He pointed out that a child in a
family setting is taken up in its mother's arms when restless and com-
forted by her warmth. As all animals shelter in the warmth of their
mothers, so an infant resting on the breast of his nurse is warmed by
her breath and absorbs the emanations she provides. A child left alone
in its crib can be exposed to a degree of heat or cold in the surround-
ing atmosphere that it cannot assimilate. As a result, the humours
needed for digestion are not stimulated.[41] "In other words, the best
remedy for this harmful malady is the breast of an attentive nurse."[42]

Doublet's point is clear: the infant needed individual attention
and loving care. Indeed, a chart prepared by Fernand Boussault (see
below) indicates that infants cared for by their own mother had a
much better chance of survival.[43]

In other words, only eighteen percent of these favoured infants
died, compared to an overall mortality rate of eighty-eight percent.

It is not surprising that thrush was the disease of foundlings.
Though it is not a psychosomatic illness, the pathetic situation of newborns abandoned to institutions like Enfants trouvés and Vaugirard
went a long way to explain why they so often lacked the will to live

Table 3.2
Mortality of infants nursed by their mothers (Boussault)

Year	Living	Deceased
1780	10	10
1781	49	8
1782	50	4
1783	56	9
1784	58	2
1785	48	12
1786	44	8
1787	68	16
1788	55	10
1789	52	12
1790	54	14

(assuming that it could make any difference with that particular illness). Ironically, the hospital that Colombier, Lenoir, Doublet, and Faguer Despérrières envisaged for curing newborns provided a setting that undermined their chances of survival – a realization that Doublet only gradually came to.

Jaundice was another ailment discussed in some detail at Vaugirard. It was attributed to the inability of infants to expel meconium from their system. Dissections revealed a blackish mass collected in the intestinal canal, a yellowish tint to cellular tissue, and an enlarged liver.

Chest ailments were especially dangerous for newborns. Sometimes simply coughs and colds turned out to be "stomach cough" or whooping cough. The remedy of choice was to induce vomiting. Emetics and laxatives, such as Glauber's salts, ipecacuanha, or kermes (an emetic based on antimony), could loosen up blockages of mucous humours in the chest, stomach, and intestinal canal. What struck Doublet (and his modern readers) was that chest problems were more common among the plumpest and apparently healthiest infants. This he attributed to overfeeding by "independent" nurses who neglected to subject charges to a strict and rigid regime.[44]

Teething was considered a disease in its own right. Convulsions (as distinct from epilepsy) were also diagnosed as a separate and highly dangerous disorder. For this, doctors prescribed treatments to calm the nervous system such as laxatives and, with more success, lukewarm baths. This latter remedy is still advised when an infant is susceptible to convulsions related to a high temperature. Doublet distinguished such convulsions from those presaging imminent death from inanition – the final stage of any number of the illnesses we have described.[45]

In the long run, Vaugirard must be evaluated in terms of its mandate and avowed purpose – saving the lives of infants with congenital syphilis. But understanding the nature of the illness was an important precondition.

BIOGRAPHICAL INFORMATION ON INFANTS OF VAUGIRARD

Origin of Infants

The records of Vaugirard hospital provide data not only on diseases but also their victims. The first group of 198 cases is for the early period when the hospital opened its doors in August 1780 until December 1781, and a second set of 307 cases pertains to the closing period of its operation from January 1788 to December 31 1789. These are the cases from which I have compiled tables 3.1 to 3.6.

The records give the age, gender, origin, parentage (legitimate or illegitimate), and fate of the infants. The names, occupations, and addresses of parents are also sometimes available. Thus, records of admission at Vaugirard included far more personal detail than those of other institutions at the time, which consisted of little more than an alphabetical list consisting of a series of names, as Charles Dickens describes in his novel *Oliver Twist*. In Spain's orphanages the saint of the day provided a convenient designation for infants who had been abandoned without a name.

In most cases (328), infants were admitted from Enfants trouvés. The next largest contingent (97) were born at Vaugirard itself, many with mothers who had been admitted from Bicêtre. Those from Hôtel-Dieu were relatively few (26), though it is likely that many newborns had been funnelled from there through Enfants trouvés. The rest came from Bicêtre (30) or were brought in by local health officials, usually through the parishes (29). Occasionally some were admitted directly by the administration.

Fate of Infants

Of course the overwhelming majority died, and it is only rarely that we can follow a child's history. One exception was François Denis

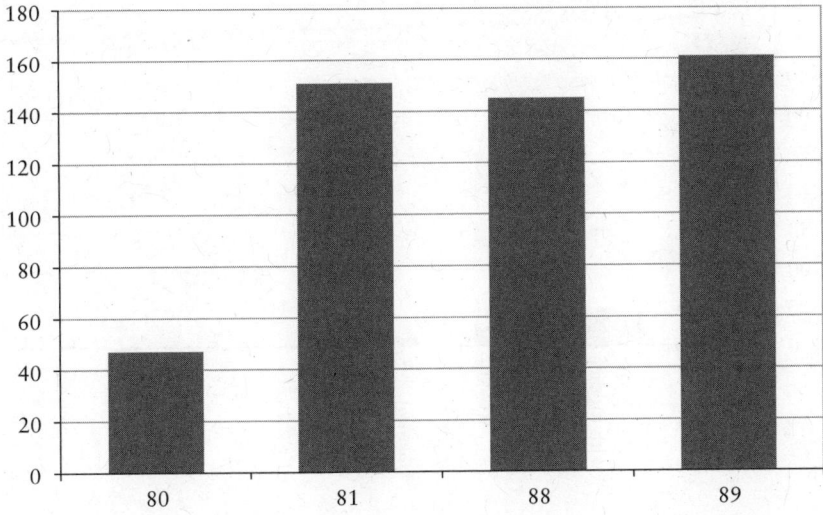

Figure 3.1
Year of admission of infants to Vaugirard

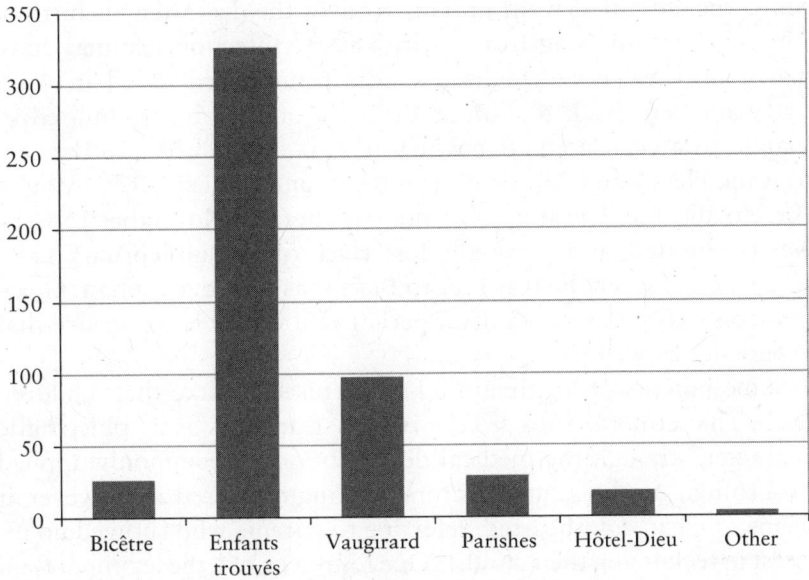

Figure 3.2
Origin of infants

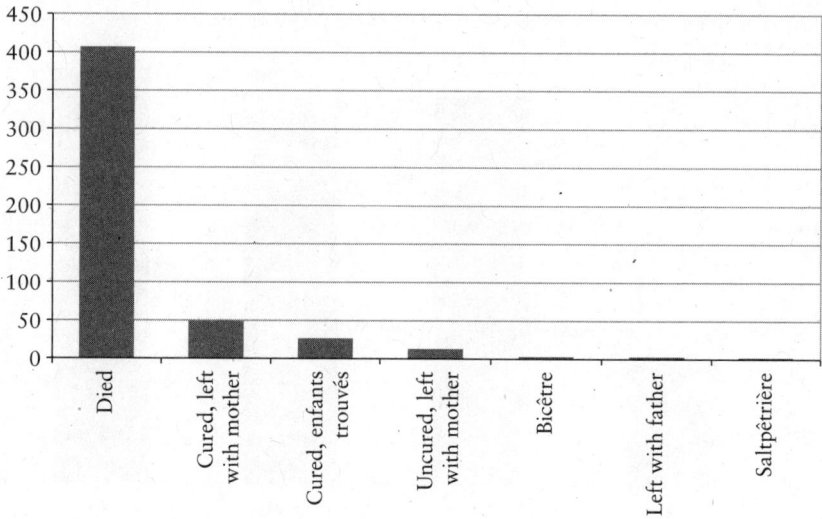

Figure 3.3
Fate of infants admitted to Vaugirard

Malherbe, admitted from Enfants trouvés the day after his birth in August 1780 suffering from a virulent eye infection. He may have had gonorrhea, not syphilis. He was pronounced cured in April 1784 and sent back to Enfants trouvés, only to be readmitted to Vaugirard a year later, after which he was dispatched into the care of Anne Fleury and J.B. Duport in the country village of Pauville in Perzeux diocese. The story does not end there. In November 1786 he was readmitted, and we finally lose track of him in February 1787 when, at age seven, he was sent to Bicêtre as an older orphan. Given François's remarkable stamina, perhaps he was able to survive that experience as well.

Some parents of legitimate infants refused to take their children back. The term *humeurs froides* usually translates as a "phlegmatic character," though the medical designation was commonly applied to scrofula. As the administrators of Vaugirard used it, however, it seems to mean cold-hearted, referring to parents who showed no interest in reclaiming their child.[46] One four-year-old, the legitimate son of a stonecutter in the parish of St Nicholas des Champs, Faubourg St Denis, was sent off to Salpêtrière after spending eight months at Vaugirard. Similarly, Claude Picard, another legitimate son of parents with "*humeurs froides*," was admitted in September 1788, then sent to Hôtel-Dieu in December with smallpox. In February 1789 he was readmitted to Vaugirard and eventually "cured." He also ended up at Salpêtrière. Joseph Marie Alexander Diverny was abandoned to Salpêtrière by his family after a sojourn at Vaugirard of almost a year, from April 1789 to March 1790. It may have been because his parents were separated. Or perhaps the marital arrangements were more complicated. The mother, Marie Louise Dumay, gave her address as rue de Verneuil, at the corner of rue de Bac; her husband, however, was an inspector at the Dépôt de Chalonne (military warehouse) in Champagne.

The case of six-year-old Marie Madeleine Bourgeois raises interesting questions. She was the legitimate daughter of a vineyard keeper near Dreux in the diocese of Chartres and had been admitted with her mother, Marie Madeleine Clairet, in April 1789 with the accompanying notation "famous." Why famous? Though I can only speculate, it is possible that the notation referred to a court case in which a wet nurse sued parents for hiring her for an infant with syphilis, which was then passed on to her own family. Such cases, which became more common as the years went on, are the subject of a later chapter.

Biographical information remains scanty because most of the subjects lived only a short time. Those with no caregivers were routinely sent to Enfants trouvés after their cure and from there were dispatched to rural nurses until they reached the age of four, or sometimes seven. The records do not usually give details for those sent out to nurse. On rare occasions a foster family would decide to keep a child, having formed an emotional attachment, but usually poor families could not afford the luxury of such sentiments, and the child was returned with alacrity to the institution when it was no longer eligible for financial support. After that, those who lived, approximately one-sixth of the original cohort, entered the hospice of La Pitié, or St Antoine orphanage, or one of the religious hospices where they were destined to be trained in some trade or sent to work in the country, or given to anyone who wanted them. A fortunate few, chosen for their looks, were accepted at the Maison de la Crèche or the hospice of St Esprit. They were then exhibited as "poster children," sometimes in public events to raise money for hospitals, sometimes in funeral cortèges. Theoretically, they were given the same education as those at St Antoine, but "they turn out much better because they have better care."[47] However, the findings of the poverty commission were not optimistic that survivors were being adequately prepared, either the physically or morally, to become productive citizens.

Table 3.3
Fate of infants, by year of admission

| | Year of Admission | | | | |
	80	81	88	89	Total
Died	41	140	109	115	405
Cured, left with mother	5	1	17	26	49
Cured, Enfants trouvés	0	10	13	4	27
Uncured, left with mother	0	0	2	11	13
Bicêtre	1	0	1	1	3
Left with father	0	0	2	1	3
Saltpêtrière	0	0	0	2	2
TOTAL	47	151	144	160	502

Table 3.4
Fate of Infants

	Frequency	Percent	Cumulative
Died	407	80,4	80,8
Cured, left with mother	49	9,7	90,5
Cured, Enfants trouvés	27	5,3	95,8
Uncured, left with mother	13	2,6	98,4
Bicêtre	3	0,6	99,0
Left with father	3	0,6	99,6
Saltpêtrière	2	0,4	100,0
TOTAL	504	99,6	

Age

One might question how accurately age could be assessed for newborns; nevertheless on admittance a date was usually assigned. The vast majority of the infants, 91.4 percent, were deemed to be less than two weeks old, and 77.2 percent less than a week old. Among the sample only fifteen infants were more than two years old.

The youngest to be registered at Vaugirard was Louis François, son of Christine Crapin from Bicêtre, who was born in September 1781 in *marasme* (inanition) and lived for only three days. He seems to have been the victim of an abortion. According to the notation beside his name he had been killed (*tué*) before term. The oldest was six-year-old Marguerite Victoire Pierre Faibess, whose father was

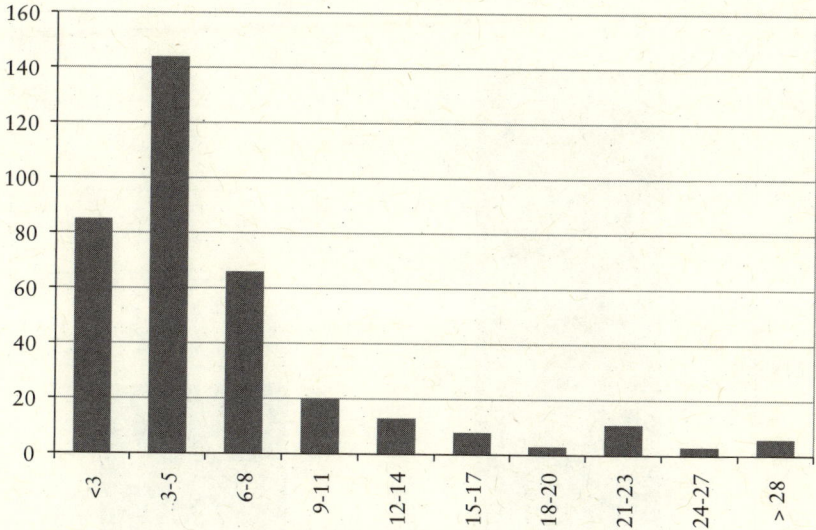

Figure 3.4
Age of infants on admission to Vaugirard (under 28 days)

a *Suisse à l'Intendance* – a soldier or guard at the quarters of the intendant. But the parents had waited too long to have her treated and she went home in March 1789, no better for two months in the hospital. Sophie Catherine Pelle, just under five years, and her sister, three-year-old Marie Julie, are unique in that they left with their father after three months at Vaugirard. There is no information about the mother, who may have succumbed to syphilis. Another four-year-old went home with her mother. In fact it was not uncommon for a married woman to bring her own older children with her when she came for free treatment for the syphilis she had contracted from a nursling or a soldier-husband.

Gender

Syphilis did not respect gender. Any distinction was slight: 262 males with the disease to 244 females, which may simply reflect the slightly larger proportion of males born in the general population. In most years of admission, more boys were admitted than girls, except for 1788 when there were noticeably more girls – eighty-two females to sixty-two males. One might speculate that the distress of the poor was exacerbated by the harsh conditions of 1788 that culminated in

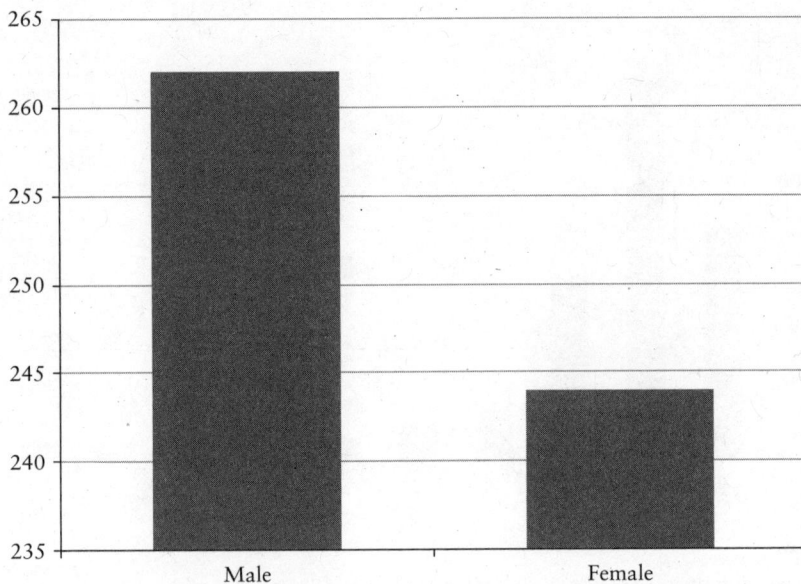

Figure 3.5
Gender of infants in Vaugirard

Table 3.5
Gender of infants

	No	%
Male	262	51.8
Female	244	48.2
TOTAL	506	

Table 3.6
Year of admission of infants, by gender

	Male	Female	Total
80	28	19	47
81	85	66	151
88	63	82	145
89	84	77	161
TOTAL	260	244	504

Table 3.7
Origin of infants, by gender

	Male	Female	Total
Bicêtre	15	11	26
Enfants trouvés	174	152	326
Vaugirard	44	53	97
Parishes	15	14	29
Hotel-Dieu	8	10	18
Other	2	1	3
TOTAL	258	241	499

Table 3.8
Fate of infants, by gender

	Male	Female	Total
Died	220	187	407
Cured, Left with Mother	23	26	49
Cured, Enfants trouvés	9	18	27
Uncured; Left with Mother	5	8	13
Bicêtre	3	0	3
Left with Father	0	3	3
Salpetriere	2	0	2
TOTAL	262	242	504

the events of 1789. Under such circumstances it is possible that poor families may have made the difficult choice of reducing the number of mouths to feed by packing girl children off to a foundling hospital. Nevertheless 1789 does not show signs of such a distinction on the part of parents.

Overall, more boys were admitted both from Bicêtre (fifteen boys, eleven girls) and Enfants trouvés (174 boys to 152 girls). The numbers among children admitted from parishes (fifteen boys to fourteen girls) and from Hôtel-Dieu (eight boys, ten girls) were not significantly different.

There is little evidence that one gender was favoured over the other when it came to families taking back an infant, a circumstance in itself unusual. Girls actually had a slight advantage of eight to five, which might only reflect that more of them lived to be cured (twenty-six girls to twenty-three boys). In accordance with the overall pattern of

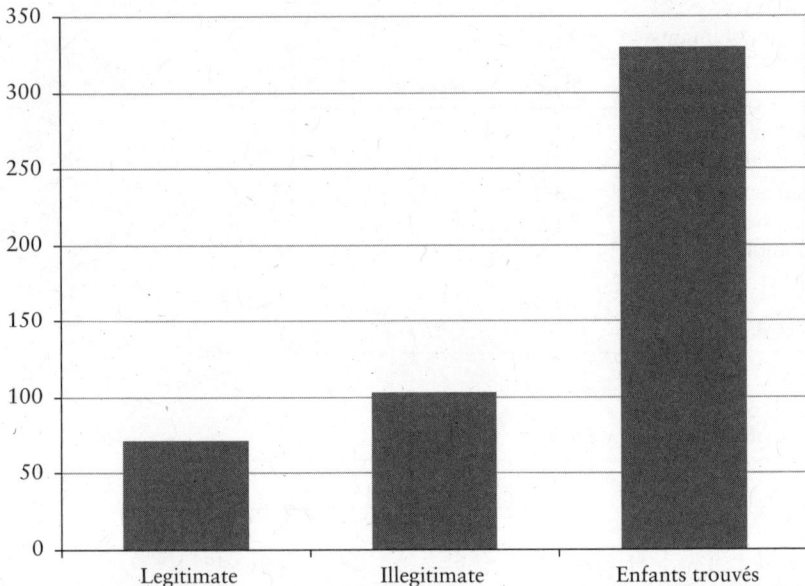

Figure 3.6
Legal status of infants

the population, more male than female infants died (220 to 187). On the other hand, the proportion of girls returned to Enfants trouvés was considerably higher – eighteen girls compared to only eight boys in the small sample of twenty-six cases. This could be interpreted as reflecting the relative value assigned to males in the society of the day, but overall the differences in terms of gender were too few to justify any significant generalization, other than that gender was not an important factor for the infants of Vaugirard.

Status

Infants of legitimate parentage made up only seventy-two cases in the sample, or 14.3 percent. This meant that 103 infants were explicitly termed illegitimate. On the face of it, however, this is misleading. Parentage data for admissions from Enfants trouvés were not usually given because it was the policy in such hospitals to protect the identity of single women. The rationale was to encourage abandonment as an alternative to abortion or infanticide. Therefore, I have separated those at Enfants trouvés from those whose status was clearly designated.

Table 3.9
Legal status of infants, by gender

	Male	Female	Total
Legitimate	39	33	72
Illegitimate	44	59	103
Enfants trouvés	178	152	330
TOTAL	261	244	505

Table 3.10
Legal status of infants, by year of admission

	Legitimate	Illegitimate	Enfants trouvés	Total
80	3	3	41	47
81	12	41	97	150
88	24	25	96	145
89	33,0	33,0	95,0	161,0
TOTAL	72	102	329	503

Table 3.11
Legal status of infants, by origin

Origin (hospital)	Legitimate	Illegitimate	Enfants trouvés	Total
Bicêtre	7	17	2	26
Enfants trouvés	3	6	317	326
Vaugirard	18	77	2	97
Parishes	28	1	0	29
Hotel-Dieu	9	2	7	18
Other	1,0	0,0	1,0	2,0
TOTAL	66	103	329	498

Throughout the decade, there were few changes in the legal status of the infants admitted. One exception was 1781 when the proportion of illegitimate to legitimate was noticeably higher (forty-one of the 153 infants admitted were illegitimate compared to only twelve legitimate infants in the admissions registers). Otherwise numbers remained stable and similar throughout the decade. Attention to status was scrupulous; it was even noted when a newborn was legitimized by its parent's marriage, no matter how long "after the fact" of its birth. When twenty-seven-year-old Louise Michel married her soldier of the guard, for example, the infant born in May 1782 was

categorized as legitimate by means of an amended notation of the
register of March 1788.

In estimates for foundling hospitals the proportion of legitimate
to illegitimate children is difficult to ascertain. In an earlier study
of abandoned infants, I estimated that in some years the numbers
could be almost the same for both groups.[48] This was most likely to
hold in periods of crop failure, war, or times of exacerbated distress
among the poor, whether married or unmarried. That is, as the price
of wheat rose, so did abandonments. The assumption is less likely to
hold at Vaugirard. One might expect that unmarried women would
be likelier than married women to produce a syphilitic infant. In
fact, when leaving the hospital, a single woman had to supply evidence of a support network before being allowed to take her child
with her. Today's welfare system, which encourages single mothers
to keep their children, reflects a more generous attitude.

Women admitted from parishes were more likely to be married
women whose charges had given them syphilis, which was then passed
on to their own families. These women, who were supplementing the
income of a poor family by wet nursing, were treated at the expense
of the city administration. This would account for the larger proportion of legitimate infants in that cohort. Similarly, as we have noted,
women married to soldiers were treated free of charge.

CONCLUSION

Dealing with syphilitic infants in large numbers in a specialized institution may have fulfilled the thirst for medical enlightenment in
the physicians involved, but it did little for their newborn patients
during the short term of their hospitalization at Vaugirard. Most infants with congenital syphilis died, and Vaugirard did little to change
that, though statistics indicate a slight improvement in the mortality
rates during the hospital's ten-year history. Since saving lives was
Vaugirard's raison d'être, how could it justify its existence when it
had so little impact on mortality rates?

Of the infants who survived, many ended up where they had started, at Enfants trouvés. There was little reason to be sanguine about
their eventual fate. Older infants without family could look forward
to a dismal future at the hospices of Salpêtrière, Bicêtre, or Pitié, or
the orphanage of St Antoine.

The success stories, mothers who left with their own infants after a cure, were usually married women who had been hired as wet nurses for syphilitic infants. Can we assume, as Doublet reluctantly did, that having a caring nurse, mother, or mother substitute had a greater impact on an infant's chances of surviving than the efforts of the physicians who were treating the infant's symptoms? At the very least it must be acknowledged that a clean, warm, and protective environment, however strictly regulated, in which both the mother-nurse and infant received a healthy and adequate diet, could only be beneficial.

On the other hand, mercury in any form was harmful. Inhalations were especially dangerous. It was assumed, in the scientific understanding of the day, that the amount of mercury ingested by the infants in their nurses' milk was relatively innocuous (that is, the proportion of mercury in the nurse's milk would not be sufficient to effect a full cure) and it was taken to be so throughout Vaugirard's term. For this very reason Doublet insisted that, in desperate cases, the mercury in nurses' milk should be amplified with doses by mouth. The result could be seen in digestive upsets, which then required a series of laxatives or emetics in order to mitigate the effects of the mercury. The opportunity to try any number of herbal and chemical remedies – sarsaparilla and marshmallow combinations were among the mildest – left the infants vulnerable to all the side effects that we now associate with new drugs and clinical trials. Admittedly, the prospects for these infants were not good under any circumstances.

So we are left with the question, was Vaugirard a worthwhile venture? For a dispassionate and reasonable summary of the Vaugirard experiment we have La Rochefoucauld-Liancourt's report to the poverty commission of the Constituent Assembly in 1790. The information was based on material supplied by Doublet himself. He pointed out that of the ninety infants who could be accommodated eight were unable to nurse, forty-two were being treated, thirty-seven were convalescing, and three were weaned and cured.[49]

The figures for mortality were harder to assess. Doublet claimed that two-thirds of the deaths at Vaugirard could be attributed to thrush, which made nursing impossible, or to congenital weaknesses other than syphilis. Almost one-quarter of all the infants treated at Vaugirard died during the course of treatment and one-third perished from one of the other childhood illnesses. Doublet insisted, however, this should not be seen as discouraging, because in the alternative settings of Salpêtrière or the Crèche, all the children died. And, as he pointed out, the survival rate at Vaugirard did in fact improve over the years.

Though Doublet did not say so explicitly, the numbers make it clear that the technology on which the hospital was based could not be adequately evaluated, given conditions at Vaugirard. That is, for the almost two thousand infants admitted over the years of its tenure, only slightly more than one-half (1,171) were able to nurse. Thus, the project on which the hospital was based, mercurialized breast milk, could not in itself be evaluated. And among the nurses only about half were well enough themselves to fulfill their nursing duties. Even within the hospital itself, the Vaugirard experiment had a limited impact.

In the manner of bureaucracies, the questions raised and conclusions arrived at by the poverty committee of 1790 zeroed in on the financial aspects of Vaugirard. Its final assessment was harsh. "At a cost of 500,000 livres ... the hospital has been able to save only 371 lives. But of those one-half, or perhaps two-thirds, will not reach an age to be of service to society ... to save more would double the cost, and then what kind of men would society acquire as a result? One can judge from the immoral and degenerate [abbatardée] race that emerges from the hospices." [50]

The negative, almost cynical tone of the conclusion handed down by the members of the poverty committee in 1790 stand in marked contrast to the high expectations that greeted the founding of Vaugirard in 1780. The reader may well agree with the committee's assessment, but before coming to a definitive judgment we must look at the other half of the human equation at Vaugirard – the wet nurses. Individual infants may not have been helped by the Vaugirard project, but from the standpoint of health, wet nurses fared much better. For many wet nurses, however, Vaugirard had serious and harmful consequences that unfolded throughout the nineteenth century. In the next chapter we will discuss the women who were a major factor in the experiment.

4

The Wet Nurse as Technology

The wet nurses at Vaugirard were of different ages and disparate backgrounds, but they shared two qualities: poverty and syphilis. In this chapter I look at the women whose bodies served as instruments for the advancement of medical science.

The wet nurses of Vaugirard were employed in an experiment to deliver mercury in their milk. They became receptacles for the prescriptions that were administered through them to infants with congenital syphilis. The Spanish physician Ruiz de Luzuriaga cogently described them as *"instrumentos animados"* (living tools).[1] Their role in this controversial exercise did not come to an end with the closing of the hospital. Throughout the nineteenth century, there were instances of wet nurses being victimized by families who hired them as human siphons, and by doctors who collaborated in the process. At Vaugirard they were also patients in their own right and received treatment accordingly, even if the principal focus was on the infants. There were numerous instances of nurses succumbing to puerperal fever at Vaugirard. As we shall see in this chapter, Doublet's approach to this malady as related to wet nursing seems to have been characteristic in France at the time, but not elsewhere. The term "medicalization" popularized in the work of Michel Foucault, Ivan Illich, and others has come to mean more than an event that first occurred in France at the end of the eighteenth century.[2] For Foucault medicalization evokes the growing power of physicians and surgeons over broad aspects of care, including the beginning as well as the prolongation of life. In the past, women had played a conspicuous role in health services as herbalists, midwives, bone-setters, and religious sisters who functioned not simply as nurses in hospitals but often as caregivers in the general community. This was particularly the case in rural France where their ministrations threatened the prestige and the pockets of trained medical practitioners.[3] But as physicians asserted their claim to scientific expertise over "amateurs," all this would change.

Obviously, women have benefited from the technological advances of modern medicine, but feminist historians have pointed out certain negative aspects. They argue that as doctors and surgeons began promoting their professional credentials, they manipulated, controlled, and reinforced a view of women that centred on their biological role as child-bearers[4] – a view that was by no means exclusive to the medical profession at the time.

What has gone unrecognized is the long gestation of the invasive technology of using women's bodies as an instrument for treating infants, as was done at Vaugirard. Women not only played a key role in the Vaugirard experiment but in a very real sense they became the technology. While the treatment process, particularly the passing on of mercury in their milk, was carefully monitored in the hospital setting, eventually it had serious health consequences for the women who became purveyors of this project in nineteenth-century France.

WET NURSING IN THE HOSPITAL

Nurses and Milk

Wet nurses were controversial figures in the plans envisioned by Enlightenment thinkers for a healthy and progressive France. Maternal breast-feeding played a significant role in their projections. They clearly believed that mothers who transferred their nursing function to a paid surrogate went against "Nature's" law and risked their own health and that of their offspring. Medical experts described paid wet nurses as unhealthy immoral women who profited from their milk at the expense of their own infants. It was assumed that through their breast milk nurses also passed on psychological traits (such as bad character) and the physical weaknesses that were often due to the poverty of their circumstances. Consequently, wet nurses were castigated for producing debilitated and degenerate citizens.[5] Nevertheless, wet nursing remained common in Europe and America until the advent of safe pasteurized milk at the end of the nineteenth century. The practice seems to have been more widespread and lasted longer in France than in other western European countries.[6] Hired nurses were the custom, not only for the well-to-do bourgeoisie but also for the working woman whose child depended on the milk of a woman who may have been only slightly lower on the economic scale. In nineteenth-century Lyon, for example, where large numbers of women were employed in the silk-weaving industry, seventy-five percent of newborns were placed by their mothers with rural nurses. Evidently, the number of women who nursed their own children was negligible.[7]

Despite the forceful critique of women who sold their milk, doctors had to take into account actual practice. For the well-to-do, the employment of a mother-substitute usually included consultation with the family doctor in an attempt to mitigate the dangers supposedly posed by the milk of a hired stranger. As a result the medical literature of the time, while encouraging maternal nursing, also gave advice to families on how to choose the ideal wet nurse. Along with physical qualities, her age, appearance, general health, and that of her own infants were evaluated, as were her moral qualities and character. Blondes were singled out as unsuitable because of their "excitable nature," which was apt to alter their milk; altered milk, in turn, had "been known to produce the death of the infants." Redheads too were rejected as being subject to sanguine humours that made them unfit nurses for young infants.[8] The doctor and the wet nurse were inextricably connected.

The pervasive denigration of wet nurses that suffused medical texts required modification, however, for Vaugirard's purposes. Doublet found himself exercising a form of mental acrobatics to make a virtue of necessity. In his revisionary script, the nursing experience itself was extolled as capable of producing feminine benevolence. He proposed that the very act of presenting a delinquent woman with a helpless newborn could bring to the surface the latent instincts it was assumed all women shared with lower animals. Milk – in this case mercurialized into medicine – was to become a healthful source of healing and renewal, not only for the syphilitic infant but also for the woman. Using debauched women as wet nurses could bring about their rehabilitation. Technology could transform both infants and their nurses into healthy productive citizens. The hospital, the infants, and society in general were to become the beneficiaries of the Vaugirard experiment.

Clearly, Vaugirard had moral as well as medical pretensions. Doctors at Vaugirard proposed controlling minds and hearts, not just bodies. In Doublet's words "they must be warmed by feelings of maternity ... inspired with zeal and affection, without which obedience to rules is only illusory." Severe treatment, he recognized, only irritated these undisciplined women. "Fear discourages them, but gentleness in applying rules, and persuasion that the good of the infants is in their own best interests ... are the means to *develop sentiments* without which the promise of the hospital cannot be attained."[9] Technology could modify and adapt what nature had produced and thus generate an improved and improving wet nurse. Vaugirard was to be the workshop for this new model of nurse.

Training the Wet Nurse at Vaugirard

The decade 1780-90, which ushered in the events of the French Revolution, has been depicted by scholars as the beginning of our modern age. Although it has inspired almost as many revisionists as historians, however, there is one group about whom we have more to learn – women of the poor. Olwen Hufton, Jane Abray, Natalie Zemon Davis, Harriet Applewhite, Darlene Levy, and, of particular relevance to this chapter, Rachel Ginnis Fuchs, have done much to expand our understanding of the lives of women of the French working poor. Nevertheless, there is still a great deal to be gleaned about women whose lives were not dramatized in the theatre of the streets.[10] For this largely anonymous group, life was a private struggle to keep themselves and their infants alive – a challenge they won or lost on a daily basis. If they were sick that struggle reached a point of crisis.

Doublet's account of the work at Vaugirard, along with the records of the hospital available in the archives of the Assistance publique in Paris, provide data that are not normally accessible, as they are for women of the French upper classes, or for women who were politically active. Because the women at Vaugirard were part of a clinical experiment, intimate details from their lives become available after two hundred years.

I have done an analysis of 302 of the 772 women who made up the complete contingent at the hospital. The first group were admitted during August-December 1780 and January-December 1781; the second were admitted in the last years of Vaugirard's tenure from January-December 1788–89 and January-March 1790.[11] Registers 6.1, 6.2, and 6.3 give names, ages, the institution from which a

woman was admitted, addresses, and occasionally the woman's occupation and that of her parents or husband. In exceptional cases,
i.e., those concerning women who were markedly better or worse
than the average, the records note their physical and mental health
and character, even their temperament and behavior. They also record dates of arrival and departure and give the reasons for leaving. A
woman may have been cured and her term of nursing completed, or
she might simply have refused to stay. Other women were dismissed
as unsatisfactory on any number of grounds, from being physically
unable to nurse to exhibiting incorrigible behaviour. Those who died
were as likely to be victims of puerperal fever, which often accompanied childbirth in maternity wards of the day, as from venereal
disease or its treatment. The fate of the deceased's newborn was
noted as well. This information, supplemented by Doublet's account
of his interaction with the nurses, in particular his *Observations* of
1785, have left brief but vivid vignettes of a few days or months in
the lives of a group of poor women in Paris at the end of the eighteenth century.[12]

As Doublet was in a position to know, using women to further
medical progress could be frustrating. The women he described with
considerable insight were not passive entities following a fixed routine of medication and waiting patiently for the outcome. But for the
doctors of the hospital, the problems presented by the *animados* in
the experiment provided a challenge, not an obstacle.

The vaunted rehabilitative quality of women's milk (theoretically
that of the mother) was to be put to the test through the nurses at
Vaugirard. Milk was depicted as having curative qualities for simple
childhood illnesses. But the ideology of the Enlightenment carried this
one step further: milk was nature's way to improve the human species. The expectation was that nursing a newborn would produce (or
reproduce) the motherly virtues that were part of "Nature's" design.

Natural instincts, however, were not easy to foster in a setting that
was far from natural. As we have seen, while Vaugirard operated as an
innovative clinic, it continued to incorporate the punitive apparatus
that characterized hospices of the day. A rigid routine could bring out
the worst in women who were ill-adapted to a life of rules and regulations. In such a situation, how could one generate enthusiasm and
dedication? In monastic fashion each activity of the day was marked
by a bell. From rising at 5:30 A.M. in summer or 7:00 A.M. in winter
to bedtime at 9:00 P.M., the nurses were under constant supervision.

They were forbidden access to the patios or kitchen or anywhere vigilance could not be maintained. Time away from infants was taken up with household tasks: sewing, or knitting stockings (for which they were given a slight compensation amounting to the value of the product). Recreation consisted of the gentle exercise of walking in the garden or in the enclosed promenade for an hour after their main meal and supper. The young ones had to be restrained from running about. Outside visitors were permitted only with a signed form from the administrators. There was little in the daily routine to promote a sense of fulfillment or responsibility; rather, it was a round of onerous chores centred on a succession of diseased and dying infants.

The medical men involved with Vaugirard had bought into a highly unrealistic set of expectations: that women suffering from the effects of misery, often with concomitant degradation, could become caring and careful wet nurses. An idealized mother-child model was inappropriate from the start. Nurses were exposed to a series of infants, many with symptoms that were frightening as well as physically revolting. Watching a nursling waste away and die did little to foster the sentiments Doublet had hoped to find in his wet nurses. Even the Spanish doctor Ruiz de Luzuriaga, an enthusiastic supporter of the project, recognized that a woman with a succession of newborns dying at her breast was unlikely to gain from the experience a sense of self-worth or confidence.[13] Where was the incentive to form attachments to infants that were likely to die despite their efforts? Doublet was forced to admit "with horror,[that]some women have fallen to such a degree of deprivation that maternal sentiments, innate in all women and animals, have been eradicated from their hearts, or so weakened as to have the same effect."[14]

Doublet's observations scarcely gibe with the account written by René Bertin in 1810 about the venereal diseases hospital in the Faubourg St Jacques, which continued the practices used for infants at Vaugirard. Bertin describes the wet nurses as "tender, gentle and sensitive, devoting all their time to their own infants and those assigned to them and overcoming disgust and repugnance to mourn the many deaths that occurred."[15] Is it possible that Bertin had an ulterior motive for producing a more positive evaluation of the wet nurses at his hospital?

In Doublet's experience, "when infants are strangers to the nurse, when hideous and disgusting symptoms repel them, or when a nurse of little strength and intelligence has several infants die at her breast, it can be impossible to revive her courage and hope."[16] Unwed nineteen-year-old Marie Elizabeth LeBrun, admitted by Doublet personally in December 1789, left in despair after she lost her own infant at birth and then the foundling she had nursed for over two months. Madeline Vacquez was described as "having become insane" after a term of eight months and was sent to Hôtel-Dieu for treatment. Twenty-three-year-old Elizabeth Latouche, married to a soldier, was described as "depressed" and would not stay after her newborn died at two weeks. Catherine Houdin, aged twenty-seven, gave birth to twins in 1783 both of whom died within two days. She slipped under the barrier and threw herself into the well of the garden where she drowned.[17]

For someone already physically stressed, an environment devoted to the care of dying infants was hardly conducive to mental health. It was not unusual to be assigned a series of foundlings from Enfants trouvés, only a few days old, and have one after another die before the week was out. On occasion, one woman might have the care of three who were too weak to take the breast, but the usual procedure was to nurse her own and one other. Many simply refused to stay. One evening in October 1782 Rosalie Petitjean, daughter of a grape grower in the diocese of Senlis, went over the garden wall at 6:00 P.M. Two nights later twenty-one-year-old Madeline Tissoriot did the same thing. Twenty-eight-year-old Elizabeth Saulnier from Bicêtre "escaped" after six days. Others left as soon as their child was born. Some took less-direct routes: Louise Anne Fouquet received permission to leave to settle her affairs and then did not return. Rather than confront authority directly, many chose a form of passive resistance and lost their milk.

There were those who allowed an infant, even their own, to die from neglect. Whether a woman had done so overtly or surreptitiously, the consequences of being found out could be serious and the woman sent back to the unspeakable conditions of Bicêtre, or the prison-hospice of Salpêtrière. This happened to eighteen-year-old Marie Francoise Alboret, whose newborn died at three months from lack of care. Marie Lalire was dismissed in January 1789 and a note appended to her record stating that she should never again be admitted to Vaugirard under any circumstances, because she refused to nurse her own newborn.

About thirty percent of the women left as soon as their symptoms disappeared and they were deemed cured; only twenty percent saw out an eighteen-month term. Ten percent left on their own and almost as many, seven percent, were dismissed as unsatisfactory, either because physically they were unable to nurse (two percent) or because the matron and staff found them too insubordinate to deal with. In other words, only about one-half of the women admitted to the hospital were able to "be of some use to the matron"[18] by fulfilling the expectations of the hospital and functioning within the paradigms outlined by the medical and administrative staff.

In 1937 Fernand Boussault, in a study of abandoned infants in France that made use of the archives of Vaugirard, listed the reasons why nurses left.[19] Table 4.2 shows some overlap between nurses who were dismissed as incorrigible (*mauvais sujet)* and those sent to other institutions for any number of reasons including an inability to nurse, or a need for more intensive treatment for syphilis. Women who were too weak to nurse or who needed stronger therapy were sent back to Bicêtre. Others, deemed too difficult to control, were dispatched to Salpêtrière or to the prisons of Santé or St Martin. At that, many may have found it psychologically necessary to distance themselves from their distasteful and depressing charges. Nor was this difficult to do when given care of a foundling – a stranger already rejected by its own mother.

Having reconciled himself to his failure to arouse maternal feelings in his wet nurses, Doublet invoked a more materialistic approach. Administrators at Vaugirard found that rivalry had a more salutary effect on difficult or recalcitrant wet nurses than scolding and reproaches. There was more success with competition where women attached much value to compliments on their zeal, courage and cleanliness. Competition was encouraged by a system of rewards and punishments. "Nurses who cared for infants other than their own were recompensed at seventy-two livres per month at the end of their terms, with an additional forty sols per month for a second infant. They were also given fifty-two sols monthly for those with one infant and eighteen sols monthly for a second infant to recompense them for small expenses needed for cleanliness for the infant."[20] A summary prepared under the chairmanship of La Rochefoucauld-Liancourt for the poverty committee of the constituent assembly in 1790 explicitly credited Doublet as the source for its information on Vaugirard.[21]

Table 4.1
Fate of nurses admitted to Vaugirard 1780–82 and 1788–90

	0	80	81	82	88	89	90	Total
Died	0	1	8	1	1	7	1	19
Cured	0	14	39	33	7	24	3	120
Sent away	0	2	6	8	1	2	2	21
Term complete	1	0	1	2	21	22	11	58
Unable to nurse	0	0	1	1	12	8	8	30
Wanted to leave	0	0	4	8	4	13	5	34
Remained in hospital	0	0	3	3	0	1	0	7
Became insane	0	0	0	1	0	0	0	1
TOTAL	1	17	62	57	46	77	30	290

Table 4.2 (Boussault)
Wet nurses of Vaugirard Hospice, 1780–90

Year	Nurses	Bad Character	Sent elsewhere	Escaped	Cured	Died	Stayed as employee
1780	19	2	0	0	14	1	2
1781	62	5	2	1	39	10	5
1782	56	8	5	3	34	2	4
1783	76	7	9	2	50	5	3
1784	78	5	15	6	44	6	2
1785	73	7	6	1	49	6	4
1786	71	7	8	0	49	4	3
1787	97	4	5	2	74	8	4
1788	74	2	0	0	69	2	1
1789	84	4	1	1	69	7	2
1790	79	3	2	0	67	5	2
TOTAL	769	54	49	16	558	57	32

There were also women for whom the hospital refused recompense because their work was deemed unsatisfactory. Elizabeth Claude Bouchard, a twenty-year-old embroiderer of lingerie who was herself a foundling, was refused pay because she was "indocile and impertinent," despite having taken care of seven infants, two of whom lived. When she left in March 1782 after finishing an eighteen-month term, she was still not cured of syphilis nor her bad attitude. Attempts to "train" the wet nurses were unsuccessful for the most part.

Table 4.3
Origin of nurses, by year

	80	81	82	88	89	90	Total
Hôtel Dieu	3	34	40	22	31	13	143
Bicêtre	12	9	3	6	8	4	42
Santé	1	1	3	0	0	0	5
Parish	2	10	8	18	33	11	82
Saltpêtrière	0	4	1	0	2	1	8
Pitie	0	2	0	0	0	0	2
Saint Martin	0	1	0	0	0	0	1
Other	0	0	1	3	6	2	12
TOTAL	18	61	56	49	80	31	295

Doublet's Account of the Wet Nurses

Some nurses adapted to the system to the point of identifying with the authorities and chastising their weaker sisters, but they were an insignificant minority. In his account of 1785, Doublet presented detailed insights into the day-to-day operation of the hospital. He slotted the fifty to sixty-five women he estimated to be in residence at any one time into five different groups, only one of which approached the ideal type he envisioned. The actual numbers he cited do not necessarily correspond with those in the admission registers. Thus, according to the figures in his account for the poverty committee, the number of nurses admitted over the whole period came to 703; the admissions registers of the hospital total 772 or 769 in Boussault's account.[22]

The first group came from the lowest strata of society. A debauched way of life (thanks, presumably, to prostitution) had taken its toll on their physical condition and morals. Despite their youth – the women in this group were all under twenty-five years of age – many had undergone mercury treatment on more than one occasion. They were often unattractive and ill-natured as a result of neglect and poor health. A few were vicious, others merely thoughtless and careless. Physically, they might vary from lazy and listless to strong and energetic. Mentally, they exhibited similar diversity: some were intelligent and proficient, others stupid and dull. But they were all hard to control. They were disrespectful of the matron and several were expelled, having been deemed more trouble than they were worth. There were women in this group who had themselves been abandoned at birth. One such, Madelin Nessir, had been raised by a farm family in the Dauphine. Though not cured, she was unwilling to stay at Vaugirard and was described in the records as vain and lazy. Of course, there were women in this category who did not conform to type. If someone was fortunate enough to have her own child survive, or if she had become attached to a foundling, then she might turn out to be a good nurse. This raised hopes among the administrators that a few of the 112 women in this group who were admitted each year might yet become respectable.[23]

On the other hand, the hospital had absolutely no success with the few women (an average of eight per year according to Doublet) who were admitted from the middle class. Disowned by their families, their lowered circumstances were reflected in their state of mind. While a privileged upbringing enabled them to present an accommodating facade, they were far from dependable. Gentle and compliant throughout their pregnancies, they showed no interest afterwards in contributing to the hospital. They concocted excuses to get out of their tasks, and their superior airs and complaining made them insufferable to their companions. Accustomed to a comfortable standard of living, the nourishing meals and security of Vaugirard did not compensate for confinement and burdensome chores. These nurses were so repelled by the infants with their disfiguring symptoms that they could not bring themselves to care for them. Some just took off without warning. In the end the hospital had to resign itself to doing without middle-class women as wet nurses.[24]

The women in Doublet's third category made no pretence of cooperating with the authorities at Vaugirard. They were homeless (vagabondes), dull girls from some rural backwater (villageois stupides). Many had spent time in hospices, which had done nothing for their character. They were either incapable of nursing or unwilling to try. Appeals to their self-interest ended in frustration: being treated well seemed to make no difference to them whatsoever. They were willing to put up with the discomfort of overloaded breasts rather than relieve them by nursing, and they could not be persuaded that this practice risked serious illness.[25] They were hopeless in every sense of the word. Perhaps exhausted by the mercury treatments that many had already been subjected to at Bicêtre, they delivered infants that were often premature or stillborn. They themselves sometimes wasted away from puerperal fevers. Their numbers were mercifully small – only a dozen annually.[26]

Those who fulfilled Doublet's highest expectations were also rural women, many admitted from Hôtel-Dieu where they had given birth. They had been driven to the capital by economic need, or to escape the shame attached to some indiscretion. In Paris they found low-paying work, often as servants – an occupation that in itself could expose them to sexual exploitation. For such victims of some un-fortunate liaison, or perhaps rape, the wholesome diet and routine of the hospital provided a temporary relief. These women viewed their confinement as an opportunity to regain their health, and with it, their natural good spirits. Neither likely to be chronically diseased nor morally corrupt, they were anxious to be cured. Doctors were understandably enthusiastic about them. They were gentle, careful, clean, and responsible. They were able to feel tenderness for their miserable charges, and to be saddened when they died. Some took on infants that others had rejected and spoon-fed them for weeks at a time. Doublet singled out women from Alsace for their particular ability to transcend their environment and even demonstrate some gaiety. Julienne Fleith, a twenty-three-year-old who went on to nurse seven infants after her own died at eleven days, was an example of how hard-working such nurses could be. We can assume they were exceptional among the poor, unhealthy, and disadvantaged who largely made up the contingent. Fortunately for the hospital, the women of this group, willing to be generous with each other, their superiors, and their unfortunate charges, numbered about twenty to twenty-five, approximately one-third of those in the house at any given time.[27]

While they may have benefited from the hospital experience, the competence of these women owed little to it, though Doublet had hoped otherwise. He was sensitive to his subjects' faults and vir-tues; but he was also blinded by his faith in medical progress and his commitment to the methods employed at Vaugirard. He could not see that the characteristics that made this cohort successful had nothing to do with Vaugirard and its methods. They were the result of basic good health, a willingness to work hard, and the ability to adjust to difficult living conditions, circumstances to which many rural women were accustomed.

In sharp contrast was a special group of women who were com-pletely unsuited to the hospital environment. Married to artisans, soldiers, or day labourers, they had contracted syphilis from their husbands, or from an infected infant they had been hired by a family to nurse. Their expenses at Vaugirard were paid for by the army, the town, or their local parish, and they were under no obligation to take on another charge. They came with their own infants and sometimes with their older children as well. Though treated with consideration, they often became despondent and homesick. Institutional rules, incompatible companions, and a weakened condition induced in them a profound melancholy. By Doublet's account, only four or five of these unhappy women were admitted over the course of the year. Few of them stayed, probably because they had the option of returning to a family. Their contribution to the hospital was minimal.[28]

Given the variety of personalities and backgrounds assembled in confined quarters, it is not surprising that tensions were high. Disputes arose between factions and individuals; women from Bicêtre, for example, often had to be segregated from their more "respectable" sisters. There were quarrels over status and over the few privileges that long-term residents might gradually gain. There was also rivalry for some of the healthier and more appealing infants. The success of the Vaugirard project depended very much on cooperative wet nurses, but there were serious problems in finding women ready to carry out difficult and unpleasant duties in an exacting and rigid environment. Only about one-half to one-third were capable and willing to nurse, which in itself subverted the aims of the hospital.[29] According to the La Rochefoucauld-Liancourt report, the hospital could accommodate sixty-nine women at a time. Of this number, thirteen might be pregnant, twenty-nine in treatment, twenty-four convalescing, and three sick and incapable of nursing. As the report also pointed out, however, the actual number of women accommodated at Vaugirard at any given time averaged closer to fifty (slightly more in the winter). Of those fifty, only twenty-nine were capable of nursing. This number could be responsible for around forty-two infants, which meant that most women had only one nursling at a time. Infants were weaned at eleven to thirteen months, but the women's treatment usually lasted four months, so the few infants who completed their terms at the breast would have been taken care of by more than one nurse.[30]

An essential component of the Vaugirard experiment, the nurses could also be a major impediment to its success. Nevertheless, those few who adjusted and became good nurses left the hospital with a certain confidence and attractiveness, and with their vitality and *fraicheur* (freshness) restored. Perhaps because their health was closely

monitored, Doublet credited Vaugirard for making it possible for a
small segment of disadvantaged women to take up their lives again
with serenity and self-respect.[31] The experiment may have had a
positive impact on a few of the wet nurses subjected to the system
set up by Colombier and his colleagues to mercurialize their milk.

BIOGRAPHICAL INFORMATION

The 302 notations from the admissions registers are in two sets,
covering the 135 nurses admitted in the opening period from August
1780 to 30 December 1782, and the 160 admitted during the closing
years from 1 August 1788 to 30 November 1790. The last admission was on 29 March 1790, though a few supplementary details
were recorded after the official closing, as for Marie Marguerite
Caillet, for example, wife of a soldier of the guard. She had been
admitted on two occasions with syphilitic infants, one who died on
29 December 1788, and another who succumbed in January 1791.
In general, the women had a much better chance than their infants
of surviving. The numbers involved, while not valid from a statistical
viewpoint, provide additional information of an anecdotal nature
on the women and flesh out the categories that Doublet described in
more general terms.

Origins

Hôtel-Dieu. Almost half of the admissions to Vaugirard (143) came
from Hôtel-Dieu's maternity wing for poor women. They had already delivered syphilitic infants and were unavailable for the prep-
aratory treatment on which the medico-clinical experiment was
based. The vast majority of this group (seventy-five percent) were
single and of those who were married, four were widows. They were
young, some of them very young, with two-thirds aged nineteen
to twenty-nine and only one-sixth in their thirties. Twelve of the
women in this group were deemed too weak to nurse, but more
than half (thirty-eight out of sixty cases) were considered in good
physical condition. This gave them an advantage over the women
from Bicêtre who had already undergone debilitating treatment.
They were also in better health than those who came from parishes;
it is possible that syphilis had been detected in the maternity ward
and was not well advanced.

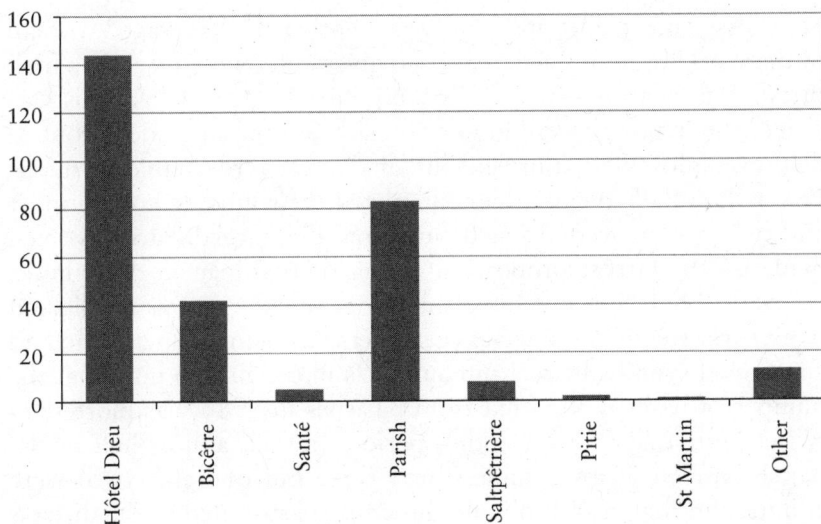

Figure 4.1
Origin of wet nurses 1780–82 and 1788–90

Thirty-three of the women in this group finished out their term of nursing, fifteen refused to stay and did not complete treatment, and twelve had to be dismissed as unsatisfactory for reasons other than health. Forty-two left cured. On the other hand, more than half those who died at Vaugirard were from Hôtel-Dieu – not disproportionate given their overall numbers. As discussed below many deaths may have been the result of puerperal fever for which Hôtel-Dieu was notorious.[32] Their numbers peaked in 1782 when they made up almost three-quarters of admissions. Dora B. Weiner discusses the Port Royal Maternity Hospital in Paris which was set up in the renovated former Oratory and monastery of Port Royal between 1796 and 1797. There conditions for pregnant women were much improved over Hôtel-Dieu. Nevertheless only 13.8 percent of newborns in Napoleonic France went home with their mothers after delivery, compared to twelve percent in the prerevolutionary period. This was unquestionably related to the high rate of illegitimacy at the time.[33]

Parishes. The second major cohort of eighty-two women, or 27.5 percent, came from various rural and urban parishes. Their backgrounds may have been relatively stable, since they were not usually homeless. They came closest to representing the "average" woman of the working poor. They had been given references by their parish priest or a local official such as the police. In cases where this was noted, the majority were in good health but, in an evident contradiction, almost half (thirteen out of thirty) were unable to nurse. Fewer than half (twenty-one) completed their nursing commitment and twenty-four were deemed cured and discharged. Parish women made up the largest proportion of married women in the sample, i.e., almost half. It is not surprising, since the hospital was obligated to give free treatment to wives of soldiers, or to any woman who had contracted syphilis by wet nursing. It is interesting to note that the number of women admitted from parishes in 1789 was more than twice the number for any other period. In fact, almost half of the parish women in my sample (thirty-three out of eighty-two) were admitted in that year. Probably this can be attributed to the distress of the poor, including the married poor, compounding the stress already felt by syphilitic women. It raises the question why there might be more syphilis among the general population during a year of such political significance.

The numerical records from the sample of the archives indicate that there were far more admissions from parishes than the four or five per year specified by Doublet. In one respect, however, the two versions are consistent: these women made up the largest contingent of those who refused to remain. Perhaps the married women had some independence, and an alternative to confinement. They were similar to the women from Hôtel-Dieu: neither had the characteristics for which women were originally to be recruited, and they were therefore ineligible for the experimental aspect. They often arrived shortly after or just before delivery, sometimes bringing along their older children and were among the group Doublet considered to be of little use to the hospital.

Bicêtre. When Lenoir and Colombier drew up their plans for Vaugirard, the model they had in mind for their wet nurses were women from Bicêtre. Faguer Despérrières had been its *gagnant maitrise*, or senior surgeon in charge of students. As we have seen, he was credited with conceiving of the Vaugirard project as a solution to the difficulties he experienced in treating pregnant women and syphilitic newborns under the conditions that prevailed at Bicêtre. Though making up only 14.2 percent of the sample, these women were in many ways the control group and could be monitored from their admission at seven months. They were already undergoing treatment for evident symptoms and were not free agents, since their only option was to return to Bicêtre. But that rarely dampened their spirits. Street-smart and toughened by their way of life, the women in this group were the hardest to manage, and many posed discipline problems for their superiors. Even the healthy ones who were fulfilling their duties often had "good nurse but impertinent" on their record. One woman was described as making "*sottises*," indulging in silly or insulting behaviour. "*Mauvais sujet*" (bad character) was a common annotation. Sent back as incorrigible were Catherine Bernard, who lost her milk "through her own bad will," and Catherine Bouchard, who was described as "dirty both personally and with infants, quarrelling with comrades and causing an uproar in the whole house." We have already met Marie Lalire, who was dismissed for refusing to nurse her own infant, and who was never to be readmitted to Vaugirard. Louise Henriette Mea, a married twenty-five-year-old, was too fond of wine (to indulge this taste in the hospital setting required some ingenuity on her part).

The women from Bicêtre tended to be younger than the other nurses: six of the sample were under the age of nineteen, only four were over thirty, and none were older than thirty-two. Most were unmarried (thirty-three out of forty-one). Physically they were in relatively good health; only four were unable to nurse, four died, and almost half were cured. But clearly they did not live up to the hopes of the founders. Some women were said to have become "institutionalized"; that is, they had adjusted so well to the secure and sheltered environment of the hospital that they chose to remain at Vaugirard as servants or laundresses. No one from Bicêtre took that option. Completing a nursing term meant a ticket to freedom, an objective that only one-quarter of admissions from Bicêtre attained.

The hospices of Salpêtrière and Pitié, the prisons of St Martin and Santé. The sample from these places was small. Those with actual criminal records were from St Martin or Santé, while Salpêtrière was a virtual prison for homeless women. Marie Marguerite Morin, who "stole underwear and clothing," was sent to the "*maison de la force*," or prison section of Salpêtrière. None of these women were married. Their overall health was generally good: only one was unable to nurse, and five of the eleven left cured, "*allaitement fini*" (their term of nursing completed), their period of restriction over, and free to go.

Table 4.4
Reasons for leaving, by origin of nurses, 1780–82 and 1788–90

	Died	Cured	Sent away	Term complete	Unable to nurse	Wanted to leave	Remained in Hospital	Became Insane	Total
Hôtel Dieu	11	60	12	26	12	15	4	1	141
Bicêtre	4	22	3	7	4	2	0	0	42
Santé	0	3	1	0	0	0	1	0	5
Parish	2	24	3	18	13	15	2	0	77
Saltpêtrière	1	2	1	3	1	0	0	0	8
Pitie	0	2	0	0	0	0	0	0	2
Saint Martin	0	1	0	0	0	0	0	0	1
Other	1	6	1	3	0	2	0	0	13
TOTAL	19	120	21	57	30	34	7	1	289

Character

Character was a matter of importance to the administrators of Vaugirard. Notations in the registers allowed the matrons to vent their frustration, particularly when a nurse deliberately refused to cooperate by neglecting to nurse her own infant. One senses the irritation in such remarks as *"mauvais sujet,"* or even *"très mauvais."*[34] Occasionally, as we have seen, there was the further injunction "and never admit her again under any circumstances." This happened with Jeanne Huygeny, who arrived in December 1781 at the age of twenty-two but left in her ninth month, uncured. When she reappeared in September 1784, again eight and a half months pregnant, she was turned away. Women who purposely lost their milk were expelled, even when their cure was not complete.

In some cases a nurse who was lazy and uncooperative might be tolerated, apart from the note by her name. With Charlotte Quenón, for example, insolence in the "good nurse" was indulged, as well it might be; for after losing her twins at birth, she wet nursed two foundlings and dry nursed ten for a record number. (All of her charges died.) Allowances were also made for Jeanne Meygannie, who was a "good nurse but muddle-headed." Less generosity was shown Marie Anne Tetrault, who was described as "weak both mentally and physically." Boussault's account lists fifty-four out of 769 nurses as *mauvais sujets*. In my smaller but more detailed sample, more than twice that many, i.e., fifty-nine of the 302, were given bad

Table 4.5
Reasons for nurse leaving, by year

	80	81	82	88	89	90	Total
Died	1	8	1	1	7	1	19
Cured	14	39	33	7	24	3	120
Sent away	2	6	8	1	2	2	21
Term complete	0	1	2	21	22	11	57
Unable to nurse	0	1	1	12	8	8	30
Wanted to leave	0	4	8	4	13	5	34
Remained in hospital	0	3	3	0	1	0	7
Became insane	0	0	1	0	0	0	1
TOTAL	17	62	57	46	77	30	289

notices. More women were deemed unsatisfactory and "sent away" in the first period, 1780–82, than in the second – sixteen individuals as compared to five. This may have balanced out with the numbers who voluntarily chose to leave. Thus, in the heady days of 1789 only two nurses were dismissed, but thirteen took their fate in their own hands and found means to depart.

Three of the women in the house from September 1782 to April 1784 were specified as "good nurses but subject to drink." Married thirty-six-year-old Angeline Duvau was too fond of eau de vie, and thirty-one-year-old Anne Marie Rigolet was able to "smuggle alcohol with the help of comrades."

In all fairness, the director also recognized the "good nurses," or even just a "good nurse for her own." In exceptional cases there might be a note such as "good nurse, very sweet."

Age

The vast majority of women admitted to Vaugirard ranged in age between twenty and twenty-nine: two-thirds of those in this category were from Hôtel-Dieu, and one-third from Bicêtre and the parishes. Many teenagers were from the parishes. They were single, usually on their own in Paris, having been attracted to the city from some rural area.

Of those under twenty, the youngest was seventeen. This group had the most difficulty adjusting to the hospital routine. Eighteen-year-old Marie Ann Debudé from Hôtel-Dieu, seven months pregnant, was

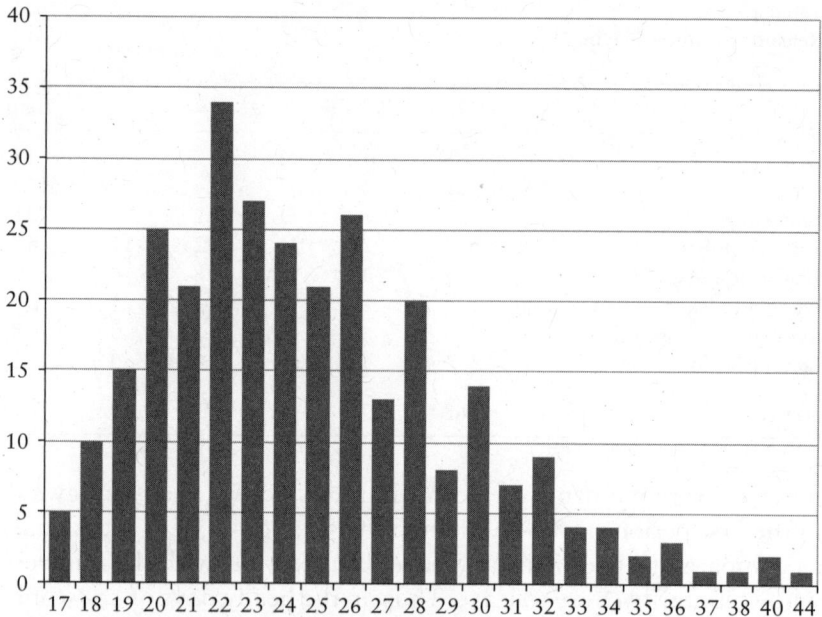

Figure 4.2
Age of nurses on admission to Vaugirard, 1780–82 and 1788–90

sent back to Bicêtre immediately after delivering a stillborn infant. Marie Derablée left on her own as soon as her infant was born, as did the "*très mauvaise et insolente*" (insolent and extremely difficult) Victoire Horsner. Eighteen-year-old Marguerite Constance Gruel was sent away because she refused to nurse a foundling after her own was stillborn. The servant, nineteen-year-old Marie Jeanne Villette, would not care for her own newborn. Impertinence was noted in seventeen-year-old Marie Rose Basse from Bicêtre, but she finished her nursing and left cured after a year with seventy-two livres in pay. One nineteen-year-old was not pregnant when admitted in December 1789; unusually there were no details given, but she remained for five months. Only five of the sample of twenty-eight women under twenty earned the designation "good nurse."

Marguerite Laurent, the oldest at forty-four years, married, and admitted by police order, was not expected to nurse. She spent three months and left cured, as did forty-year-old Marie Madelon Girot, who came with two children. At thirty-eight, Jeanne Dumont, wife of a *terrassier* (construction worker), was the oldest woman to deliver an infant at the hospital and was described as a "good nurse for

Table 4.6
Age of nurses admitted from Hôtel-Dieu, Parishes,
and Bicêtre, 1780–82 and 1788–90

Age	Hôtel-Dieu	Parish	Bicêtre
17	3	1	1
18	3	5	1
19	7	3	4
20	10	10	3
21	9	8	1
22	15	6	11
23	14	9	3
24	13	7	3
25	12	1	3
26	19	6	2
27	4	4	3
28	8	9	
29	6	2	
30	7	4	2
31	4	3	
32	4	3	2
33	2		
34	1		
35	2		
36	2	1	
37	0		
38	1		
40	1		
44	1		

Table 4.7
Age by Origin (totals)

Under 20	Hôtel-Dieu	13/146
	Parishes	9/82
	Bicêtre	6/42
20–29	Hôtel-Dieu	104/146
	Parishes	60/82
	Bicêtre	31/42
30–39	Hôtel-Dieu	23/146
	Parishes	11/82
	Bicêtre	4/42

her own." There were many examples of women who had probably been infected by their husbands or a nursling.

For at least a few women, Vaugirard provided an alternative to the unsettled and violent life that might await them on the streets of Paris. There was unmarried forty-year-old Marie Marguerite Catherine Simmoneau, for whom the hospital proved to be a haven. She stayed as a "*sevreuse à Compter*," keeping track of weaned infants, and was commended as a "*bon sujet*" (good character). Marie Anne Cirou, herself an orphan, born in Picardy, had spent six months in Paris as servant when she was admitted with symptoms of syphilis and then found not to be pregnant. Despite being weak physically, she was kept on as a serving girl. Similarly, thirty-five-year-old unmarried Catherine Morel, though incapable of nursing, stayed on to work with weaned infants. Twenty-five-year-old Madeline Voilant could not nurse because of "putrid fever" but after recovery she too remained to do ironing. Not all those who stayed on were older; Augustine Champaigne was only twenty when she opted to continue in the hospital as a servant in the sleeping quarters.

Others were not free to make such a choice. Twenty-six-year-old Marie Louise LeFêbvre had spent eight months in St Denis working in a hostelry when her father insisted she leave with him. She had only been at Vaugirard a month when her mother died and, sick or well, her father had once again insisted that he needed her at the farm. Perhaps the women who gave false names were hoping to forestall such an eventuality, or possibly, like Marie Veronique Cignières, daughter of a schoolteacher in Picardy, they might be attempting to protect the good name of their family.

Occupation

Occasionally nurses listed an occupation – servant, laundress, seamstress, employed by a lawyer or businessman – but most had no such notation and were probably either prostitutes or unemployed.

Marital Status

By far the majority of wet nurses were single. Around ninety percent of the women from Hôtel-Dieu and Bicêtre were nominally single. As noted earlier, the largest proportion of married nurses were admitted from parishes, a contingent that was likely to include women who had been employed as wet nurses and been unfortunate enough

Table 4.8
Occupations of nurses

Blanchisseuse	(laundress) (2)
Bl. Gazier	(laundress of stockings, lingerie)
Brodeuse	(embroiderer) (2)
Couturier	(dressmaker) (3)
Cullotière	(breeches-maker)
Cuisinière	(cook) (3)
Domestique	(household servant) (2)
Femme de chambre	(maid-servant)
Fil à crêper	(thread or yarnmaker or perhaps hairdresser)
Fruitière orange	(orange seller)
Garde malade	(nurse, caregiver)
Lavandreuse(sic) à chambre garni	(laundress in lodging house)
Ouvrière en linge	(linen worker)
Servante	(waitress or barmaid)

to contract syphilis from an infected nursling, or from a husband (often a soldier). The records were much concerned with legal status; hence those adjustments to the records, written years after the fact, noting that a relationship had become regularized and thus officially recognized by church and state, or the refusal to allow a woman to leave with her own infant if she could not show means of support from a family or spouse. Even during the brief period in which the government of the Revolution recognized illegitimate children as "*enfants de la patrie*" (children of the state), the single mother had few resources she could turn to for assistance. There was no revolutionary legislation recognizing "*mères de la patrie.*"

NURSES AS PATIENTS

Symptoms and Treatment of Syphilis

Vaugirard hospital can be seen as a prototypical example of the practice of clinical medicine at the end of the eighteenth century in Paris. Under the aegis of Colombier, Doublet, and Faguer Despérrières, it represented a stage in the evolution of the clinic of today. Women's syphilis was observed carefully, and as with the infants, other signs of illness were also scrutinized. The symptoms detailed in the records of admission under the name of the woman, date of admission, conditions under which she left, etc. are presented in table 4.10.

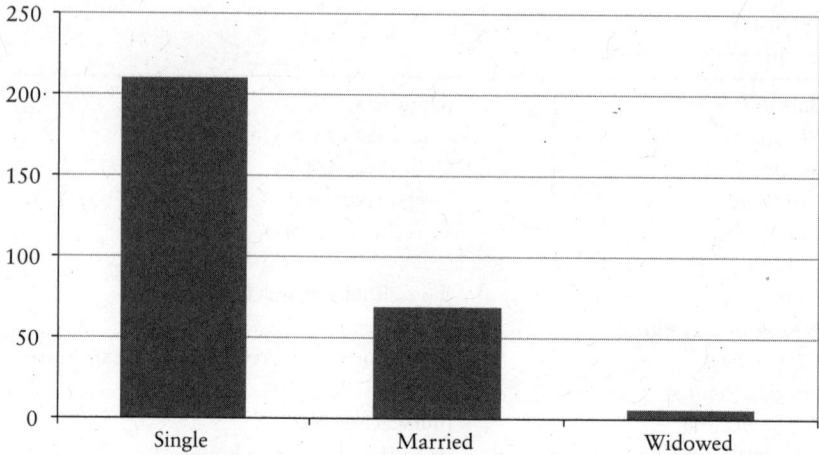

Figure 4.3
Marital status of wet nurses, 1780–82 and 1788–90

Table 4.9
Marital status of nurses, by origin

	Single	Married	Widowed	Total
Hôtel Dieu	103	29	3	135
Bicêtre	32	7	1	40
Santé	3	2	0	5
Parish	53	24	0	77
Saltpêtrière	7	0	1	8
Pitie	1	1	0	2
St Martin	1	0	0	1
Other	7	6	0	13
TOTAL	207	69	5	281

Even those in relatively good health provided a challenge to the doctors. In the registers of admissions there were 115 notations concerning nurses' physical characteristics. Sixty-six of the women with notations, or 57.4 percent, were considered healthy. The meaning of that is open to question since all were suffering from syphilis. For Doublet, it meant that they were well enough to care for infants and make a positive contribution to the work of the hospital. Close to one-half (forty-eight women, or 41.7 percent) were in a poor state. They were enervated by misery, poverty, and the illness itself. Doublet performed his own triage, classifying their conditions

Table 4.10
Symptoms of syphilis in wet nurses

ANUS total cases	65	Nymphes-suppurating of	1
Inflammation	17	labia/minora	2
Chancre	2	Uretha (urinary inf.)	1
Poireaux (vegetations or		Flat pustules	16
wart-like excrescences)	6	Crêtes	
Choufleurs (vegetations or			
wart-like excrescences)	4	MOUTH total cases	17
Ulcerated pustules	12	Inflammation	4
Crêtes(sic) execrescences		Swollen tongue	1
resembling a cock's comb	16	Glands	4
Bubons (buboes, open sores)	8	Tonsils	5
		Throat	3
BREAST total cases	11		
Inflammation	4	PAIN total cases	4
Chancre	1	Inflammation	4
Ulcerated pustules	3	SKIN total cases	25
Abscess	1	Inflammation	3
Tumor	1	Poireaux	4
Buboes(open sores)	1	Ulcerated pustules	1
		Buboes	1
FACE total cases	7	Scabs	2
Inflammation	3	Pustules on body	10
Inflammation of eye	2	Gales (itchy rash)	4
Eyelids	1		
Nose	1	GONORRHEA cases	190
GENITALS total cases	175	Inflammation	185
Inflammation	38	Virulent discharge	5
Chancre	48		
Poireaux	26		
Choufleurs	7		
Ulcers	36		

as *febrile* (fever), *saburres* (maladies indicated by foul granular matter in the stomach, contracted from vermin and lack of hygiene), and *faiblesse* (overall weakness).

The first group were subject to intermittent fevers that might last throughout their term of pregnancy, despite treatment with laxatives of bitters or quinine. *Saburres* were indicated by loss of appetite, nausea, and diarrhea. Women thus afflicted were treated with rhubarb, light purges, and emetics of one and a half grains of manna and ten grains of ipécacuanha. A third group suffered illnesses of general debilitation: convulsions, digestive obstructions that might cause swelling and diarrhea, and chest ailments producing "*ca-chexie*" (probably tuberculosis). Women in this group were consti-tutionally incapable of nursing. Treatment relied on strict cleanliness and nourishment, occasionally supplemented by absinthe, rhubarb, quinine, or the lancing of ulcers. Many more women were unable to nurse in the second period (twenty-eight out of thirty) than in the first, when there were only two. This might simply reflect the distress experienced by the poor in Paris in the years 1789–90 (see table 4.2). Boussault's account of mortality figures, however, indi-cates that mortality was highest among nurses at Vaugirard in the year 1781 (ten deaths among sixty-two women). Doublet took pride in the fact that the number of deaths declined as the years went on.

To improve the overall health of the women for safe childbirth and subsequent nursing, Doublet advocated gentle remedies – *ana-lyptiques fébrifuges* (restorative roots like sassafras) and tisanes (herbal teas) – but did not exclude massages or plasters of mercury. He resorted to bleeding when blockages, hemorrhaging, or high fe-ver called for it. Sometimes he prescribed, sensibly, additional meat for those in a depressed frame of mind.

But not all births went well. Loosened wombs had lost their elasti-city. Many deliveries were premature and proceeded quickly because infants were small. Stillborns were common among those suffering from depression, or *langueur*. Doublet blamed imprudence in the young and active as a factor in miscarriages.[35]

Then there were specific problems related to venereal disease. Ulcers and large tumours in the vagina could cause pain so disabling that the woman could not walk or sleep. They made childbirth atrociously painful, even dangerous. Doublet had some success with applications of mercurial ointment, but when strong doses were required it was hard to prevent salivation, indicating that the amount was danger-ous for pregnant women.[36] Other symptoms that were apparently less frightening could be more serious. These were flat black pustules and venereal scabs, swollen glands, throat ulcers, or gonorrheal dis-charge, accompanied by a rapid pulse, dry skin, and stomach upsets. The routine massages and mercury baths, if they were of more than normal intensity or if the woman was weak, could cause abortion. Bitters (herbs or roots in alcoholic spirits) and anti-scurvy tonics were considered safe. The afflicted women were often too weak to nurse or lacked energy to try. In any event, Doublet feared that their humours had been so corrupted that their milk would do the infants no good.[37]

Doublet and Faguer Despérrières remained absolutely convinced of the value of mercury, though they were willing to experiment with the dose. Mixing mercury with sea salt yielded *sublimé corrosif*, its most potent form, which was considered useful for very stubborn outbreaks of a large hard slow-growing tumour called *Squirreuses* (scirrhus), a cancerlike form of sclerosis in which the tumour contracts the cellular tissue. "Some can be cured with three-four ounces of mercury, others required stronger doses, or additional remedies along with the mercury."[38] Treatment began with baths, followed by frictions. Women with strong fibres, indicated by dry skin and a cold temperament (again in humoural terms), were afflicted with a nervous or irritable disposition. Frequent mercury baths were prescribed. That these sometimes caused headaches and pain in the eyes or kidneys was not taken as a disincentive. Tonics were found more appropriate for women with soft, weak fibres. Other remedies were plasters or liniments to melt tumours and decrease swellings at the anus and vulva. Doublet mercifully allowed time for such outbreaks to dissipate gradually, instead of attacking them with scissors or a caustic solution.

The basics of treatment were described as "mixed," i.e., mercurial baths or massages with mercury ointment, other sudorifics, and laxatives. Doublet provides the recipe for a sarsaparilla tea he found successful when the virus did not respond to a long regime of mercury. It consisted of large portions of aromatics, purgatives, honey, and sugar, mixed to the consistency of syrup. Usually at the end of four to six months of this regime the women were considered cured and no longer given syphilitic infants to nurse. For the remainder of their term they "dry nursed" infants who were so generally debilitated that they were too weak to take the breast.[39]

The cure could be as traumatic as the symptoms. One married woman exhibited a variety of outbreaks, the most dramatic being a hard tumour on her jaw the size of two fists. She did not take her medicine quietly. When *emplastrum de Vigo cum mercurio* (a mercury poultice) was applied she became impatient after three months and removed it. On exposure to the air the tumour hardened, though her other symptoms had responded to treatment. When the poultice was reapplied the tumour shrank, but in its place came an explosion of new outbreaks. This time she was given a series of "mixed treatments" for a month. After that she submitted, only reluctantly, to a third application of the poultice, which she viewed, not illogically, as

having activated the symptoms. This time the tumour was successfully extirpated, but not without some recurrence of other eruptions.
On this occasion they were minor and she was deemed cured.[40]

With simple abscesses due to inflammation, rather than tumours,
as they would normally be characterized today, the relentless cycle
of one symptom after another might signal that the infection was
resurfacing. However, according to to-day's practitioners, the rationale for the mercury poultice as treatment for a hard tumour remains
as difficult for the modern reader to understand as it was for the
patient herself who found the treatment unhelpful to say the least.

Doublet described another case of heroic treatment. Marie, a single
woman from the Champagne region and a "good nurse," had a chancre on the roof of her mouth and a gonorrheal discharge. Ointments
brought on an abundance of acrimonious outpouring but after several months this "salutary" release stopped and the chancre reappeared
in a more virulent form. Five weeks of mercurial baths, skin treatments in the strongest form of sublimates, and gargling with turpentine only weakened the patient more. The ulcer spread over the entire
upper part of her mouth and into the pharynx. Nevertheless she did
not give up nursing, and finally Doublet's other option, the sarsaparilla syrup, produced renewed evacuations that had some impact on
the ulcer. Swallowing became easier; in two weeks she was able to
take solids and a month later she was pronounced cured.[41] Marie
could be considered one of the success stories.

Puerperal Fever at Vaugirard

An assessment of the hospital must also take into account the lives
of the women it could not save. Their deaths were usually attributed to phthisis (consumption) or to hydropsy [dropsy], or, most
commonly, to a difficult delivery or to puerperal (putrid, or childbed) fever.[42] The latter often occurred among women who had given
birth at Hôtel-Dieu. This was consistent with the insights of Ignaz
Semmelweiss of Vienna and Alexander Gordon of Scotland, who saw
a pattern of contagion among patients of *accoucheurs* practising at
lying-in hospitals or, less frequently, among patients of midwives.[43]

Before the role of bacteria came to be understood by Louis Pasteur
and Joseph Lister, doctors and medical students moving from dissections in the laboratory to patients in crowded maternity wards
often spread "childbed fever." Modern medicine ascribes the disease

to a bacterial infection (Beta haemolytic streptococcus, Lancefield Group A).[44] Among its symptoms are fever, abdominal pain accompanied by nausea, vomiting, diarrhea, delirium, and a drying up of milk.

Vaugirard gave Doublet the opportunity to observe and experiment with illnesses other than syphilis in wet nurses as well as infants. His diagnosis of puerperal fever depended not only on the usual humoural explanation but on his first-hand experience with post-mortems carried out at Vaugirard. As Irvine Loudon points out, continental theorists in the early eighteenth century believed that puerperal fever was due to the suppression or retension of the lochia, or postpartum discharge. This explanation was gradually replaced by the theory of "retropulsion," also called "milk metastasis," or the "translation of the milk," which seems to have gained solid confirmation in the winter of 1746 during an epidemic of puerperal fever in the lying-in wards of Hôtel-Dieu in Paris that killed almost all the women who contracted the disease. As at Vaugirard, post-mortems at Hôtel-Dieu revealed a substance in the womb resembling putrified milk.[45] It was assumed that the staunched humour had not been able to make its salutary progress from the womb to the nipples, a malfunction that was attributed either to the woman's being too weak to nurse, or to her wilfull rejection of her lactation function out of vanity, ignorance, or sheer perversity.[46] Nursing with mother's milk was considered a logical scientific and medical requirement for the health of both mother and child.

Retropulsion has a long history going back at least to the medical texts of the Renaissance. Illustrations of the time, and one vivid depiction of the female anatomy by Leonardo da Vinci, show veins or tubes running from the uterus to the breasts. Their purpose was evidently to allow for the transformation of menstrual blood into milk during pregnancy for the nourishment of the embryo. After delivery, this same source became the "white blood" of the lactating mother in order to continue its health-giving role for the newborn.[47] As late as the end of the eighteenth century Antoine Petit (1722–1794), a respected professor of medicine in the Paris Faculty of Medicine, described the infant as a parasitic plant sucking blood for its development. In his words the embryo "milks the womb" in order to prepare the organisms of both mother and child for the postnatal lactation process.[48]

Long after post-mortems had discredited the existence of a direct route between the womb and the breast the theory continued to

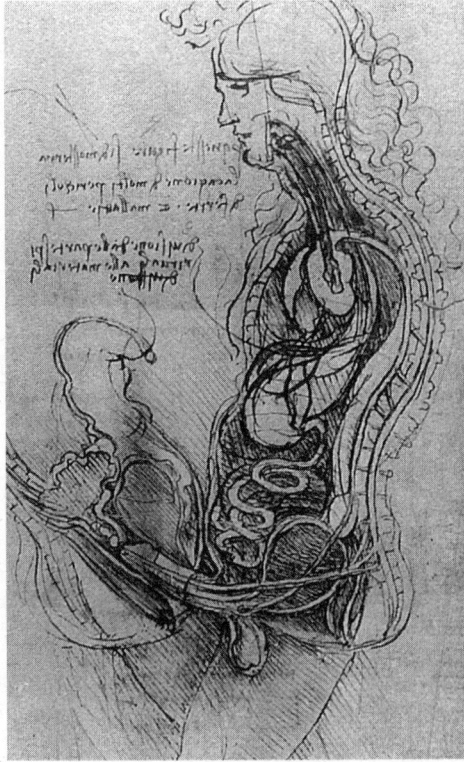

Coition of a Hemisected Man and Woman (c.
1492), by Leonardo da Vinci, depicting veins
connecting womb and breasts of woman.
(Coupe verticale du coït ©Luc Viatour www.
lucnix.be)

resonate. In the later interpretations chyle (fluid consisting of lymph
and digested food material from the intestine) was considered to
be the source of nutrition for the infant, distributed through the
woman's anatomy through the circulation of the blood.

Medical literature from the seventeenth century was based on a
mechanistic view of the body that can be traced to the influence of
the French philosopher René Descartes and the famous Leyden medical
professor Hermann Boerhaave. Boerhaave had trained many physicians
throughout Europe, including England and Scotland.[49] At the time of
the establishment of the medical faculty at the University of Edinburgh
in 1726, all five medical professors were former students of his.

Perhaps the most explicit working out of mechanistic physiology is found in the writings of Boerhaave's pupil Julien Offray de La Mettrie, author of *L'Homme Machine*.[50] But the *femme machine* was no less impressive. As Boerhaave described it, the female circulatory system was a kind of hydraulic device consisting of a complicated set of canals and tubes bearing fluids for reproduction, nutrition, elimination, and lactation. In this context, puerperal fever was considered to be the result of a "blockage" in the flow of milk in the postpartum woman. In the female machine, milk drove the motor.

Doublet's analysis attempted to discern a clear set of principles – in keeping with the humoural theory of the time buttressed by the mechanistic thinking of Boerhaave – for the cause of puerperal fever. He concluded that it was related to the role played by lacteal humour in the postpartum woman.[51] Of course, Doublet was already convinced that the source of the illness was "a retropulsion of the lacteal humour." He had performed enough dissections to know that tubes or veins directly connecting uterus and breasts did not exist. Like most French physicians, however, he believed the woman's circulatory system provided the route of humours between the breast and uterus. By a mechanistic interpretation of the body, this was not illogical. As a result of his diagnosis Doublet focused on stimulating the (re)appearance of the nursing woman's milk. This was consistent with one of the humour's essential attributes – its mobility.[52] This presupposition was to send him off relentlessly tracking symptoms wherever and however they showed themselves. It would take a radical rethinking to turn the focus from the woman's physiology as a milk-producing entity toward the doctor as a bacteria-bearing entity. It is more than likely that Doublet himself was the source of contagion as he visited the postpartum ward after one of his sessions in the dissecting room.

In 1781 an eighteen-year-old nurse became a victim of Doublet's hunt for symptoms. Her milk dried up ten days after delivery and a breast tumour caused breathing difficulties. A month of treatment decreased the size of the growth, and in keeping with the retropulsion theory, some of the humour took the course of a milletlike eruption on the skin, while some found its way into the urine. An (unspecified) "imprudence" halted this beneficial development, and a breast tumour reappeared. Doublet took drastic measures, even by today's standards. He performed an operation that opened up the lumbar (spinal) region to allow drainage of "lacteal pus." He credited this dangerous procedure with saving her life, but recovery was slow. It was two months before she could leave her bed, and her thigh and leg were still affected. Doublet was encouraged to see that the nurse's urine remained milky. Finally, a rash of red and flour-coloured eruptions assured him that five months of heroic treatment had succeeded. Only a young, relatively strong woman could have endured and survived the procedure.[53]

Doublet brought a similar diagnosis to a condition that he described, rather oddly, as a "plethora of milk." Anne, a healthy twenty-three-year-old, gave birth on 2 February 1782. The next day found her seated on her bed, in poor condition, her face red, her eyes inflamed, her head aching, burning with strong fever, short of breath, and suffering a sharp pain in her side. Doublet immediately began bleedings but without complete success. He redoubled his efforts, however, and the next day her milk appeared in abundance and she broke into a heavy sweat. The stimulation that induced her milk, he was convinced, succeeded in breaking her fever before it developed into what he had presaged to be a full-blown, perhaps mortal, case of puerperal fever.[54]

For Doublet, nursing was absolutely essential for the postpartum woman's health. But despite his urging, given the condition of the afflicted woman, nursing was sometimes beyond her strength. In several nurses, infection had infiltrated their lungs and they suffered other painful symptoms, including vomiting. Acceding to Doublet's exhortations required a great deal of courage. He was convinced, however, that perseverance in nursing could save his nurses' lives.

Rose C. bolstered Doublet's case for the maleficent effect of retropulsion based on his observations at Vaugirard. "Seized with disgust," Rose had difficulty in nursing. Cuts on her breast (conceivably to encourage the milk to rise) only increased her repugnance. Fever developed, accompanied by diarrhea and nausea, but she still showed no enthusiasm for nursing. Though the illness made slow progress, she died on the thirty-third day after delivery. A post-mortem verified for Doublet what he had expected to find, i.e., the presence of several pints of milky substance containing cheeselike flakes in the abdomen.[55]

In August 1782 the breasts of Marie M. remained empty after birth, though she attempted to nurse her infant. Finally, she succeeded and her milk returned, though she still had to endure a long convalescence. In another typical case, a thirty-year-old woman, sanguine and attractive, had a happy delivery when the postpartum discharge suddenly diminished. Some women were called in to assist in bringing on milk by suction, and medication was also given. The latter brought on spasms and pains in her lower stomach. By the third day she was in mortal straits. For this, her foot was bled and she was given laxatives. On the seventh day, sweat broke out, producing discharges from all parts of her body, until "other symptoms" (presumably benign) and the lochia returned.[56]

Such a regime required not only fortitude and a strong constitution on the part of the woman but considerable stubbornness on the part of the doctor, as one set of symptoms dissipated, only to be replaced by a new cycle of symptoms. It is interesting to note that doctors today believe that an insistence on nursing is a reasonable course of action in the case of breast abscesses caused by inflammation.

While advances in medicine have discredited the retropulsion theory as an explanation for puerperal fever, Doublet nevertheless earned his footnote in the history of the illness. J.J. Leroux, author of the third volume of *Cours sur la généralité de la Médecine pratique et sur la philosophie de la Médecine*, had himself attended many of the examinations and post-mortems Doublet held at Vaugirard. The author credited Doublet with showing that very few cases could be described as "putrido-adynamique" (exhibiting suppurated outbreaks and debilitation) but were usually highly inflammatory, reacting to infection with irritation, redness, and swelling. Inflammation called for bleeding and anti-phlogistines (calming solutions), rather than the purges and emetics that were usually administered at Hôtel-Dieu.[57] In this context, Doublet counselled moderation and warned against using leeches on the abdomens of women in a debilitated condition.

Leroux's letter to Doublet's grandnephew in 1825 acknowledged that attributing puerperal fever to a deflection of milk was an error. At the time, however, it was an understandable error since a chemical analysis of the affected membranes in the abdominal deposits indicated certain similarities to soured milk. What Doublet observed at Vaugirard in the post-mortems carried out on women who had succumbed to puerperal fever led him to mistaken conclusions. His methodology in coming to this conclusion was based on dissections, which provided the scientific basis for the analysis of puerperal fever in treatises of the late eighteenth and early nineteenth centuries.[58]

On issues other than puerperal fever, Doublet was on firmer ground. As we have seen, he brought an insight that would have important ramifications when it came to the nineteenth-century debate on the contagious nature of congenital syphilis. He pointed out that about one-third of women admitted to Vaugirard from the Parvis of Enfants trouvés (the section of Hôtel-Dieu devoted to abandoned infants) arrived with an ulcer on the breast and noted, among other things, if a healthy nurse suckles an infected infant, the first sign that she had contracted the illness was a suspicious outbreak on her nipple. With considerable prescience he stated, "These considerations could perhaps throw some useful light on medico-legal questions relative to this subject."[59] The implication is that as early as the 1780s there was perhaps already some legal controversy over the issue of contagion between infants and nurses. In fact, Doublet in 1785 had pinpointed the crucial symptom that was to become an important factor in the debate dividing prominent members of the Paris medical community in the 1850s.

Doublet also claimed that at Vaugirard he was able to disprove certain "popular errors" that worked against the use of purges on women during the last months of pregnancy. He himself saw nothing wrong with administering emetics as early as eleven to twelve days after childbirth, in order to prepare women for anti-venereal medication. This presumably referred to the custom of waiting for the period of "churching" of postpartum women who suffered from "unclean" humours.[60] He had no patience with "childish ideas" based on a religious interpretation of the woman as "unclean" that prohibited medical interference after childbirth until the lochia ceased.

In general, Doublet's practices at Vaugirard concerning puerperal fever were typical of the "enlightened physician" in France, but they differed considerably from what went on in Britain. Among French doctors and in French treatises the emphasis on the role of milk was pervasive. Irvine Loudon points out in his collection of the principal treatises on puerperal fever that, just as Doublet did, "accoucheurs of France believed puerperal fever was a variant of milk-fever, due to 'milk metastasis' (because putrifying milk from the breasts was carried in the bloodstream to the abdominal cavity)." But, he adds, "although the French held to this until at least the end of the eighteenth century, it never took hold in Britain."[61] This is borne out in a recent article by Christine Hallett discussing the influence of inflammation theory on the understanding of puerperal fever in eighteenth- and early-nineteenth-century Britain. In an extensive survey of the British medical literature, Hallett found no evidence relating puerperal fever to lactation problems. The only citation that could obliquely be interpreted as referring to the milk thesis occurs in a footnote that mentioned William Fordyce's suggestion in 1777 that putrid fever (among other causes) "might simply be the result of the suppression of fluids or of obstructed perspiration."[62]

The sources consulted by Hallett do not include references from France except for the two that had been translated into English: Jean Astruc (1684–1766) and François Mauriceau (1637–1709).[63] Astruc's and Mauriceau's contributions are not explicitly referenced, moreover, since they did not play a major role in British treatises dealing with puerperal fever. The question remains, why did the fixation on women's lactation coalesce into a recognized medical construct in France while playing no role in the medical analysis of the illness in Britain?[64] Why were Astruc and Mauriceau, though available in English in numerous translations, discounted by British authors?

Astruc has given one of the earliest accounts of the symptoms and course of the disease. His observations do not differ markedly from those in numerous later treatises by *accoucheurs* in both France and England.[65] "Milk fever" was taken to be a normal, if transitional, phenomenon as milk entered the breasts of the postpartum woman. But on some occasions it became a life- threatening "real disease," commonly known as puerperal fever.[66] Section 16 of Astruc's treatise on diseases in women discusses accession of milk to the breast and the problems that could arise:

Stage 1) breasts swell gradually (no pain or fever). Stage 2) the flow more becomes more abundant as breasts swell more quickly with milk. Gradually after pain from tumefaction and tension, a fever develops [a sign of a "real disease"]. Stage 3) progression to a third stage is dangerous. It commences with brisk shivering, followed sometimes with a shaking fit, then culminating in a burning fever, as breasts become full, hard and painful. If the fever lasts 24–30 hours longer it has developed into a double tertian fever which returns every 24 hrs. This is accompanied by considerable urine and stool evacuations And milky lochia.[67]

Astruc has depicted a classic case of puerperal fever. He goes on to explain how this was related to the connection between the breasts and the uterus: "Since the veins of the uterus and the milky vesicles of the breasts have great affinity for each other ... they receive in common the lymph which comes from neighbouring parts [of the woman's body]. During pregnancy the lactiferous vessels of the uterus ... discharge milk and chorion into the placenta for the nourishment of the embryo. In a similar way the lactiferous canals of the breast dilate and provide a means to nourish the child when it shall be born."[68] In some cases, however, the milk intended for nursing "steals off below" to the womb where it stagnates, causing inflammation in the intestines and abdominal area,[69] i.e., the disease of puerperal fever.

Astruc explains how nursing ideally operates to synchronize the female system. "If milk does not rise for any number of possible reasons, the consequences are to turn the milk acidic and bring about inflammation."[70] The conclusion is evident. Milk played a major role in the functioning of the female machine and nursing was a prerequisite for the health of a postpartum woman.

François Mauriceau's treatise of 1728 was the other major work on puerperal fever to be published in English. Mauriceau blamed "the stopping of the lochia for causing an inflammation to the womb which is a very dangerous disease and the Death of most of the Women to whom it happens."[71] This came about because "at the beginning of Child-bed the Woman's Milk is not well purify'd due to the great commotion her Body suffer'd during Labour, and is then mixt with many other Humours ... convey'd to Breasts in too great abundance this causes an inflammation."[72]

The innovative part of Mauriceau's treatise was his rejection of the idea that milk had descended to the womb. "If they are acquainted with Anatomy they would know that there is no Passage which hath to this purpose a Communication between the Breasts and the Womb."[73] He also criticized the "white blood" theory. "Until late it was always believ'd that the blood was the Matter whereof the Milk was made in the Breasts, but it is much more probable that the *Chyle* only is the true matter out of which all the Blood of the Body is made."[74] Neither insight was attributed to Mauriceau by British medical theorists.

Despite the authority it retained in France, there was an almost unanimous dismissal of "milk theory" among British *accoucheurs*.[75] Nevertheless they upheld the importance of nursing and prescribed that, where a mother lacked strength or interest, the milk should be "drawn." Thus, at the Westminster Lying-In Hospital, John Leake insisted that every patient should suckle her own child, though he explicitly rejected the theory on which it was based and observed that nursing alone could not secure them from the fever.[76] More generally, the collection of essays on puerperal fever written before the end of the eighteenth century by Fleetwood Churchill illustrates the pervasive confusion among physicians in the discourse on puerperal fever and "the utter failure of all attempts to arrest [the fever's] progress or prevent its fatal termination."[77]

One characteristic of puerperal fever that is largely absent from the French accounts is the terrible pain suffered by afflicted women. There are numerous references in the British treatises to the "outrageous behaviour" of women who sometimes had to be strapped down in their beds as they reacted to their suffering.

MORTALITY OF WET NURSES IN VAUGIRARD

The horrific medical procedures to which he subjected women with puerperal fever make it difficult for the modern reader to evaluate Doublet's accomplishments dispassionately. But clearly, the loss of life among syphilitic wet nurses while they were in Vaugirard hospital itself was relatively insignificant. One caveat must be kept in mind – recovery from syphilis is impossible to estimate in the long term because symptoms might very well recur.

Overall, the registers listed fifty-nine deaths in total (fifty-four in Boussault's account).[78] Women often died during childbirth, sometimes before receiving mercury. Other deaths were attributed to illnesses other than syphilis, especially puerperal fever. The registers that record mortality provide the dates on which women succumbed. Comparing the date of the woman's death with that of her child's birth makes it possible to estimate the number of deaths from puerperal fever. Women dying a few weeks to a month after delivery were likely to have succumbed to puerperal fever.

At that, survival of the syphilitic women may have depended less on the medical treatment they received than on a wholesome diet, cleanliness, and a routine in which work, though stressful, was shared in a communal if uncongenial setting. At Vaugirard some women from the lowest strata of French society were given a respite, however brief, from disease and destitution.

Table 4.11
Mortality of wet nurses in Vaugirard

Livre de mortalite des nourrices	Puerperal fever	Child birth	Total deaths
6.8 August 1780–August 1783	9	2	11
6.9 August 1783–August 1787	8	6	14
6.10 September 1787–5 March 1791	5	11	16
6.11 after official closing			
Total related to childbirth	22	19	41
Deaths presumably due to puerperal fever (within month after childbirth)			22
Deaths in childbirth			19
Other			18
Total deaths			59

The inquiry into the hospital carried out by La Rochefoucauld-Liancourt for the Comite de Mendicité de la Constituante (poverty committee) in 1789–91 is based on Doublet's account. But one can assume that the conclusions were not given in his words. That the final assessment was harsh[79] can be attributed largely to Vaugirard's failure in saving the lives of infants. That is understandable, since the hospital's mandate was to find a treatment to do just that. The report showed relatively little interest in the outcome for the syphilitic wet nurses who were treated at the same institution.

A last word, and a complimentary at that, comes from the same Rochefoucauld-Liancourt report. "It is claimed that nurses take more interest in caring for these infants, than is the case with healthy ones [perhaps because they both suffer from the same Illness]."[80] We have seen that Bertin, writing in 1810, described the nurses as "tender, gentle and sensitive."[81] He dealt with similar women at the venereal diseases hospital who carried on the practices initiated at Vaugirard. This did not correspond with Doublet's view that much of the failure at Vaugirard could be blamed on the poor quality of care, which depended on nurses of inferior health and character.

Wet nurses remained an essential, if vilified, component of the operation at Vaugirard hospital. Administering medication through women's milk, however, had repercussions for hired wet nurses long after Vaugirard had closed. As we shall see in the following chapters, it was not until the legal-medical controversy over syphilitic contagion arose in nineteenth-century France that wet nurses were able to insist on a degree of self-assertion and force some doctors and the legal system to recognize their claims for respect and fair treatment as individuals. They were finally to be taken seriously as individuals on their own terms, not merely as "*instrumentos animados.*"

5

The Wet Nurse and the Law

The Vaugirard experiment in treating syphilitic infants with mercurialized milk was deemed a failure by La Rochefoucauld's enquiry for the Comité de Mendicité and the hospital closed in 1790. But the experimental method of giving infants mercurialized milk had taken on a life of its own. As noted earlier, it was used at the new venereal diseases hospital in the Faubourg St Jacques.[1]

In the private sector it was not unusual to hire a wet nurse for a syphilitic infant. The medico-legal literature of nineteenth-century France makes numerous references to civil court cases brought by wet nurses against families that had knowingly exposed them to contagion from a dangerous disease. Abraham Colles's observation that, while a mother was immune, a stranger nursing an infant was inevitably susceptible to infection became established as "Colles Law" in 1837. The likelihood of a healthy wet nurse contracting syphilis from a nursling was common knowledge from at least the end of the eighteenth century. Doctors were compromised because the hiring of a wet nurse may have occurred on the advice and with the compliance of the family physician. On occasion this could mean giving the infant mercurialized milk (see cases 1 and 2, below), though usually the child was treated with mercury administered in alternative form. This differed from the Vaugirard model. And in the original experiment the nurse already had syphilis and therefore she was not at further risk of contagion. For a healthy woman, however, nursing a syphilitic infant could have serious consequences.

Dr Paul Diday, the expert on congenital syphilis, though acknowledging in his treatise of 1854 the problems that could result, was willing to countenance (with reservations) the hiring of a healthy woman to nurse a syphilitic infant. His standard advice was to have a mother nurse her own infant. "If the practitioner believes it is necessary to prescribe specific remedies, he will not meet [from the mother] with either opposition or ambivalence[as he might from a mercurialized hired wet nurse] in carrying out a treatment which, though often insufficient for the cure of the child, is always a valuable auxiliary to remedies administered directly to it."[2] Mother's milk was not always available, however, because sometimes the syphilitic woman was unable to nurse her own child. In such circumstances, "with a healthy nurse, mercurialized for the sole purpose of treating the child, the aggregate of elements favourable to this mode of treatment would be realized."[3] In his discussion of serious cases in which he advocated giving the infant mercury by "direct" means, it is clear that "indirect" means, i.e., the Vaugirard method, were still used on occasion. He stated, "A great number of children ... would infallibly succumb if we endeavoured to treat them exclusively through the medium of the medicated milk of the nurse."[4]

Obviously, hiring a healthy woman to nurse a syphilitic infant could raise legal and medical issues for the doctor, "especially if there was no [alternative] nurse at hand who requires or consents, to take mercury." But if a (healthy) nurse was hired without involving him in the transaction, then "one can be happy for the child." Diday insisted, however, that in such cases the nurse should be carefully observed and treated as soon as she presented any visible symptoms. The doctor must also point out to her the signs by which she could recognize the onset of the illness. "It would be highly repugnant to me to sacrifice a highly respectable woman in the prime of life to the very problematic future of a child ... because of the infection which it suffers."[5] Diday was evidently aware of the risk to the woman's health, and though attempting to mitigate problems that might arise, he tolerated ways that would allow her to operate within the terms of her contract with the family of the infected infant.

Actions brought against families that incidentally involved their doctors brought issues of jurisprudence to the fore. Measures originally intended to safeguard the infant eventually called attention to the predicament of the wet nurse. There is very little in contemporary historiography about the controversy. The reasons are complicated and involve legal and social factors as well as confusion among some physicians over contagion in congenital syphilis. The wet nurse, the family that hired her, and the doctor were linked in a

series of lawsuits on matters of public health and private and professional behaviour. This chapter will address these issues and their
impact on French jurisprudence and offer possible explanations for
the gap in the historiographical record.

LEGISLATING WET NURSING

Largely because of high rates of infant mortality and a pervasive ten-
dency in the medical literature to blame hired wet nurses as a contributing factor, legislation in France had long supervised the occupation
of wet nursing.[6] Under eighteenth-century laws the parish priest was
to serve as an intermediary between rural women who were willing
to be wet nurses and four employment bureaus in Paris. He was responsible for certificates as to her character, marital status, number
and ages of her children, and the condition of the resident infants in
his parish. But for all practical purposes, the business was run by approximately sixty *meneurs* (drivers) who recruited rural women and
transported them to Paris and back to their homes with the infants.
The meneurs then delivered pay, clothing, and messages to the women
monthly, while reporting back to the parents on their child's welfare.
The employment bureaus' use of these men as subcontractors invited
abuse. Legally, for example, a nurse could not have more than one
charge at a time, or rent out a child to a neighbour on her own initia-
tive – rules that could be circumvented by a cooperative *meneur*.

Initially, the doctor's role was minimal. It was only after 1762 that
medical personnel became formally involved with wet nurses. Then
a doctor was employed by the canton to visit any nurse who had
not been hired through the bureaus and submit regular reports on
the health of her charge.[7] In 1769 there was an attempt to centralize
the system under one office. It failed, because local entrepreneurs
offered wet nurses higher subsidies.[8] Over the years government
surveillance increased. The nurse was to provide data on her own
infant and any other nurslings in her charge. She was responsible for
obtaining a doctor's certificate vouching for her good character, age,
address, the occupation of her husband, and finally, a birth certificate
for the client's infant. All this information was to arrive at the local prefecture of police within eight days of her employment. Given
the paperwork involved, wet nurses continued to favour regional
meneurs, and often parents found it easier to work through personal
contact or private agencies.[9]

Gradually in the course of the nineteenth century, a series of measures culminating in the Roussel law of 1874 reasserted government control. Committees under the mayor or prefect of the town included two respectable matrons, a doctor-inspector, a curate and, where relevant, representatives from the Protestant presbytery and Jewish consistory.[10] Problems remained with unscrupulous drivers, and with parents who were unable to keep up payments to the nurses. As with many bureaucracies, conditions were not always adequately monitored. Critics claimed that the law was ignored as much as enforced.

Infant mortality continued to be of serious concern as a matter of public health throughout the period. Indeed, it took on greater intensity as the century progressed thanks to fears about a decline in population fostered by the conflict with Prussia. Alfred Fournier, the renowned expert on syphilis, did nothing to discount these fears. In 403 pregnancies in his practice, he reported, hereditary syphilis could be attributed to the father, and either abortion or death shortly after birth occurred at a rate of one out of four cases. If the mother was infected as well, "the resulting mortality can only be described as terrible." In the latter instance he found that infants died in forty-three out of forty-four cases. "No other disease can compare to it as an agent in depopulation."[11]

The prevalence of congenital syphilis was taken into account by Assistance publique, the governmental agency supervising the foundling hospitals in France. It took measures to protect nurses from the threat of contagion. After 1852 there was a requirement that the nurse should be medically certified free from syphilis before being given an infant. A foundling was examined on arrival at the hospital to verify that it was not tainted. If the child had congenital syphilis, the woman was instructed not to nurse the child but to feed it "artificially." That meant either spoon-feeding or having the baby suck from a rag or sponge soaked in the milk of a goat or cow, or giving the milk from one of the awkward but commonly used *biberons*, or nursing bottles, made of glass, metal, or clay. Given the sanitary conditions of the time, diarrhea was a major factor in infant deaths, especially during the summer months. Nominally, if not always in practice, the child was to be examined monthly in the first few months for the appearance of signs of syphilis. A decree of 27 February 1877 stipulated that when the child's parentage was unknown, a visit must occur no later than two months after the first examination to avoid any threat of communicating syphilis to its nurse.

Indeed, if a resident nurse at the hospice in Paris did contract syphilis she was entitled to compensation.[12] On 24 February 1893 an appeal court confirmed a judgment of the Tribunal Civil de la Seine condemning Assistance publique for not taking adequate measures to safeguard a nurse from a syphilitic infant.[13] In this rare instance of the courts finding negligence on the part of Assistance publique, the nurse was awarded twelve thousand francs in compensation, plus expenses.[14] This particular decision was the most generous remuneration for any case of an infected nurse I have found.

The Roussel law of 1874 extended protections to infants and nurses in the private sector that were similar to those in the public system.[15] It again required doctors to make monthly visits to infants sent out to rural areas. It is possible that this played a role in educating the nurses, not only instilling basic principles of hygiene and infant care but raising their awareness of threats posed by a syphilitic infant. The fact that nurses were being monitored by the local doctor cannot be discounted as a factor in the increasing number of legal cases reportedly being brought by wet nurses in the period following passage of the Roussel law. The wet nurse, the families that hired her, and the doctor were linked in a series of lawsuits.

CONTAGION: THE SCIENTIFIC CONTROVERSY

Contagion from secondary symptoms in congenital syphilis was the basic issue in legal cases that impugned not only the families employing a nurse for a syphilitic infant but also their doctors. It was not only family doctors whose reputations were at stake. The dispute over contagion and secondary symptoms involved the most · famous venerologist of the day. Philippe Ricord's place at the summit of medical prestige came under siege over his interpretation of contagion in congenital syphilis. The complicated nature of secondary symptoms sometimes made it difficult to defend the innocence of the wet nurse. Arguments that were largely based on Ricord's reputation as an expert had to be appraised and either accepted or rejected on scientific grounds.

Like John Hunter, the British physician who carried out many experiments on syphilis and was the author of a seminal treatise on the subject, Ricord believed that direct contact with a primary symptom, the hard chancre, was the source of contagion not only in adults but also in infants. Ricord had made important findings about the nature of syphilis by distinguishing between gonorrhea (of which he recognized several varieties) and syphilis. In particular, he had developed a technique of inoculating a subject with the pus from a primary symptom, or chancre, in order to confirm the existence of the illness. He also determined the existence of a "third stage" that usually took the form of severe pain in the joints and ostosis, commonly known as tabes.[16] As we have seen, however, legal tribunals were making decisions in favour of nurses at the very time that Ricord's reputation at the Hôpital du Midi was still at its high point.[17]

Ricord's ability to deploy his erudition in an accessible manner, wedded to a rhetorical gift for wit and satire, made him a formidable opponent in debates at the Paris Academy of Medicine. His combination of flamboyance and incisive intelligence had served the profession admirably on the issue of syphilization,[18] when he had rallied opposition to an attempt to immunize subjects by means of a series of injections with pus from a primary chancre – a procedure modelled on smallpox vaccination. However, the prestige he brought to his controversial stance on contagious nature of secondary symptoms meant that simple matters of fact based on a plethora of observation were disputed for much longer than warranted.

Ricord disparaged the notion that contagion was transmitted from a secondary symptom via the mouth of an infected infant to the point of impugning the cleanliness, character, and sexual practices of wet nurses. He suggested some ingenious alternatives – the soiled fingers of the nurse, genital contact causing an outbreak on her breast, or the possibility that someone else with syphilis had been allowed to fondle the infant's genitals.[19] The transcripts of a debate in the Academy of Medicine in 1852 show how effectively, with his talent for sarcasm, he denigrated not only the nurses but medical colleagues who supported them. Ricord could make an opponent appear naive to the point of stupidity. In response to the claims of rural nurses that they had been infected by infants they had brought from the city, he argued, "It is interesting that all those stories of whole villages being infected by a syphilitic infant occur only in the country. But why not Paris? It is in Paris that the disease is supposed to originate, or in nearby garrisons, but it only leaves the city to follow certain [i.e., rural] nurses."[20] He warned, moreover, that "it is important not to readily accept the evidence of those who can profit from deceiving us."[21]

Ricord's scepticism about the comportment of country folk is not surprising in someone whose practice made him familiar with attempts at concealment in sexual matters. It seems to have bred in him a degree of cynicism towards women in general. As he explained to Diday in a letter, "Induced by my long practice [I have come to the conclusion that] the virtue of women may always be more or less doubted."[22] On the character of wet nurses in particular, this bias was evident in his sarcastic disclaimer that he was in no way impugning "their morality, innocence and respectability ... in fact, no one respects them more than I do." But, he insisted, the debate over contagion had come full circle, to the point where now "nurses alone are depicted as the subject of unjust suspicions and false accusations."[23]

The Ricord-Hunter thesis was buttressed by the observations of another important syphilologist, Auguste Cullerier (1805–1874), chief surgeon at the Lourcine hospital, who presented his findings at the Imperial Academy of Medicine in 1852.[24] On the basis of eleven cases, Cullerier claimed to show immunity to secondary symptoms between nurses and infants. He cited infants in his sample who had not contracted the virus, despite being nursed by syphilitic women or by women who remained healthy but whose children had contracted syphilis.

Cullerier evinced little sympathy for nurses exposed to contagion from a nursling. "She claimed that she had contacted her present malady from a hired infant she had nursed in the months of November and December of 1849," but, he added in italics, "*she nursed at the same time her own infant and this child was healthy and had never had signs ... nor was sick a single instant during all his stay at the hospital.*"[25] He gave three other examples of the same type. As further evidence for his point he cited a different type of incident. "The patient, questioned several times, declared that she had acquired her syphilis from a nursling. But her husband, when he was questioned, claimed she had contacted the disease from a man whom he could perhaps name ... He seemed firmly convinced that his wife had deceived him ... moreover her child was untainted and remained so when both were discharged from the hospital."[26]

Another of Cullerier's examples, described in considerable detail, echoed the allegations already noted in Ricord's letters on syphilis. It relied for its credibility directly on Ricord's hypothesis that a syphilitic outbreak on the breast of a wet nurse could come from the soiled fingers of her husband as a result of "abnormal" sexual relations. Such practices, Ricord had insisted, were not unusual where an unwanted pregnancy would serve to interrupt the woman's lucrative nursing. "I do not wish to call into question the morality of the nurse," he explained, "but it is likely that the husband had contracted syphilis 'outside the home' i.e., from an illicit encounter, since it is usual for such married couples to abstain from sexual relations to ensure that the woman does not lose her income by becoming pregnant."[27]

In Cullerier's example, Joneau Pelagie, wife of a farmer day labourer of Ferté-Villeneuve, had complained bitterly on her admission to Lourcine in May 1851 about the parents who had hired her, "deploring the lot of poor peasants like her who had been poisoned by the infants of Parisiens." She changed her tone when confronted with Cullerier's diagnosis that the secondary symptoms in the infant were not contagious and that therefore the source of infection must, in this case, have been a third person – i.e., the husband of the wet nurse. His conclusion: the primary chancre on the breast of the nurse probably came from her own fingers, soiled by accidental contact with the pus of her husband's primary chancre. Of course this was pure conjecture. As far as Cullerier was concerned, however, the fact that it could not be confirmed because the husband refused to be examined merely corroborated his suspicions. His conclusion, that "physicians must exercise prudence and great reserve in coming to judgment," carried considerable weight with his colleagues.[28] This, despite the criticism voiced by a few sceptics that all his citations could be interpreted to support either side.[29]

It was Paul Diday, in his 1854 treatise, who convincingly demolished the position on contagion of his old friend and teacher, Philippe Ricord. Most persuasively, he quoted Hunter, the original source for Ricord's opinion.

A lady, delivered September 30, 1776, and having a large quantity of milk, suckled her own child at one breast and a neighbourhood child at the other. At the end of six weeks the breast given to the latter became diseased: several small ulcers formed around the nipple and ultimately destroyed it. The glands at the axilla became swollen, but their tumefication was resolved. The strange child had apthae [mouth ulcers] and hurried respiration. It died of phthisis [tuberculosis], with outbreaks on the rest of the body. The mother, after having suffered pains in various regions, had an eruption of spots on the arms, legs and thighs, some of which became ulcerated.

[The sequel informs us that] three years later, this lady had a child with symptoms of constitutional syphilis, under which it sank at the end of nine weeks, after having communicated it to a nurse, who also expired; (nose and palate exfoliated, she died tabid.)

Hunter dismissed this case as one of the "new instances rising up every day very *similar in many ways to venereal disease.*"[30] Clearly, however, it describes the transmission of syphilis to a nurse from a nursling. For Diday, "the evidence against Hunter's opinion appears to be conclusive," i.e., that constitutional syphilis could in fact be transmitted from the child to its nurse.[31]

As for Ricord's claim that syphilis among the general population was not unusual in rural areas, Diday pointed out that, unless related to nursing a strange infant from the city, "general observation proves that in the country, beyond a circle from 15–20 leagues around the large cities, syphilis is extremely rare."[32] However, he was able to give an example of a "whole village" – Alsenburg, Belgium – that suffered a veritable epidemic of syphilis in 1852 after becoming infected by a nursling with congenital syphilis from Brussels. A woman in the village developed an outbreak on her breast and was unable to nurse. She turned to the ministrations of her ten-year-old son to relieve her loaded breasts of their milk. "He succeeded so well in this that several women, having occasion to take advantage of his talent, used him for the same service. Many of them became infected in the same manner ... A doctor passing through the commune and informed of the disease which was preying on the inhabitants, submitted all those affected to a strict and minute examination, and found the source to be the boy; originally, like his mother, the victim of the syphilitic foster child."[33]

Granted, the terms in which Diday defended the virtue of rural nurses were far from chivalric. He alluded to "a collection of hideous and loathsome creatures, all however nurses, [and] subjects of constitutional syphilis as a result of the lactation of infected children ... Assuredly, in the face of such repulsive objects, the suppositions of ultra-Ricordians [that these women were sexually promiscuous] would involve the most improbable gallantry."[34] Less pejoratively, Diday noted that, in his experience, none of the infected women bore signs of a previous primary chancre; the original lesion appeared on the nipple, and only later on other parts of the body. This was a characteristic that Doublet had already observed from his experience at Vaugirard.[35]

Ricord had qualified his position in a way that allowed for a degree of uncertainty and left open the possibility that contagion could be passed from infant to nurse: "It is important to note that I do not absolutely reject the mode of transmission from foster-child to nurse and from nurse to foster-child. I only say, without leaving the field of strict observation and exact analysis of the facts, that the existence of this transmission is not yet proved."[36] Diday conceded the qualification. But in his view the caveat that went with it carried little weight in the face of the evidence that had accumulated to the contrary. Diday judged, "If *conclusive* facts be wanting, *probable* facts abound ... [and] if there be a doubt, the safety of families would be far better served by my solution."[37]

Diday was not alone; most of his colleagues had come to the consensus that Ricord was simply wrong. A series of debates and critical articles, in particular a report based on a set of ethically controversial human experiments carried out by Dr Camille Gibert and Joseph Alexander Auzias-Turenne, verified for the sceptical that secondary symptoms were contagious. In 1859 the academy secured a reluctant retraction from Ricord.[38]

This was followed in 1861 by a formal enquiry of the Academy of Medicine, which was meant to drive a stake through the heart of the argument.[39] Joseph Rollet of the hospital of Antiquaille in Lyon, who had himself written several prominent studies of the disease, was commissioned to deal with the transmission of syphilis from nurse to nursling. Rollet provided doctors with exact and comprehensive material on the contagion issue that was especially useful for physicians who had been called to appear in court as expert witnesses. Basically, he described three types of case: in the first the nursling had secondary syphilis and the nurse primary; in the second the nurse had secondary symptoms and the nursling primary lesions; and in the third both exhibited the same symptoms.[40]

The first type was the most common, and Rollet considered such cases relatively simple to adjudge. Lesions of a secondary type around the mouth of the infant meant that it had inherited syphilis from a parent. A primary chancre on the nurse's nipple and on the glands under her arm could come only from the infant. If the source were a husband, lover, or another nursling, it would be the infant who had the primary chancre. The history of the infant's parents had also to be investigated for a record of miscarriages or stillbirths. While they did not furnish conclusive proof, a succession of such incidents could rouse suspicions that syphilis was already present in the family. To sum up this first example, when the nurse had a primary chancre (usually on the nipple) and the infant suffered from constitutional syphilis but bore no signs of a primary chancre, there was no doubt that a nursling had communicated syphilis to the nurse.

Cases of the second type involved a primary chancre on the infant and a secondary symptom on the nurse. If neither parent had syphilis, the object of suspicion must be the nurse. She might have been treated in the past, or perhaps her disease had progressed to the second stage. A primary chancre on the infant, with a concomitant secondary symptom on the nurse (usually on her mouth, lips, tonsils, or tongue), indicated that the nurse had given syphilis to the infant. There was a caveat – the infant's primary symptom could have come from someone other than the nurse who had kissed, fondled, or cleaned the child.

The third situation, in which both infant and nurse exhibited a primary chancre or both had secondary symptoms, was more complicated. It called for a close examination of all parts of the infant's body, and an intense examination of the nurse with a speculum to look for the presence of a chancre or scarring from a previous outbreak. The object was to ascertain the "age" of the symptoms in both parties. The assessment could be difficult if the infant had died, or if parents refused to allow an examination.

Rollet reiterated the numerous sources for infection by secondary symptoms. These could be children or adults who had had contact with the infant by touching or feeding it. The infant could have been given the breast by another woman who needed stimulation to produce milk for a different nursling, or to discharge milk, or even for "depraved" enjoyment. The smallest detail could raise questions about the source of contagion. Rollet's analysis became the basic manual for doctors as experts or as expert witnesses. More detailed studies by Etienne Lancereaux and the later work of Charles Vibert owe much to his account.[41]

From that time on, with this imprimatur from the Paris Academy of Medicine, the theory that syphilis could be transmitted from nursling to wet nurse via secondary symptoms, usually from the mouth of the infant to the breast of the nurse, was no longer a matter of scientific controversy but an accepted fact. Nevertheless, it was not a fact that all doctors were ready to insist upon when dealing with their patients with syphilitic infants. As late as 1875, Camille Appay, in his book *De la Transmission de la Syphilis*, set out seven detailed observations on the medical aspects of some oft-cited cases. Appay claimed that the doctor could be excused for having failed to warn the nurse about contagion since he had acted simply as an intermediary between the family and the wet nurse; or that alternatively, she could have contracted syphilis from a previous charge.[42] His conclusion: "One can see the need to proceed carefully and look at the slightest piece of evidence from a medical point of view ... as much as medico-legal."[43] At that point, the scientific issue became an ethical and legal issue.

THE ETHICAL CONTROVERSY

The experience of Paul Diday illustrates the ethical dilemma involved in the wet nurse/family/physician encounter. In 1854, though he chose his words carefully, Diday had unreservedly dismissed the kind of excuse that Appay had held out to doctors. Ignorance could not be condoned. Diday was well aware of the legal pitfalls that threatened a family doctor who prescribed mercury for an infant who was being wet nursed by someone other than the mother. If a family knowingly hired a nurse for a syphilitic infant, he warned, "you [the doctor] can be the family's confidant, but never their accomplice."[44] Diday made it clear that the practice of nursing a syphilitic infant, with or without mercurializing the milk of a healthy woman, was highly problematic for family doctors, who could be accused of putting the health of the wet nurse at risk.

We have seen that public hospitals had conceded the risk and taken a more open course. "On giving a nurse a child suspected of having syphilis she is to be warned of its condition and acquainted with the symptoms which may develop. She feeds it artificially and brings it to the hospital as soon as it presents visible symptoms." But, Diday acknowledged, "if this is the most moral course, it is far from the most advantageous for the child."[45]

In private practice, Diday noted, the situation could be more complicated for all parties. A hired nurse either lived with the family or returned with the child to her own home. The first option provided a controlled environment, which simplified things for everyone. The doctor could observe the infant carefully during its first months. If symptoms occurred, he had time and opportunity to cauterize them and give general treatment immediately. This could usually be done

without interrupting lactation – and without arousing the suspicions of the nurse. Only incidentally does he evince sympathy for
the healthy woman who has been hired to nurse a syphilitic infant.
His prime interest was to protect the doctor from the threats of in-
crimination in such cases.

If the nurse returned to her village with the infant, the same resources were not as easily available. Should the doctor ensure the
health of the nurse by telling her of the dangers to which she was
exposed? Diday's response was a resounding "No." With the permission of the parents, he advised instead writing to the local medical man, "confident that his professional discretion and respect for
secrecy, would provide a sufficient guarantee. Have him examine
the infant frequently. If symptoms which he is unable to neutralize
occur, then have lactation cease."[46]

In order to demonstrate how this could be carried out in practice,
he cited an example from his own experience with a cooperative
colleague.

> To alarm the nurse less, the doctor used various pretexts for the
> frequency of visits, such as running into the child on the street, as
> if by chance. He used silver nitrate to cauterize mucous tubercu-
> les at the mouth of the infant and cautioned her not to give the
> left breast when the nipple became a little excoriated … In short,
> the child was thoroughly cured, thanks to the intelligent inter-
> vention of my colleague, without having ceased for a single day
> to be suckled by its nurse who remained healthy.

However, he had to admit, "few families, few practitioners and few
writers take the interests of nurses so seriously. On the other hand,
some women, finding pecuniary advantage in nursing a suspicious
child, took on voluntarily the dangers of contagion, while seeking to
minimize them [by avoiding breast feeding as much as possible], to
the misfortune of the child."[47]

At the same time as he was admonishing doctors who put the
health of wet nurses at risk, Diday nevertheless struggled to allow for
the prescription of mercurialized milk for their nurslings. At the very
least, this left his ethical stance open to a charge of inconsistency.[48]

As a form of compromise in treating an infected infant, Diday
made a distinction between direct and indirect mercury injections.
The direct method he proposed did not necessarily involve a wet

nurse. In life-threatening cases, he advocated giving mercury by mouth to the infant. He prescribed mercury and potassium iodine in twelve parts gum arabic and ten parts sugar, diluted in 375 parts boiling water, and administered in spoonfuls of milk, broth, or pap, if the infant's gastro-intestinal system could tolerate it. If not, he proposed ointments rubbed on the skin. The direct approach he considered absolutely necessary in cases of "galloping syphilis," which otherwise would inevitably prove fatal.[49] But he had to acknowledge that this method achieved only minimal success.

If the child survived this heroic regimen or was afflicted with a milder form of syphilis, then he had recourse to the indirect (or Vaugirard) method, i.e., giving mercury in the milk of a hired wet nurse. "With a healthy nurse, mercurialized for the sole purpose of treating the child, the aggregate of favourable elements would be realized."[50] Diday went so far as to prefer a healthy wet nurse to an unhealthy mother. "A nurse free of syphilis, if she be willing to perform her duties conscientiously, will always be much better than one (even the mother) whose organism has been debilitated by syphilis … in fact, one should give up altogether on mercurialized milk, rather than purchase it only because she has syphilis."[51]

How could this advice be justified coming from a respected physician writing sixty years after William Buchan's prescient warning against allowing a healthy woman to nurse a syphilitic infant, and almost twenty years after the Colles's conclusions on the same issue had earned the stamp of "law"?[52] The only possible explanation was Diday's confidence in monitoring any outbreaks before they became full-fledged syphilis – a confidence that was completely unjustified. Despite having presented a cogent critique of Ricord's position on contagion from secondary symptoms, Diday was himself a prime example of the profession's stubborn adherence to mercury in the face of the risks involved in using a healthy nurse for a syphilitic infant.

Because he had not sorted out his own conflicts, Diday in the 1850s eagerly grasped at the controversial procedure of syphilization as a way out of the medical morass. It involved injecting a healthy subject with a series of inoculations of pus from a primary chancre. As noted earlier, the object was to induce syphilis, and eventually immunity, following the model of smallpox vaccination with cow-pox virus. Poor women, he explained, could then nurse syphilitic newborns without risk. "Thus, any infant with suspicious symptoms could find a syphilized nurse … and with the encouragement

of administrators [of foundling hospitals] women who had been persuaded to undergo this useful operation [would then be available]."
He suggested that hospital authorities should encourage paid nurses
to undergo this experimental operation, in order to ensure "breasts
for all those little beings, innocent victims of the faults or credulity
of others."[53] Syphilization did not work and was never accredited in
France despite intense debate in the Paris Academy of Medicine. But
it was taken up in Russia and Norway and as late as 1867 attracted
supporters in Britain.[54]

Diday's odyssey epitomized the ethical dilemma faced by one doctor, and one with significant prestige and influence as an expert on
congenital syphilis, struggling to accommodate the Vaugirard technology, or the hiring of healthy women for syphilitic infants. How
could the perceived advantages of nurse's milk be utilized with minimal risk to the nurse, infant, and doctor? There were no clear an-
swers. Meanwhile families continued to employ wet nurses, with or
without their doctor's collaboration.

THE LEGAL CONTROVERSY

Even though medical dissidence about contagion from secondary
symptoms had been resolved, the legal ambiguities involving the wet
nurses on one side and the family and family physician on the other
remained. On the strictly legal side, the issue was complicated by
two contradictory precepts. The first, set out in articles 3682 and
3683 of the Napoleonic civil code, made the doctor, like other professionals, responsible for any overt harm and the victim eligible for
reparations. The second, contained in article 378 of the penal code,
decreed that patient-doctor confidentiality must be respected and
that anyone who violated that trust could be punished by imprisonment for one to six months and subject to a fine of one hundred to
five hundred francs.[55] Granted, the privilege of confidentiality could
be abrogated if the doctor became a defendant in a court case, or
if he was called as a witness or an expert.[56] But a physician could
invoke confidentiality in his defence and claim that his first loyalty
had been to the family that had employed him and trusted him to
look after their interests.

The patient's right to privacy had traditionally been respected
by tribunals and in legislation. Doctors, moreover, had taken the
Hippocratic oath, and it was part of the oath that "anything I see or

learn in the exercise of my profession, or even outside, I will treat as secret and keep silence." The physicians' claim to independence on ethical matters included their own judgment as to what they deemed was owed in loyalty to their patients. The inviolability of confidentiality even in the court of law was closely tied to a practitioner's reputation for honesty and discretion. Indeed, France had no formal code of medical ethics before 1936 (the code was formulated in legal terms in 1947).[57] Alex Dracobly has termed confidentiality the most important medico-ethical issue in nineteenth-century France.[58]

Confidentiality was the basis of trust in the doctor-patient relationship. The "secret," as it was termed in French medico-legal literature, could make ambiguous an otherwise straightforward formulation of a doctor's ethical responsibility. A family's right to confidentiality was given added weight in the atmosphere of heightened anxiety posed by the war with Prussia. The *heredos,* children who survived congenital syphilis but were unable to procreate or to serve their country in the army, were seen as examples of degeneracy in France.[59] In Fournier's words, "Syphilis is slowly but surely sapping the strength of succeeding generations."[60] In this context, the physician's role as guardian of the family's secrets took on an intensified importance. Fournier, though a strong advocate of public health measures to control syphilis, argued that "we owe absolute confidentiality to our patients, even those who least merit it."[61] Nor did his mentor, Ricord, have any hesitation in the matter: "When a magistrate questions me in a civil inquiry, I only respond when I am authorized to do so by the individual [patient] who consulted me."[62] In essence, medical confidentiality allowed doctors the prerogative of refusing to incriminate themselves by invoking the sacred nature of the patient-doctor relationship.

It was not only the patient's right to privacy that the doctor was protecting but also that of the physician, especially in matters that might reflect badly on members of the profession. Dealing with families who had hired a wet nurse for a syphilitic infant left the doctor in difficult straits. This became a major theme in Diday's 1883 book *Le Peril Vénérienne* and Fournier's earlier work, *Nourrices et Nourrissons* (1878). Although it would be an anachronism to read back into the nineteenth century the publicity that incidents would receive in the press today, doctors were nevertheless concerned about good public relations for members of their profession. As late as 1953, article 1 of the Committee of Public Health of France lists as a condition of the practice of medicine that "the doctor must avoid in writings or declarations any statement related to an infringement of the law [*attente*] which might call into question the honour of the profession, including all publicity [and all] that is incompatible with individual and professional dignity. He must abstain from furnishing any information that could be used for these ends. Nor should he divulge in public a [legal] procedure insufficiently proven, whose harmlessness has not been demonstrated."[63]

In his article on medical ethics Robert Nye writes, "In matters of morality, professional independence was akin to the concept of individual autonomy in which the physician was personally responsible for his ethical judgments."[64] He points out that confidentiality applied also to a doctor's relations with his peers if it meant revealing matters that could affect the profession's general reputation for honesty and discretion.[65] The prerogative concerning confidentiality remains to this day a criterion of trust on which doctors base their relationship with each other, as well as with their patients. Its importance for members of the medical community cannot be underestimated.

Is it possible that the reluctance of the medical profession to publicize matters regarding patient–doctor relationships, especially in the matter of venereal diseases, had the effect of playing down, if not completely silencing, the reporting of cases that involved wet nurses? Is it possible that confidentiality may even have influenced members of the legal press? I have information on thirty-four cases of wet nurses suing families or physicians, but only one appears in the usual legal collections of documents.[66] While it is no justification, a reluctance to publicize such cases could explain why a dispute that caused a scandal in the medical profession of the time has left almost no trace in modern studies of medical practice in nineteenth-century France. It is tempting to conclude that perhaps the profession had more power than its members were willing to concede. If doctors closed ranks to protect one another from public scrutiny, were they also able to influence members of the press? Reporters may have seen themselves as representatives of the medical establishment, in that their work involved commentary on publications in medical journals. Even so, there were doctors who were willing to call attention to the ethical and legal issues relating to congenital syphilis and the dangers of contagion posed to wet nurses and indeed to criticize colleagues on the subject. In an article of 1988 Alain Corbin states that the subject of contamination of wet nurses much enlivened the debates on syphilis and that such cases were responsible for several judicial decisions on malpractice suits (i.e., those dealing with responsibility for contagion based on article 1382 of the civil code).[67]

Alex Dracobly has researched the literature of the period – medical journals, collections of jurisprudence, treatises of legal medicine, etc. – for his doctoral thesis on medical malpractice. In all, he was able to document only thirty-seven malpractice cases of any type between 1830 and 1870. Dracobly attributes the relative dearth of malpractice cases in France to good doctor-patient relations, professional solidarity, and a conservative jurisprudence system that depended on written law with trial before judge, rather than jury. A further limiting factor could be that the person who lost a suit was responsible for court costs. Dracobly concluded that suits against doctors were relatively rare in the period 1830–90 but increased in number during the last decade of the century. Is it possible that litigiousness in general, not just among wet nurses, may have been on the rise in France at the end of the nineteenth century? Harsin refers to four cases in which wet nurses or their families sued in the period 1898–1903.[68] This is remarkable given that the availability of safe pasteurized milk was making wet nursing less common by then.

Dracobly makes an important contribution to our understanding of the problem, but a convincing additional explanation has been offered by Eva Steiner. In her recent study of French legal practice, she found that "reporting is largely a matter of choice or discretion on the part of the courts themselves, or the editor of the particular series of reports in his charge. *This system is by no means comprehensive.* Decisions handed down by the highest courts constitute the vast majority of judgments published in law compilations, but only a small percentage of the thousands given each year by the courts are published."[69]

There is only one official source of law reports that deal with matters of appeal, the *Bulletin de la Cour de Cassation*. Among other collections of jurisprudence the most commonly cited is the *Recueil Dalloz-Sirey*, initiated by Victor Dalloz in 1845. It merged with the other major compilation, J.B. Sirey's, in 1965. Other contemporary references are *La Semaine juridique* and the *Gazette du Palais*.[70]

Members of the medical profession wobbled uncomfortably as they tried to secure a foothold on shaky moral ground. On the one hand, they were constrained by a sense of responsibility to their clients concerning confidentiality; on the other hand, they had an obligation as medical professionals to see that wet nurses were not harmed. The threat of accusations of malfeasance exacerbated their disquiet.

When Ambroise Tardieu assumed the position of chair of legal medicine at the Faculty of Medicine in Paris in 1863, he took it upon himself to counsel physicians who found themselves on treacherous ground in cases where a wet nurse blamed a family, and often the family doctor as well, for her syphilis. Despite many earlier attempts to warn colleagues of the problems thatcould arise. Tardieu had written in 1854:

> *Cases in which doctors have been accused of actions in their practice [malpractice] seem to have been increasing for some time*, and this is a matter of concern for the dignity and best interests of the profession. The law has not been precise nor jurisprudence established in these matters. Doctors need general principles in difficult situations where clear guidelines are lacking leaving them defenceless and at risk for lack of clearly defined principles ... We must keep in mind we are dealing, not with scientific problems, nor moral intentions, but with precise facts of experience ... as in a direct anatomy of an autopsy.[71]

But focusing on "precise facts" could not exclude ethical questions when nurses who had been infected with congenital syphilis came before the courts.

In 1864 Tardieu took up the issue himself. In a series of articles in the journal *Annales de l'hygiène publique et médecine légale* Tardieu examined a number of suits brought by wet nurses. "I have personal experience already in similar cases and am aware of recent writings on transmission [of contagion] by wet nursing."[72] For the historian, the paucity of examples in the legal compilations of the time makes it difficult to know exactly how many such incidents there were.[73] This is particularly frustrating because the secondary literature does not necessarily supply information on the final outcome of a dispute or the amount awarded to a nurse in damages, if she won. However, there are many other instances mentioned by high-profile doctors such as Paul Diday, Philippe Ricord, Auguste Cullerier, and Alfred Fournier, as well as J.P.M. Rollet, Eugène Bouchut, M.Lagneau *fils*, and Etienne Lancereaux. These are only the best known of the "big names" who wrote about the issue.

CASES PRIOR TO 1868

In his treatise of 1854 Paul Diday had addressed the legal problems doctors might encounter in cases dealing with the wet nursing of syphilitic infants.[74] Though he did not always provide details, Diday cited numerous examples of the disease being transmitted from infant to wet nurse, including several incidents culled from medical journals in Dublin, Edinburgh, Lombardy, and Brussels.[75] To my knowledge, Britain, Belgium, Italy, and America did not witness the same flurry of litigation as France,[76] where by mid-nineteenth century there had already been a series of suits brought by nurses against the families who had hired them. But some of the French cases were reported in British and other foreign journals.[77] Diday's earliest example concerned a demand for recompense on the part of an infected nurse in 1797. It was originally cited in the *Journal Général de Médecine* by Michel J. Cullerier (1758–1827), chief surgeon at the new venereal diseases hospital.[78] The parents had conceded that they were at fault and were willing to yield to the demands of the complainant, but Cullerier's interpretation of the evidence threw suspicion on the husband of the nurse as the source of the illness. Diday took issue with the conclusion because, although there was evidence of a tumour on the groin of the husband, Cullerier had not examined the mother of the child as well.[79]

As we have seen, much was made of observations presented by Auguste Cullerier, surgeon at Lourcine hospital and grandnephew of Michel Cullerier, to further discredit the theory of contagion through secondary symptoms.[80] His first category of observations concerned healthy infants whose mothers were being treated for syphilis. Though four of the five women involved explicitly blamed the nursing of a strange infant for their illness, Cullerier made the point that none of their own infants had contracted syphilis. This would not be surprising given Colles's findings on the subject. His second category dealt with six cases in which the mothers remained healthy despite nursing infected infants. In an article published in the journal *Union Médicale* in April 1854 and also in his treatise, Diday dismissed Auguste Cullerier's examples as unrepresentative and his conclusions as questionable: "Let us ... examine more closely these observations which furnish so strong an argument in the opinion of some writers on syphilis ... These facts, *which allow of no doubt*, which ought, it is said, to counterbalance the thousand histories of infectious lactation daily furnished by experience – these facts are *six* in number!"[81]

Diday also cites an action of 22 December 1841 in which the court of Limoges awarded damages to a claimant, pointing out that she was the second nurse to be hired by the family within a year, and that the parents must have been aware of the condition of their infant.[82] In 1851 another procès-verbal, or legal statement, of the Congress of Nantes dealt with the transmission of syphilis to three generations in the household of one nurse.[83] She blamed the family who had hired her. Clearly, by mid-nineteenth century, claims brought by wet nurses had become a serious matter.

The *Gazette des Tribunaux* is a legal journal that gives annual tables in which one might expect to find references to such suits. In a sample based on the years 1830–42 and 1868–73, looking under the listings *nourrices* (wet nurses), *dommages-intérêts* (damages), and *médecins* (doctors), I found only one new example (for 1831), and between them Tardieu and Fournier cited three others.[84] The incident of 1831 refers to a *maladie honteuse* (shameful illness) contracted from a nursling. I will quote it in detail.

> What appeared to be a fresh and healthy young woman was looking for a nurse for her newborn infant, who likewise seemed well, and in fact came with a *certificat irrécusable* [verified certificate] of good health. The child was six weeks old, and shortly thereafter signs of a shameful illness became evident. The nurse herself found on her breast unmistakable signs of the same illness. A doctor was called in and confirmed that fears were well founded. Treatment for the infant seemed impossible and it died after 15 days of nursing. An autopsy confirmed the cause of its death. The nurse required treatment for two months. This *bonne villageoise* [respectable woman of the village] has issued a legal action against *la demoiselle* Grannerie [the mother] for 10,000 francs in *dommage-intérêts*. M. Bautier, represented the nurse but Mlle.Grannerie did not even present a lawyer in her defence. As a result, a judgment by default has condemned her to damages to be fixed by the state.

No precise details were given as to the amount. The article goes on: "It is a usual practice to submit a nurse to a doctor's examination before assigning her a nursling. This proceeding of the fourth chamber of the Cour de Cassation [court of appeal] illustrates that the nurse would do well to demand a doctor's examination for the mother from whom she takes the infant."[85]

Though there are references in the *Gazette des Tribunaux* to nurses accused of fairly minor offences (such as giving a sleeping potion to an infant so that she would not be woken up for a feeding), there are few references to nurses suing families or doctors for giving her a syphilitic infant. Surprisingly, a landmark case of 1868 that is listed in the important *Dalloz-Sirey* compilation is not found in the *Gazette*.

Because of the lack of evidence in more formal sources, I have relied primarily on accounts in the secondary literature. My principal documentation for the cases is based on a series of articles by Ambroise Tardieu published in 1864 in the *Annales de l'hygiène publique et de médecine légale*. Many were subsequently published in 1879 in an expanded version entitled *Etude médico-légale sur les maladies provoquées ou communiqués comprenant l'histoire médico-légale de la syphilis et de ses divers modes de transmission* (A medico-legal study of contagious diseases taking into account the medico-legal history of syphilis and its means of transmission). In chapter 5, "Syphilis Transmitted by Wet Nursing," Tardieu cited thirty instances, not all of which ended in court.[86] His case studies make fascinating reading. The fifteen citations originally published in the 1864 articles were brought by wet nurses, and though some won their suits against families, the doctors involved were all acquitted. I have chosen six cases that illustrate typical incidents. The first two involve nurses who were given mercury without being told why or warned about its effects. In such cases doctors were usually excused by magistrates because the ongoing controversy over secondary symptoms as a source of contagion in the scientific knowledge of the time was considered to be a mitigating factor.

Case One

The first case is interesting in part because the family consulted Philippe Ricord. Some three weeks after the birth of an infant, a nurse who had been hired on 21 April 1857 found that sores had developed on the infant's mouth, throat, and genitals. She returned the infant to its family. A second nurse was hired who, after four months, developed outbreaks on her left breast. The father, himself the son of a doctor, conferred with the family physician and sent medications by rail. The nurse eventually took the infant to a local practitioner who confirmed that the child had syphilis. She informed the parents, who brought her to their country house for eleven days in November 1857. There she was treated with "whitish liquid in a spoonful of milk" and given lotions and powder for her breast. The family doctor told her that the child had a cold and eye problems.

At this point, the nurse was taken to Ricord at the Hôpital du Midi. He prescribed *deutochlorure de mercure* (mercuric chloride), but even then she was given no information concerning the nature of her illness. The nurse subsequently learned that a second infant in the same family had died at two and half months of so-called "diarrhetic choleriforme." Meanwhile, her condition worsened. She suffered ulcerations in her throat, mouth, and gums, pimples on her hands, swelling on her neck and armpits, and hair loss. At this point she brought charges against the family and doctor.

Experts could make only a retrospective diagnosis concerning the infant, who had recovered, though they established that by the time the case was heard the child had had no problems for four months, and that it had had none during its three weeks with the first nurse. On the other hand, the second nurse had been healthy when she took the infant. The family's doctor at first denied but later admitted that the liquid sent to her from the father was mercuric chloride. The court found that there was "no reason to think that he would provide an infant of only few weeks with medicine as strong as potassium iodide or [the emphasis is mine] *give to the nurse a substance as dangerous as corrosive sublimate except to combat syphilis.*" Meanwhile, the woman remained debilitated, though her sexual organs were unaffected – another indication that her syphilis came from the nursling. She sued the family for ten thousand francs in damages and received five thousand.[87]

Case Two

This incident did not involve Ricord directly but his opinion was explicitly invoked in the arguments offered by the defence. Again, two nurses were involved. Sieur B. and his physician arrived at the Bureau des Nourrices on rue Pagevin where they physically examined four nurses for a child who had been born in July 1855. They explained to the nurse who was hired that the child was suffering from excoriated gums and a slight fever that would require baths and herbal teas. The nurse accompanied the parents to their country home. In early October the family physician warned the parents of the child's syphilitic condition and *prescribed a strong mercurial treatment to be given through the milk of the nurse.* She refused this regime and left. As a result her replacement, a married twenty-four-year–old woman of good character with three healthy children, was kept in the dark as to the precise nature of the child's ailment. She agreed to what was termed a "depurative" treatment and was given strong doses of Van Swieten's liquid, as well as mercury in pill form. Nevertheless, the child remained sickly.

Within two months, mucous plaques and whitish outbreaks were found on the nurse's breast. She was assured by the family doctor that these were simple ulcers, although he doubled the dose of mercury. Meanwhile, the health of the woman deteriorated, despite the doctor's implementation of a course of strong mercury treatments. These measures, or the illness itself, left her in a deplorable state. The worried physician called in a colleague, who confirmed syphilis and insisted that she stop nursing. At this point the wet nurse's husband consulted a local doctor about her condition and then demanded reparation. The employer balked and replied, "I paid her wages, I will only pay her medical bills and 300 sous on top of this."

In a civil suit brought before the Tribunal of the Seine on 12 August 1856, the lawyer for the prosecution, M. Bertin, claimed that the incident was not the result of a mistake but a clear example of guilt on the part of the family and their doctor. "They had conspired to use the body of the nurse *as an alembic to pass on mercury to the infant in the nurse's milk,*" he argued, "but realized after their experience with the first nurse they must deceive the woman to do so."[88] As a result her health had been profoundly altered. The lawyer for the defence invoked Ricord, who had said, "I have never been able to verify a case of constitutional syphilis transmitted from a nursling resulting from conditions that were absolutely convincing … I can only be certain that that there may be simultaneity and coincidence in such examples." Ricord reiterated that "in villages where nurses are recruited syphilis is not rare."[89] The lawyer for the accused emphasized that the father of the family was a businessman and a respected citizen from an honourable family; "but before all that, have you not been a young man yourself?"[90] This appeal was designed to elicit sympathy for his clients and to remind his audience that syphilis was after all almost commonplace among young men of the "better" classes (and perhaps all classes) in Paris at the time.

The tribunal rejected this argument and awarded the wet nurse damages of five thousand francs (like the nurse in case one, she had asked for ten thousand), to be paid by the family. The doctor was acquitted because, in the view of the court, "it is not certain that the nurse, even if warned, would have been able to escape contagion, and therefore her condition was not necessarily the result of the doctor's reticence."[91]

Case Three

In another suit before the Tribunal of the Seine the doctor was also discharged. In 1857 a woman took a sickly infant to a physician who prescribed cleanliness and cooling lotions. At a second visit five days later, he found ulcers and pustules on the woman's breast. At this point he told her to stop nursing. In a few days the infant died. Subsequently the woman had a miscarriage, despite having had three healthy deliveries in the past. Meanwhile, her husband developed syphilis. His occupation as gamekeeper meant that he was outside in all weathers and his treatment left him unable to work. She recovered, but two years later he remained incapacitated. They charged both the family and the family's doctor, who had allowed her to continue nursing after her first visit and had at no point revealed the nature of her illness.

Forced to appear under a court injunction, the doctor invoked the confidential nature of his relationship with his patient. The court conceded that the state of scientific knowledge at the time allowed for uncertainty. The claim of negligence, rash conduct, and ignorance of matters on which he should be informed (i.e., voluntary malfeasance) was rejected by the tribunal. It accepted the argument that on his first visit the doctor had only suspicions of the nature of the illness and that, on the second visit, he had decided that it was already too late to prevent the consequences of the disease. He was let off, although the employer was fined three thousand francs (again, damages of ten thousand francs had been sought).[92]

Case Four

Collegiality could supercede ethical considerations in a small community where two nurses and the local curate were involved. In this case the original nurse had the infant for only a few weeks from its birth on 21 July 1854. At baptism, the priest provided the second nurse with ointments and mouth rinses for several ulcers on the child's mouth and lips, as well as for outbreaks on the genitals. The first physician to see the child, Dr Debourge (this is one of the few instances in which the doctor's name is supplied), gave evidence as to its deteriorating condition. The symptoms were copperish plaques, crusted outbreaks, ulcers at genitals and underarms, suppurated nails, and discharge from the nasal passages. After the infant's death on 16 November 1854, the doctor noticed that both breasts of the nurse were inflamed, but "since her mouth and throat were asymptomatic he did not intervene." Within a month, however, there were red spots all over her body, swollen glands, ulcers in her throat and on her tongue and lips, and she was losing hair. Meanwhile, similar outbreaks occurred on the tonsils of the first nurse, though she had had only brief contact with the infant. She also developed genital ulcers and suffered hair loss, and in September 1856 she had a miscarriage five to six months into a pregnancy. Three doctors agreed that the disease started at her nipple, not the genitals.

Two local doctors certified that death of the infant had been caused by intestinal complications, but in Tardieu's view: "There is no doubt the infant died of congenital syphilis."[93] He gave no details about legal consequences.

Case Five

This case, from the village of La Ferté sous Jouarre, near Meaux, illustrates the convoluted nature of many such depositions. It involved testimony from four physicians, five neighbours who vouched for the wet nurse's character, and the busy intervention of the nursling's grandmother. The first doctor was originally consulted by the nurse's husband in August 1849 about a chest complaint but he noticed "en passant" symptoms of syphilis in the nursling. Out of loyalty to the colleague who was in charge of the infant's case he did not come forward until he was called in directly by the maternal grandmother. Then he prescribed anti-venereal medicine for the infant and warned the nurse not to give the breast she had used for the infected child to her own infant. When symptoms appeared on her breast and throat, he treated her but still did not inform her as to the precise nature of the problem.

In October 1850 the nurse and her husband made a trip to the hospital at Meaux where she was apprised of the facts of her condition. She confronted the doctor in the village, who was now in charge of the case, and accused him of being more an "*homme de famille*" than a "*homme de médecine*." He responded that "she was in no position to understand the reasons for my reserve and discretion" and insisted that he was not certain that her symptoms were venereal, though given the condition of infant he had his suspicions. At that point, the maternal grandmother asked him to act as intermediary by offering the nurse costs for treatment and medicine plus one hundred francs in damages. This he refused to do.

The two doctors who saw the nurse at the hospital in Meaux immediately reacted to the serious nature of her condition. They found a deep ulceration in her throat that had eaten away part of her palate, and a similar outbreak on her nipple. They concluded that "syphilis was due to the nursling," and one of the consultants expressed surprise that the nurse had not been given the same antisyphilis treatment as the infant nor told of her condition. In Meaux, meanwhile, an examination of the couple found that their sexual organs were unaffected; nor did their own infant have any signs of syphilis. One of the doctors there testified that, when asked to examine the infant's parents for indications of syphilis, he had declined on the grounds that it would have no scientific value, and that it might involve a conflict of interest in a situation that seemed likely to come before the courts.

When it did end up in court, four village women testified (often at some length) to the nurse's health and that of the nurse's own child, and to the distressing state of the nursling. One of the women volunteered that the grandmother had commissioned her to deliver a bottle of medicine that was to be taken only by the nursling. According to another, the grandmother had bemoaned the state of the infant, praised the doctor for his attention, and said, "Now we have only the nurse to cure."

It was clear that the second doctor brought in for the infant had tactfully prevaricated to protect the reputation of his colleague. It took two doctors from the city to tell her the truth about her condition. More remarkable was the spunk with which she confronted the second family doctor. She sued for and received two thousand francs in damages from the family. This particular case received much publicity and was discussed later in articles by Alfred Fournier, Paul Diday, and Dr Castelnau of Meaux.[94]

Case Six

This final example shows how the health and very life of an unsuspecting woman could be altered by contact with congenital syphilis. Tardieu describes the excellent health and character of the nurse. "The conduct of this girl was irreproachable ... she has since become a nun in a Visitine convent." She had nursed a newborn whose father was a *commis voyageur* (travelling salesman). Within a month, she brought to Tardieu this infant with syphilis, while she herself now had copperish marks on her back, chest, and members, swollen neck glands, a red and painful throat, no appetite, and a large round ulcer on her nipple – all this after the family's doctor had assured her that her problems were not serious. She required mercurial treatments for six months and ongoing treatment over a period of four years.[95] As in all these examples for the period prior to 1868, the doctor was absolved.

Though the women in these cases were poor, they had been hired as wet nurses by families, usually in consultation with a family physician. In a sense, they were the elite of their profession. The pay was negotiable, and some lived with their employers for the duration in comfortable circumstances. There were other nurses, however, even more impoverished and consequently lacking the attributes of good health and appearance, who were eligible only for lower-paying situations, such as those within foundling hospitals, or those in which they nursed infants from their own, not their employers', home. Where nurslings had been abandoned by unmarried girls or families too poor to support them, such nurses were often given infants whose mothers had died in childbirth. The chances of being assigned a syphilitic infant were far from negligible. These nurses were at the bottom of the scale for remuneration and the top of the scale for risk. The foundling hospitals recognized that they must give some compensation to those who had contracted syphilis from the nursling, but only at a minimal level. The decision to take on the administration of a government-run institution was daunting, and the chances of winning in court minimal.

Tardieu and Fournier both document one such incident. In 1872 a young woman from Burgundy, wife of a very poor farmer, came to Paris where she was hired to care for a foundling by Assistance publique. Born in March, the infant was diagnosed with syphilis in June and died on 24 July. When the nurse developed symptoms, she was told to stop nursing and given treatment, but sadly it was too late to be of any help. She had a miscarriage in May 1873, but this was only the first of a series of misfortunes. The couple brought a suit against Assistance publique asking for damages of five thousand francs. The administrators acknowledged responsibility and offered recompense, but the terms (unstated) were rejected. At the trial, the defence argued that the child had appeared healthy at birth and that, once diagnosed, a doctor had treated the nurse immediately. Despite an appeal, the couple lost their suit and were fined expenses. The impact on the family was disastrous. Devastated by the costs, the husband began to abuse his wife, then he left her, taking with him their oldest child, who subsequently died from lack of proper care. Technically, Assistance publique could justify its stance, but the price paid by the wet nurse was the loss of her health, loss of her fetus, loss of her husband, loss of her child, and ultimate destitution.[96]

Under any circumstances, whether with a private family or a public hospital, wet nursing could present perilous occupational hazards. Eugène Bouchut is one of the few doctors to recommend early on that privately hired wet nurses who received their charges through a nursing bureau deserved some compensation for the dangers involved, just as Assistance publique compensated nurses who were infected by foundlings.[97]

On rare occasions, the court assigned damages to a wet nurse who brought charges against a bureau administrator. In 1853 the director of the nursing bureau in Lyon, La Veuve Boisseux, was judged responsible for having assigned a syphilitic infant to a wet nurse. As Fournier pointed out, it was unlikely that she knew of the infant's condition. In any case, considering that the nurse and her husband both contracted syphilis, the reimbursement of four hundred francs seems negligible.[98]

THE OUTCOME

Despite the distressing circumstances they endured and their failure to win claims against doctors in the courts before 1868, nineteenth-century wet nurses in France must be credited for bringing about a revision in French jurisprudence.(See appendix 3 for a brief summary of terms in which French law relates to this discussion.) In all the examples quoted by Tardieu, the doctor was acquitted, even when the family was deemed guilty, and his concurrence was not coincidental.

The original interpretation of confidentiality as it affected nurses has been amended and revised slightly over the years, but the turning point can be traced directly to the ruling by the Court of Dijon on 14 May 1868 (see appendix 2) that:

> the Doctor who knowingly does not warn a nurse of dangers
> to which nursing an infant with congenital syphilis leaves her
> exposed, can be declared responsible for harm caused by his reti-
> cence. He cannot claim to be called only to care for the infant.
> He must also take into account the danger to which the nurse
> is exposed; no system which acts against moral laws can be in-
> voked against a nurse; in such a situation, the Doctor is called
> upon to provide the same trust [for her] as he provides for the
> family of the infant.

The responsibility of the doctor for the well-being of the nurse as well as for the infant of the family under his care had been asserted as a matter of principle. But even in this instance the doctor was given the benefit of the doubt. "It is not certain that by this time ... she could have avoided contagion even if warned of the danger by the doctor and ceasing to nurse; therefore it is not shown that the *réticence regrettable* of doctor B..., has been the cause of harm ... In this case, the demand for damages presented by Protat, as caregiver for young children, against doctor B... cannot be accommodated."[99]

That doctors would be accommodated in this way seems to have become less likely as the century went on (see the table in appendix 2). As Fournier pointed out in 1878, "written law does not guide us much on this point ... but the judgments delivered in such cases throw more light on the subject. The general conclusion is that medical confidentiality [article 378] was subordinate to the more important duty of protecting the nurse from harm [article 1382]. *In many cases medical men have been reprimanded for neglecting to inform the nurse of this fact.*"[100] That is, the 1868 decision set out as a matter of principle the doctor's responsibility for harm done to the wet nurse in terms of voluntary malfeasance. Although respect for precedent does not play same role in France as in Britain, where it is part of the common law tradition, this decision of 1868 was to influence cases that followed.[101]

Similarly, in 1869 an article published in the *Annales de l'hygiène publique* advised that a doctor in such cases need not be bound by article 378 of the penal code on confidentiality; instead he should follow his conscience. He was to use his own judgment, based on justice and humanity.[102] When called to defend their actions, doctors had successfully wrapped themselves in the cloak of "the secret," terming it their duty and right to protect the patient's privacy.[103] This point of privilege was challenged and the decision pronounced: in these particular circumstances, the argument on confidentiality could be justified neither legally nor morally.

Textbooks for students of medicine unquestionably conveyed that interpretation. Albert Trebuchet's work of 1834 had made no mention of suits brought by wet nurses.[104] But after 1868 textbooks such as the *Manuel de Médecine Légale et de Jurisprudence Médicale* (1877), written by Auguste Joseph Lutaud (1847–1904), were explicit. Lutaud began by warning that the doctor must observe absolute secrecy in relation to venereal disease and congenital syphilis. In some circumstances the doctor might even skilfully dissimulate as to their nature in order to preserve harmony within the family. However, there was one notable exception: *"We are speaking about the transmission of syphilis from a nursling to its nurse and the opposite. Without advising the nurse to take legal steps, he ... need not refuse under terms of the secret, to give the woman a true and exact description of condition that he has found. [Moreover], parents must assume responsibility and agree to monetary compensation [for the nurse]."*[105] Lutaud conceded that cases in which a nurse passed on syphilis to her charge were extremely unusual. This interpretation was also asserted in Charles Vibert's basic medical textbook *Précis de médecine légale*, which went through nine editions from 1880 to 1921 and provided examples of cases that were similar to those collected by Tardieu.[106]

In other words, by 1868 for all legal purposes, the wet nurse had been vindicated. Even now, modern legislation in France concerning the employment of wet nurses reiterates the same qualification with regard to confidentiality. A contemporary revision, the Ordinance of 25 November 1960, decrees that

> imprisonment for two-six months and a fine of 2,000 N.F.- 6,000 NF, or one or other of these, is to be exacted for:
> 1) Any woman who wet nurses an infant other than her own while she is aware that she has syphilis.
> 2) Any person who knowingly allows a syphilitic infant who is in her care to be given to a wet nurse *without having a doctor warn*

her of the illness of the infant, and the precautions that must be taken.

3) Any person who knowingly gives an infant to be wet nursed without warning the nurse of the illness the child suffers.[107]

But the legal victory for wet nurses, such as it was, remained subject to the social and economic conditions governing the lives of these women. How often did the cost of their day in court damage a nurse's family financially? None of the claimants received as much as they asked for, though the damages that were awarded tended to increase over the years.[108] In any case, the price paid by a wet nurse who lost her mind or her life, or who had caught syphilis and then passed it on to her husband and children, both born and unborn, could not be measured in dollars and cents. It is likely, moreover, that there were many nurses without the resources to take their cases to court and it is most likely that there are other incidents that were settled out of court or have not become part of the public record.

Essentially, all wet nurses were at a disadvantage. They lacked the education and experience to evaluate, understand, or manipulate the workings of the legal, medical, and political system. Were there lawyers who encouraged these women to sue? If so, did they expect to get a "cut" from the damages that were assessed? Poor by any standard, how could such women afford to go to court in the first place? And when they did the odds were stacked against them. The burden of proof was on the wet nurse. Doctors tended to support each other and their client families.

Moreover, there seems to be considerable inconsistency in the way the wet nurses' right to compensation was interpreted. A measure of 1896, for example, states that wet nurses could obtain damages from a father or mother if infected by an infant but they had to establish that one or the other parent was contaminated. "Thus it has been judged that no indemnity can be given if a skilled expert has not shown that either parent had signs of syphilis nor earlier traces (Paris, 27 November 1896)." [109] This appears to call into question both the spirit and the intent of the 1868 decision by providing an out for families in actions brought by nurses. Clearly, the 1868 decision had allowed for a more generous interpretation of the nurses' right to damages. Even Fournier vacillated on this point. He admitted that from a strictly legal perspective, confidentiality as expressed in article 378 of the penal code played a subordinate role to article

1378 of the civil code. Further, he conceded that many magistrates (*jurisconsultants*) gave priority in their judgments to the wet nurse's claim that she was susceptible to harm as expressed in the decision of the Court of Dijon in 1868. After much soul-searching, however, he felt that if a wet nurse came to him and asked about the condition of the infant of a family that employed him, he could satisfy his conscience on confidentiality by telling her to consult a different doctor. And like many of his colleagues, he deemed that it would satisfy his interpretation of "principle" if he warned the father of the family of the serious risk the woman ran and the consequences that could result for him and for his doctor if a healthy woman was hired for their syphilitic infant. Fournier refers to a colloquy on the issue published in 1868 as *Mémoires et comptes rendus de la Société des sciences médicales de Lyon (Piéces justificatives)*, in which Diday expresses an opinion similar to his.[110]

Despite such reservations among physicians, there were wet nurses who succeeded in bringing public attention to the fact that they were being victimized. The next chapter deals with the reaction of the medical profession to accusations of malfeasance brought by wet nurses – how physicians dealt with the threats posed by wet nurses to their prestige, authority, credibility, and reputation.

6

The Doctor Exonerated

By the end of the century, interpretations of both the scientific and legal issues involved in cases brought by wet nurses had evolved considerably. Ricord's stand on secondary symptoms and contagion had been rejected, Rollet's summary of the methodology for analyzing cases of wet nurses and infants had been clearly set out, and the "absolute secret" in medical confidentiality, certainly with regard to wet nurses and contagion, was legally no longer tenable. After 1868 courts were more inclined to side with the nurses. Repeated warnings in treatises devoted to the subject of congenital syphilis and many articles in the *Annales de l'hygiène publique et de médecine légale* and other journals discussed the consequences of hiring a healthy woman for a syphilitic infant.[1] Doctors, to the detriment of the good name of profession, were more likely to be incriminated on grounds that allowing such a practice was scientifically, legally, and ethically questionable. As late as the end of the century both Diday and Fournier were repetitively outlining measures by which "the doctor could guard himself from allowing an infected infant to be nursed by a healthy woman (even when she consents)[2] ... or from being involved in choosing for a nurse a woman whom he will deceive as to the nature of the child's disease, and *to whom he will administer mercurial treatments disguised by another name*."[3] Fournier counselled his colleagues that by taking his advice into account, "the doctor will thus avoid the numerous surprises and dangers with which his path is beset ... [and] by obeying these principles *guard from errors or omissions which are sometimes committed by some of our colleagues in similar circumstances and which remain inscribed in the judicial records* ... in this way safeguarding the interests of the doctor and the dignity of the profession."[4]

The privileged doctor-client relationship based on confidentiality and medical assertions of scientific competence were the key grounds on which doctors claimed the right to professional self-determination and independence. In the words of one doctor, "professional secrecy was the very essence of the profession"; another referred to it as "the cornerstone of French medical morality."[5] But both professionalism and morality were to be called into question on the subject of congenital syphilis.

In concurrence with the scientific and legal issues, the doctor's authority and the honour of the profession needed solid grounding when a doctor was involved directly in such cases or called as an expert witness in court. In this final chapter we shall see how the medical profession managed and manipulated the legal, scientific, and professional aspects of a volatile situation.

THE ONGOING CONFRONTATIONS

Despite the scientific evidence against it, legal challenges posed to doctors who had cooperated with the family to hire a healthy nurse for a syphilitic infant had not disappeared. If anything, such incidents appear to have escalated over the period. Almost thirty years after his 1854 treatise on congenital syphilis, Diday published another work on the subject, *Le Péril Vénérien dans les familles*, which had less to do with treating the infant and nurse than with coming to the rescue of beleaguered colleagues who were embroiled in lawsuits. His advice remained essentially Buchan's: "Have the mother nurse her own infant. She is the only one who can do so without fear of contagion."[6] But by 1881 Diday was preoccupied with ethical and legal matters, rather than strictly medical practice.

Supposing a nurse should ask the physician for information about a patient's family where congenital syphilis was likely? Then he must tell her the truth, but he could do so in such a way as to protect both himself and his relationship with his patient:

Arrange to have her come with her husband, or a family friend, so he can explain in front of them. Then tell the employer of his duty to reply to the nurse the next day. If this is likely to involve a compromising situation, it will be the client's responsibility to prevent the nurse from coming to request information.

Three things may follow:

1) the nurse may take the infant at her own risk.

2) alerted by my resistance she decamps without the expenses for her trip.

3) she presents the family with the proposal that she bring a doctor of her choice.

Any of these eventualities would protect the doctor from the threat of being sued by a wet nurse for negligence. Diday was confident, however, that such confrontations were unlikely, since, once having been apprised of the doctor's position, the family would leave him out of negotiations.[7]

And if the doctor was confronted by a situation *ex post facto*? Given that the newborn's symptoms were not necessarily evident at birth, it was always possible that a nurse might have been engaged before the infant was found to be syphilitic. The simplest expedient, if she lived with the family, was to pay her well and send her away with some excuse about her milk being unsuitable. But since she might be incubating illness, the doctor had to take steps to protect his reputation and her health. Here Diday's counsel became more conniving than circumspect. The doctor was to caution her *in Latin* about the need for discretion; tell her (apparently in French), about the area on the breast she had to observe carefully; draw a picture, and warn her that if symptoms appeared, she should return to him immediately for free consultation.[8]

The family doctor's ingenuity was tested further if the child had been taken home by the nurse. In such cases she was to be told of the possibility of infection in front of a third person who would be able to testify later in the doctor's defence. Then she should be promised treatment and paid well. But she also had to be warned to stop nursing at the first appearance of symptoms. "Answer all questions fully ... If all is agreed upon and she is willing to go on nursing, leave a generous sum and explain it is on account, i.e., will continue." The aim was to leave the infant with the nurse, where it could be given goat's milk, medical care, and fresh air. Under ideal circumstances, the parents might be able to hide the malady from friends, and perhaps even from the nurse.[9]

Finally, in cases where the wet nurse was already infected, Diday advised the same procedure: pay her well and make sure to have her husband – or, if she was unmarried, someone of the doctor's choice – as a witness. Since she already had syphilis she might just as well keep the baby with her; in fact, bringing back a sick infant to the client meant that the rest of the client's family might be infected.[10] Note the lack of interest in the nurse's family.

In its most generous interpretation, Diday's stand could be summed up as pragmatic.[11] In cases where nurses chose to keep the child even after being warned of the danger, Diday felt that the physician was in the clear. But as a rule, the less he had to do with the affair the less likely he was to be accused of being an instigator or co-author. He should tell the family:

> "Any information you give me or ask of me must be said to everyone inside my office." Stay aloof and never dissimulate the risk and remedies required. If the parents ask you to say illness is nothing, or at any rate can be cured, be completely straight-forward in your reply. *Unhappily*, Justice for some years now has had a tendency to focus on these matters. If the nurse is infected and if (and this is almost inevitable) she goes to court, I will be as vulnerable as you to prosecution. Magistrates have a tendency to side with nurse, as distressing as this may seem.[12]

Diday's principal concern was for the physician, whose advice and behaviour had exposed him to charges of misconduct.[13]

By 1881 the tone and tenor of Diday's discourse had changed radically from his treatise of 1854. Like many of his colleagues, Diday had gone on the defensive. Why this evolution in approach in the second half of the nineteenth century? Obviously, his earlier advice to colleagues on overseeing the health of the nurse had not been enough. His interest now was in measures to be taken after the fact that infected nurses were likely to take such cases to court.

At the end of the nineteenth century Alfred Fournier, the highly respected syphilologist, differed from Diday in tone more than in content. His account is less colourful but much more straightforward. In his summary of the outcome of the landmark case of 1868, Fournier allowed no leeway for the medical profession's claims that doctors should be excused from responsibility for the health of the wet nurse on the grounds of patient confidentiality. Unequivocally, he recognized

the interpretation that had been set out in 1868 as a matter of principle for judging such cases in court. "The doctor who, called to
treat an infant, knowingly keeps from a wet nurse the information
that she is nursing an infant with a contagious disease, in the eventuality that she develops the disease, can be declared responsible for
the harm caused to her by his concealment."[14] In other words the
claim of patient confidentiality based on article 378 of the penal
code was to be subordinate to article 1382 of the civil code which
made the doctor was responsible for the health of the wet nurse.
This, Fournier pointed out, called for a clear statement of the rules
that were to be observed in fulfilling the complex duties that the
situation imposed on medical professionals. "I see, in fact, doctors
being reprimanded in 'plein tribunal' for keeping a nurse ignorant of
the [nature of] the illness of the infant."[15]

Fournier's advice encompassed families as well as doctors. For
his own protection, the doctor was called upon to play a singular-
ly active role in matters involving the family and the wet nurse. In
problematic situations, he cautioned against hiring a wet nurse for
at least the first three or four months of the newborn's life. If only
consulted after the fact, he insisted on an immediate halt to wet
nursing, brooking no excuse such as that the nurse had been warned
of the dangers she faced, and offering to pay her well. Fournier admitted that the doctor was likely to encounter resistance from the
parents, who would be understandably more concerned about their
own infant than about a hired wet nurse. He must expect arguments,
opposition, and bitter discussions and disagreements. Nor could he
anticipate gratitude or consideration for his troubles.[16] And if the
family had taken steps to warn the woman and she nevertheless
agreed to take on this task? Here Fournier quotes Julian Lanarc,
a distinguished jurist: "So far as I know courts have never had to
pronounce on the legal value of a contract between the nurse and
parents ... but they would have no hesitation in condemning it and
pronouncing it as null and void."[17]

If families refused to follow his directions, then the doctor was
left with no option but to withdraw his services. But Fournier's conscience allowed him to advise that the actual condition of the infant
should be kept from the nurse who came to the doctor privately;
she should be told only to consult a different doctor. In that way he
could preserve a form of confidentiality for his patient. If she asked
the name of the illness, the suggested response was, "It is a malady

that is contagious."[18] The implication was that even a nurse of little intelligence would understand what that "infectious malady" was. "The doctor must not by any direct intervention, engage her to continue an employment so dangerous for her and for her family."[19] Fournier's concern for his patient's predicament had to be balanced with the physician's overall responsibility to society as a whole.

In the context of the increasing importance of the public health movement, Fournier's stance was evidently complicated by a sense of duty toward his individual clients, which he found at odds with his obligation to the common good as embodied (literally) in the person of the wet nurse. If a nurse had already contracted syphilis, he recommended trying to persuade her to continue nursing, or at least to stay with the family as a dry nurse. That way her condition could be monitored and treated so that, with luck, the illness would not be passed on to other nurslings, or to her family.[20]

When it came to details, Fournier was much more forthright than Diday, and his terms more peremptory. He addressed two kinds of situation: one in which the nurse was still healthy or appeared to be, and a second, more serious, in which she had already developed syphilis from an encounter with a syphilitic infant.

How should the family doctor respond in the first eventuality? There was no ambivalence in Fournier's counsel. In his own practice he had found eighty cases in which nurses had contracted syphilis from their charge. "We do not have the right to give the disease to a nurse (which is almost inevitable in this situation), in order to save an infant."[21] Nursing should be immediately suspended in such cases, which involved persuading the nursling's father of the seriousness of the dilemma. He had to be convinced that recrimination on the part of the nurse would be the least of the dangers to which his actions had exposed him. In addition, he should be prepared for a demand for compensation from the nurse as the injured party, and ultimately, perhaps, an action at law. The result could be a public scandal that might also reflect on the medical profession.

This state of affairs could end in two ways. The parent could dismiss the nurse without giving the real reason. In that case it would be up to the two parties to agree on pecuniary compensation. Alternatively, the family could decide to ignore the doctor's ultimatum and absolutely refuse to end the nursing. If the latter occurred, the doctor would have to break off his relations with the family. The procedures he should follow in doing so were set out plainly with the clear intent to protect the doctor should the nurse subsequently become contaminated with syphilis. The doctor must prescribe *in writing* the treatment for the child and then add the following: *Absolute impossibility of continuing nursing by the wet nurse, dated and signed.* He must also *absolutely refuse to continue to attend the case.* "In this way his obligations to the nurse could be ensured without violating medical secrecy ... [and thus he could] avoid the errors sometimes committed by colleagues in similar circumstances, which remain inscribed in judicial records."[22]

While this process was dramatic, the second set of circumstances Fournier described could be even more traumatic for the parties involved. These were the cases in which the nurse had contracted syphilis, and in such a way that there was no doubt as to its origin. It was in such cases that actions at law between nurses and parents of the newborn were most likely to occur. As Fournier put it, "The situation abounds in difficulties of all kinds and has several times occasioned unfortunate errors which some of our colleagues have expiated in the law courts."[23]

Such cases called for a high degree of diplomatic skill on the part of the doctor. His initial duty was to prescribe treatment for both infant and nurse. Then, and this was often the hardest part, he must convince the parents to employ every means possible to keep the nurse for their child, while at the same time insisting on the family's openness and honesty. On the family's part it would involve revealing all the facts of the situation to the nurse, confessing their deception, and then convincing her that for her own health she should continue nursing their infant under the care of their doctor. At this stage the doctor should do nothing to make this easier for the family. He must not allow himself to be complicit by calling the disease eczema, "heating of the blood," etc., nor disguise the remedies by calling them innocuous tonic pills or "pills for milk." Such actions could only end up compromising him as well as the family. *"If we are approached by parents to sacrifice convictions on this point it is our duty to retire from the case."*[24]

Anger, dismay, and a sense of betrayal on the part of the nurse was only to be expected. The best outcome would be to persuade her to stay, thereby decreasing the likelihood of any subsequent legal action. The first step by the family was to confess, and the second to compensate the nurse. Fournier advised doing so at once in order to avoid both further expense and the publicity of an action at law.

All too often, however, the nurse may have been frightened by her symptoms or the nursling's and might even have left before the doctor appeared on the scene. Or the woman may have learned from other sources and already threatened action for damages. For all concerned, the doctor had to try to induce the family to be resolute in following the line of action he set out. Otherwise there could be only harmful results for infant, nurse, perhaps her family, and for any other nursling she might take on. And of course, underlying all of this was the threat of the legal problems she might cause the family. For the sake of all involved the family must spare no effort in following the doctor's directions strictly, uncompromisingly, and honestly. Even so, as Fournier admitted, the nurse often left after being informed of the true state of affairs, despite all the promises and inducements the family might supply.

Fournier's earnest attempts to mitigate the issue were usually unsuccessful.[25] His best hope was to avoid such conflicts by convincing his colleagues of the absolute necessity of recognizing and being guided by the scientific, legal, and ethical implications of allowing a family to hire a healthy nurse in the first place for a syphilitic infant. His conclusion: "*In all cases in which there is the least uncertainty as regards the safety of the wetnurse, the prohibition of suckling is a rule of conduct which is imposed on the medical man.* One could even call it a duty from which he should not depart."[26] In other words, the legal, scientific, and moral action imposed on the physician was clearly on the side of the wet nurse.

But how often did the social obligation prevail in the courts? The decision of 1868 clearly gave priority to protecting the nurse. How did that play out in practice?

RESOLVING THE PROFESSIONAL DILEMMA

One way around the quandary facing the nineteenth-century physician was to focus on a different aspect of the legal process. The Napoleonic code of criminal procedures routinely invited medical experts into court. While this applied most directly to the examination of cadavers in cases of violent death, less-tangible matters were also involved. That is, the doctor was regularly called into court as an expert by virtue of his scientific qualifications. On occasion, the court empowered physicians to write "reports" for the edification of the magistracy, and when two or more of these reports conflicted a group of physicians could be summoned to address themselves collectively to the problem, constituting a "medico-legal consultation."[27] For Tardieu, Rollet, and Fournier, one way of mitigating problems faced by doctors when called into court as witnesses or defendants would be to concentrate on their credentials as specialists.

We have seen that one commission of the Academy of Medicine of Paris had as its aim to clarify the controversy over contagion between infant and nurse. Tardieu reiterated this emphasis in numerous articles on legal medicine in which he discussed the role of the doctor as expert.[28] Thus, the doctor as "friend of the court" could project an image of the man of medicine as an authority – a learned, academically qualified scientist called to enlighten uninitiated judges on matters of medical knowledge. Focusing on the notion of the unbiased, objective, unemotional doctor elucidating matters of fairness and justice in a courtroom rife with fractious elements could be effective. Assuming the role of expert could only bolster the doctor's professional prestige. In her discussion of the development of psychiatry in the nineteenth century, Jan Goldstein notes that among doctors practising psychiatry, providing expert testimony in legal matters before the court was seen as a means of gaining recognition and respect for their innovative field.[29] The same could be said of medical professionals in general.

What were the facts that Tardieu considered relevant when consulted as an expert in matters that had gone to court? First, he pointed out that any discussion of the morality of the nurse was irrelevant: "It has nothing to do with the material considerations that the doctor is called upon to adjudge."[30] Nor should the court seek to determine the origin of the illness; its only concern was to establish a direct connection between the syphilis of the infant and that of the nurse. This meant that Tardieu also dismissed any examination of the parents. Obviously, if the infant had congenital syphilis, it must have come from the parents, and he recognized that inquiring into extramarital parentage would be impossible.[31] For the rest, the expert should concentrate on the guidelines set out by Rollet dealing with the nurse's present condition, and the history of her health and that of her children. When possible, the inquiry should involve an examination of the infant. One can only assume that judges were grateful for a few clear rules to assist them in unfamiliar matters.

Calling upon lawyers and witnesses to stick to the bare facts had an obvious appeal in situations that brought out volatile emotions on both sides. It could clear the ground of extraneous and distracting detail. Although lawyers acting for wet nurses might prefer to bring as much evidence as possible to bolster their suit, cutting through the amount of material could only appeal to magistrates by simplifying the court's task. An incidental side effect would be to deflect attention from the woman's miserable state of health, or the imbalance between her social status and that of her opponents. Nor was there any overt recognition of a conflict of interest in the presentation of facts by an "expert" who was also a colleague of the defendants'.

We can only extrapolate from Tardieu's writings as to the success of arguments for the defence. The cases he documents seem to present air-tight evidence against family doctors and their clients. Nevertheless, the damages assigned to the guilty parties (when they were not excused altogether) were much smaller than what the nurses had sought. That they were awarded damages in the first place spoke to the credibility of their case. That the awards were less than demanded spoke to the proficiency of the medical profession at damage control – at playing down the seriousness of the charges. We can speculate that arguments supported by the medical expert could have the effect, intentional or not, of softening the impact of the nurses' testimony and weakening its weight.

For his thesis on the topic of wet nursing and syphilis Fernand Aurientes found only sixteen cases in all of France between 1886 and 1905, and in most of them the nurse's complaint was rejected. However, he quotes a statistic from the records of the Assistance publique for the period 1890–99 stating that there were sixty-eight cases of contaminated nurses in the Department of the Seine alone. He also refers to 136 examples of nurses being contaminated in a treatise of Dr H. de Rothschild for the period 1894–96.[32] Aurientes's assessment is supported by the commentary of Professor A. Pinard in the *Revue d' Obstetrique et de Pédiatrie* of May 1905. He declared indignantly, "Nothing has been done from the legal point of view against the boundless egotism of syphilitic parents who have the cynicism to hire healthy women to nurse their own outcast progeny." In his account, "Even at the present time, when a nurse has been contaminated it is not certain that she will obtain financial damages."[33] Aurientes concluded that it was very difficult for a nurse to substantiate her accusation because jurisprudence was too inconsistent. As late as 1902, for example, some tribunals found parents guilty only if one or two traces of syphilis could be found to verify that they were the source of the infant's illness.[34] This, despite

Tardieu's observation that examination of the parents was both impractical and meaningless. "The disease evidently comes from the parents. Indeed, I must insist on the absolute uselessness of visits to examine the parents of infected infants [which can only] produce difficulties and tend to obscure the issues at stake."[35] How were charges brought by wet nurses against doctors and families to be resolved, given the ambiguities and inconsistencies they threw up?

Aurientes's findings tend to contradict the dire prognostications of Diday, Fournier, Ricord et al. and their professions of alarm about the record numbers of nurses who were successfully bringing their cases to court and receiving compensation. Given the odds stacked against them in the social climate of the time, however, it should not be surprising if the number of cases won by wet nurses was relatively small.

Still, an overall survey of the evidence indicates that there were a number of wet nurses who succeeded in calling attention to their plight. Certainly, the foundling hospital was desperate for nurses and had to make do with women, always poor and often unhealthy, who were themselves desperate for employment. As we have seen, Assistance publique was willing to offer some compensation to an infected nurse. It remains impressive that such women were able to win attention for their complaints concerning their treatment by families, doctors, and hospital administrations.

THE WET NURSE AS ACTIVIST

Wet nurses in France present an anomaly when compared to other countries where legislation did not become an issue. Were wet nurses in France, or perhaps French women in general, more politically sophisticated than women elsewhere in western Europe? The answer to that question must take into account a long history going back to the French Revolution when studies have shown that women, even and especially poor women, actively asserted their rights.[36]

In the tumultuous years of the 1790s hospitals often could not keep up payments to nurses or else gave them paper money that was seriously devalued by the time they tried to use it to buy food. The result was a veritable revolt on the women's part. Valerie Fildes, in her history of wet nursing, has documented examples of feisty wet nurses in France who did not quietly allow themselves to be exploited. Particularly during the disastrous winter of 1795–96 that aggravated civil and economic unrest, infants were being abandoned in increasing numbers. In the districts of Haute-Marne and Cevennes, besieged administrators complained that children were dying of neglect, or being returned to the hospital from which no one was willing to retrieve them. In Metz, infants were being brought back at a rate of six a day. There were examples of wet nurses demonstrating in the streets outside hospitals, demanding decent pay. In Montpellier, employees of the hospital were actually attacked by aggrieved women. In other towns, they threatened strikes.[37] Nevertheless, in Fildes's account, which goes into detail for Dublin, London, Russia, and America, there is no record of the kind of militancy that was displayed by French wet nurses, even where conditions were equally appalling – as they were in Dublin, for instance, where there was 99.6 percent mortality rate in the foundling hospital at the end of the eighteenth century.[38]

I have not found similar examples of militant wet nurses for nineteenth-century France. For the caricaturists of the period, a wet nurse was unlikely to be seen as a threat to the authorities. The events of the 1871 Commune, however, illustrate the enthusiastic participation of women of the working poor in ways that were reminiscent of the active role women played in the events of 1789 and after. Gay Gullikson and Edith Thomas have left numerous descriptions of *cantinistes* (food and drink suppliers), *ambulencières* (women who cared for the wounded), and women fighting as volunteer soldiers, some in uniform. The most memorable illustration of women's participation in those events was the *pétroleuse*, the fire-bearing virago figure. She remained burned into the collective memory as a frightening threat to the bourgeois ruling class, although only five women were ever tried for the crime, and there was no convincing evidence that the fires had actually been set by women. Nevertheless, the dramatic and intimidating image of the *pétroleuse* came to symbolize the passion and anger in women that revolution could unleash.[39]

In a manner that was less sensational but sometimes more successful, the wet nurse used the legislative system to secure some modicum of personal respect and financial compensation for her victimization as a member of the working poor. Poor and powerless women had forced members of the legal and medical establishment to recognize the justice of their cause. Moreover, neither the exceptional nature of their suits nor the absolute number of cases that they managed to win diminishes the importance of their accomplishment. From the point of view of the law, the wet nurse could claim victory. The

sacred status of medical confidentiality had been modified in her favour, no small achievement in the closed circle that encompassed the
rights of the bourgeois family in nineteenth-century France.

Wet nurses had their day in court. Their contribution to legal history and to the development of medical ethics was important. They
had forced doctors to back down from their elevated claims as arbi-
ters of their clients' management of their infants' welfare. Lawsuits
initiated by wet nurses, moreover, were not part of a short-term
trend. The fact that, according to the literature we have examined,
large numbers of nurses were still becoming infected at the end of
the century is of particular note, given the introduction by then of
pasteurized cow's milk.

THE DOCTORS' REBUTTAL

There is no question that wet nurses secured a victory in principle.
But as with most encounters between the powerful and the powerless,
it was a qualified victory. By the end of the nineteenth century, wet
nursing was becoming a thing of the past, even if congenital syphilis was not; the woman's breast was being replaced by the bottle.
When opportunities arose for work in factories, women inevitably
chose alternative employment to wet nursing. Industrialization was
providing women with opportunities to sell their labour instead of
their milk. As the number of wet nurses declined, the challenges they
offered to the medical and legal profession were becoming irrelevant.

In summary, the medical profession emerged relatively unscathed
from its encounter with wet nurses. In the process of being called
into court, physicians were able to defend themselves in many cases,
often by emphasizing their role as experts. Collegiality among members of the profession, claims to scientific objectivity, and society's
traditional respect for privacy epitomized in patient-doctor confidentiality worked to their advantage in the court of law and public
opinion. The proof of that is the difficulty facing historians today in
tracking down the actual details of such cases. We know from the
anecdotal literature that their numbers were large; we know that
the outcome often favoured the wet nurse. Nevertheless, the concrete details of most of these suits have not made it into the basic
legal documents of Dalloz and Sirey, or into many of the medical
summaries of the time, which record the authoritative history of
legal practice in France.[40] During a tumultuous period of medical

litigation in the nineteenth century, despite the questionable practices brought to the attention of courts and the public in general, the reputation of the family physician emerged intact. Doctors, for the most part, had succeeded in protecting themselves. Their claims to professional respect did not suffer any serious set-back. And if Diday is any example, the machinations to which some physicians resorted to protect their reputations from threats brought by wet nurses were nothing less than remarkable for that time, or indeed for any time.

In the end, the challenge these women posed to the medical profession has for all practical purposes been expunged from the record. Nineteenth-century medical historiography tends to promulgate a theme of progress over death, disease, and dysfunction that would do Condorcet proud. By and large, it is true that medicine has followed a triumphant course and come to merit the powerful and respected role it occupies.[41]

Nevertheless, wet nurses influenced the course of both law and medicine in nineteenth-century France. The Vaugirard experiment in the short term victimized many poor women hired as wet nurses for syphilitic infants, but in the long run they were vindicated. In medical science, questioning contagion by secondary symptoms in congenital syphilis was discredited after Rollet's report to the Academy of Medicine in 1861. Ricord's grip on the issue was loosened and the relationship of secondary symptoms to wet nursing clarified. Vaugirard had medical as well as legal repercussions.

AFTERWORD

The legacy of the Vaugirard hospital and its experiment in mercurialized milk has had a long and complicated history with implications for the twenty-first century. The Vaugirard experiment used poor women as medical instruments in a procedure with dangerous implications for their health and well-being. It can be seen as an early example of human experimentation in medical practice.

Like HIV/AIDS, syphilis still presents problems to medical researchers who have been unable to find a vaccine. Penicillin can treat the symptoms, but there is no cure in the full sense of the word. If penicillin becomes over-prescribed (and there is a genuine danger of that occurring), today's physicians may find themselves facing similar problems to those of their eighteenth- and nineteenth-century colleagues.

Despite penicillin, syphilis continues to make inroads among young people, and particularly in the gay community. Infants born of parents with sexually transmitted diseases are still victims. Since 1993 the disease has increased approximately twentyfold in China, where it is part of a more generalized problem affecting heterosexual men and women. "Even more disturbing, the rate of congenital syphilis leapt by almost 72 percent from 1991–2005." [42] Researchers emphasize that such numbers almost certainly underestimate the actual extent of the problem. This has been compared to a similar outbreak in Russia following the collapse of the Soviet Union. Dr John Zenilman, a professor of medicine at Johns Hopkins University who was not linked to the China study, has speculated that such problems could be related to the breakdown of rigid societies, coupled with lower investment in public health. Dr David Fisman, a public health expert at the Hospital for Sick Children in Toronto, stated in *The Lancet* that "You have a vast pool of people susceptible to syphilis who have no natural or acquired immunity … It's like the 15th century all over again."[43] Closer to home, in the Canadian province of Alberta with its booming oil industry, there were four syphilis cases in 1995 and more than two hundred confirmed cases in 2006. Moreover, "the government is increasingly alarmed by the number of babies being born with congenital syphilis."[44]

Confidentiality remains a matter of controversy today. Patient-doctor confidentiality is of concern where computers offer relatively easy access to an individual's medical history. This is particularly relevant for people who have been tested for HIV/AIDS. Can an accommodation be achieved between the individual's right to privacy and the public good? Balancing the patient's right to privacy with the ethical and moral responsibilities of the doctor to the community at large calls for constant overseeing and adjustment in the light of changing circumstances. Openness and vigilance are critical aspects of ethical medical practice.

I began this story with the role played by milk in the transmission of syphilis. I end on the same note. Mercury in the breast milk of Inuit and native Indian women is a matter of concern for health advocates today. It was once thought that disease could not be passed on through milk, but with the emergence of HIV/AIDS it has been found that disease can in fact be transmitted to the infant through breast milk. For this reason, the Human Milk Banking Association of North America does not accept contributions from subjects with syphilis.

Today Health Canada cites mounting evidence that minuscule levels of lead and mercury exposure increase the risk of miscarriage, stillbirth, and premature delivery and lead to problems ranging from lower intelligence to behavioural and learning disabilities, developmental delays, blindness, and seizures.[45]

Finally, it should be noted that in today's culture where mothers often work outside the home and may have undergone breast surgery or had implants, hired wet nurses are making a minor comeback in the United States.[46] Perhaps for medical practitioners there are insights still to be gained from the experience of wet nurses and infants at the hospital of Vaugirard.

APPENDICES

APPENDIX

Case Sources

Throughout the book I reference dozens of incidents where wet nurses contracted syphilis from infants infected with congenital syphilis, and a number of incidents in which wet nurses brought lawsuits against families and doctors, seeking damages. The medical and legal literature suggests that many such cases of infection went unreported, although it is impossible to know how many.

One of the earliest references to wet nurses contracting syphilis from a syphilitic infant is found in Joseph Raulin, *Conservacion des enfan(t)s*, 2 vols. (Paris, 1768). He describes an incident where forty people were infected by a nursling cared for by a nurse in the village of Nerac, Guienne, in 1751. This is also cited by Ambroise Tardieu, *Annales de l'hygiène publique et médecine légale,* vol. 21, 2d series (April-June 1864): 152.

Ambroise Tardieu, "Etude médico-légale sur les maladies accidentellement ou involontairement produites par imprudence, négligence ou transmission contagieuse comprenant L'histoire médico-légale de la Syphilis," *Annales de l'hygiène publique et de médecine légale,* vol. 15, 2d series (1861) and vol. 21 (April-June 1864), especially 129–31, and *Etude médico-légale sur les maladies provoquées ou communiquées comprenant l'histoire médico-légale de la syphilis et de ses divers modes de transmission* (Paris: J.B. Baillière et fils, 1879). See chapter 5, article 2, «Syphilis transmise par allaitment» (Syphilis transmitted by nursing), 153–274, especially 183–4.

There is a third publication with the same title and author that follows on (*suite et fin*) the topic in later issues of *Annales* and refers to cases sixteen to twenty-seven but does not give them in the same detail as in the references cited above. For this reason, I have for the most part depended on the publications of 1861–64 and 1879.

Another early incident (1797) is described by Michel J. Cullerier (1758–1827), chief surgeon of the new venereal diseases hospital in the *Journal Général ou Receuil de la Société de Médicine*, vol. 55, p.32. It refers to a case where a family was willing to yield to the demands of the complainant, but Cullerier's interpretation threw suspicion on the husband of the nurse as the source of the illness. It is not clear whether the case came to litigation. It is cited by Paul Diday in his *Treatise on Syphilis in Newborn Children and Infants at the Breast* [1854], translated by G. Whitley, MD (London: New Sydenham Society, 1859), 157.

Similar examples can be found in an account by Auguste A. Cullerier (1805–74), surgeon at the Hospital Lourcine, "Mémoire sur la contagion syphilitique entre les nourrices et les nourrissons," an excerpt from *Union Médicale de Paris* (Paris: Felix Malteste, 1854), 11–32. He describes four instances in which the nurse explicitly blamed the infant for her contagion, and six others in which the woman remained healthy despite having nursed an infected infant.

There is only one official source for law reports, the *Bulletin de la Cour de Cassation*, which deals with matters of appeal. Another resource is *Droit Français, Guide des Sources Juridiques imprimées (Legislation-Jurisprudence-Doctrine)* (Paris, Bibliothèque Cujas de Droit et de Science Economiques, 2007 edition). Under the heading *Receuils de Jurisprudence* (Collections of Jurisprudence) the subjects and principal characteristics of judicial decisions are listed. Significantly, however, it notes that only a small percentage of the thousands of judgments rendered each year by the courts are included: "All decisions are not published. Each editor makes his own selection" (p. 24). On this issue see Eva Steiner, *French Legal Method* (Oxford University Press, 2002), 100.

Compilations of legal records supply data on cases based for the most part on decisions handed down by the highest courts. The most commonly cited is the *Recueil Dalloz-Sirey*, initiated by Victor Alexis Desiré Dalloz in 1845. In 1965 Dalloz's *Recueil général des lois et des arrêts* (Paris: Bureau de l'Administration, 1872) was merged with the other major compilation, J.B. Sirey's *Codes annotés de Sirey contenant toute la jurisprudence des arrêts et la doctrine des auteurs* (Paris: P. Gilbert, 1873). Dalloz refers to the landmark case of 1868, which states that the physician is responsible for the health of the wet nurse of the family that hired her and the family physician cannot be excused on grounds of confidentiality. This meant that "in principle" article 1382 of the civil code was given priority over article 378 of the penal code, which made any professional violating confidentiality liable to imprisonment for one to six months and subject to a fine of one hundred to five hundred francs.

Other contemporary legal references can be found in the journals *La Semaine juridique*, the *Gazette du Palais*, and the *Gazette des Tribunaux*. The *Gazette des Tribunaux* provides annual tables where one might expect to find references to suits brought by wet nurses under the headings *nourrices* (wet nurses), *dommages-intérêts* (damages), or *médecins* (doctors). However, in a sample based on the years 1830–42 and 1868–73 I have found only one new example (1831), although there were three other references that had been cited by Tardieu and Fournier.

Drawing on the medical literature and the records of civil tribunals, I was able to document twenty-two lawsuits brought before the court by wet nurses or their survivors seeking damages from families and doctors between 1831 and 1906. These cases are itemized in the table below. Because of the difficulty in finding legal details in formal compilations or legal journals, the table depends for the most part on accounts by doctors in articles and treatises of the medico-legal literature. My principal sources of information for these lawsuits are as follows:

Fernand Aurientes, *Nourrices, nourrisons et syphilis*, thesis for his doctorate in medicine, Faculty of Medicine, University of Paris, 1905. Also published as "Etude médico-légale sur la Jurisprudence actuelle à propos de la transmission des maladies vénériennes," *Prophylaxie Médicale* 3, no. 475 (Paris: A. Michelon, 1906): 27–90.

Eugène Bouchut, "Mémoire sur la transmission de la syphilis des nouveau-nés aux nourrices," an excerpt from the *Gazette médicale de Paris* (Paris: Felix Malteste, 1854), 285–99. The excerpt is among the pamphlets in the Drake Collection, Thomas Fisher Library, University of Toronto.

Paul Diday, both his *Treatise on Syphilis*, cited above, and also *Le Péril Vénérien dans les familles* (Paris: Asselin, 1881).

Valerie Fildes, *Wet Nursing, A History from Antiquity to the Present* (Oxford: Basil Blackwell, 1988).

Drs Fortin, Buisson, and Saint, "Rapport médico-légale sur un cas de transmission de syphilis d'un nourrison à sa nourrice" (Report of a medico-legal case of infant transmitting syphilis to a nurse), in *Union Médicale*, new series (1866): 4–7.

Alfred Fournier, *Nourrices et nourrissons syphilitiques* (Paris: V.A. Delahaye, 1878). This was originally a series of lectures later published in *Union Médicale*. A version in English is entitled *The Treatment and Prophylaxis of Syphilis* [1905], 2d ed., translated, revised and enlarged by C.F. Marshall, MD, FRCS (London, New York: Rebman, 1906).

Joy Harsin, "Syphilis, Wives and Physicians: Medical Ethics and the Family in Late Nineteenth-Century France," *French Historical Studies* 16, no.1 (Spring 1989): 72–95. The author refers to cases reported in *Annales de l'hygiène publique et médecine légale*; see 80n31 and 88n68.

Ambroise Tardieu, chair of legal medicine at the Faculty of Medicine, University of Paris, who published a series of articles entitled "Etude médico-légale sur les maladies produites accidentellement ou involontairement," *Annales de l'hygiène publique et médecine légale*, vol. 21, 2d series (April-June 1864), and *Etude médico-légale sur les maladies provoquées ou communiquées comprenant l'histoire médico-légale de la syphilis et de ses divers modes de transmission* (Paris: J.B.Baillière et fils, 1879), 153–274. The latter includes many of the same cases found in the *Annales* of 1864.

Charles Vibert, *Précis de Médecine-légale* (Paris: Bailliére et fils, 1917). "Assistance publique has revealed that in ten years between 1890 and 1899 there were sixty-eight cases of contamination of nurses from nurslings in the Department of the Seine alone" (805n1).

Claude Quétel, *History of Syphilis*, translated by Judith Braddock and Brian Pike (Baltimore: Johns Hopkins University Press, 1990).

Dora B. Weiner, *The Citizen-Patient in Revolutionary and Imperial Paris* (Baltimore and London: Johns Hopkins University Press, 1993).

Rachel Fuchs, *Abandoned Children: Foundlings and Child Welfare in Nineteenth-Century France* (Albany: State University of New York Press, 1984).

Joseph Pierre Martinez Rollet, "Commission set up to Demonstrate the Transmission of Syphilis from Nursling to Nurse, 31 May 1861," *Gazette hebdomodaire de médecine et de chirurgie*, 13 September 1861, 588–94. See also *De la transmission de la syphilis entre nourrisons et nourrices au point de vue de médecine légale* (Paris: Victor Masson et fils, 1861).

Etienne Lancereaux, *Treatise on Syphilis Historical and Practical* (London: New Sydenham Society, 1868–9), vol. 2, "Legal Medicine," 352–62. Also Charles Vibert, *Précis de Médecine Légale* (Paris: J.B.Baillière et fils, 1917).

P.A.O. Mahon, *Recherches importantes sur l'existence, la nature et la communication des Maladies Syphilitiques dans les femmes enceintes, dans les enfans nouveau-nés et dans les nourrices* (Paris: Chez Buisson, n.d.).

René Joseph Hyacinthe Bertin, *Traité de la maladie vénérienne chez les enfants nouveau-nés, les femmes enceintes et les nourrices* (Paris: Chez Gabon, 1810).

Alex Dracobly, "Disciplining the Doctor: Medical Morality and Professionalism in Nineteenth-Century France," 2 vols., PhD thesis, University of Chicago (Ann Arbor, MI, UMI Dissertation Services, 1998).

A.B. Marfan and H. Lemaire, *Précis d'Hygiène et des Maladies du Nourrisson* (Paris: Baillière et fils, 1930), 355.

See also J.E. Moore, *The Modern Treatment of Syphilis*, 2^d ed. (Springfield, IL, Baltimore, MD: C.C. Thomas, 1941).

The table below outlines the twenty-two cases I have documented that occurred between 1831 and 1906, in which wet nurses or their survivors brought lawsuits against families and doctors. The table gives the date of the court decision when full details are available, or the date of the charges brought by the nurse. The location refers to the civil tribunal or court that judged the suit (if this information is available), or to the town or city in which the family that hired the wet nurse lived. The source refers to the author of the account or bibliographical references concerning the suit. Damages refers to the sum of money to be paid by the guilty party to the victim according to the terms of the court decision. References to cases that did not go to court or for which precise information is not given have been addressed in the text.

TABLE OF CASES THAT WENT TO COURT

Date	Location	Source	Damages
1831	Tribunal de la Seine	*Gazette des Tribunaux,* 18 August 1831, no.1875, p. 984	Parent guilty
1841	Tulle , Tribunal of Limoges	Diday, *Treatise,* 189, 90	No legal details
1848	Lyon (La Charité)	Bouchut, case 5, "Mémoire," 295–9 (pp. 9–10 in *Gazette Médicale de Paris,* 1850)	No legal details
1848	Lyon (La Charité)	Bouchut, case 6, "Mémoire," 295–9 (p.10 in *Gazette Médicale de Paris,* 1850)	No legal details
1851–52	La Ferté sous Jouarre, Tribunal of Meaux	Tardieu, "Etude" (1864): 138–40, *Etude* (1879), 203–11; Diday, *Treatise,* 315	Family guilty; 2,000 francs
1853	Lyon	Tardieu, *Etude* (1879), 198– 9	Administration of Bureau des nourrices guilty; 400 francs. Appealed (see Sirey, vol. 2, p.474)
1854	Court of Amiens	Tardieu, "Etude" (1864): 116–20	No legal details
1855	Illier (Eure et Loire)	Tardieu, "Etude" (1864): 146	Family guilty; 5,000 francs
1858	Tribunal of the Seine	Fildes, *Wet Nursing,* 239n99	Family guilty; 7,680 francs
1859	Bordeaux	Tardieu, "Etude" (1864): 142–4, *Etude* (1879), 211–14	No legal details
1859 (2 cases)	Sainte-Agreve (Ardèche)	Tardieu, 2 cases, "Etude" (1864): 147; *Etude* (1879), 216–19	No legal details
1860	Tribunal of the Seine	Tardieu, "Etude" (1864): 134–5, *Etude* (1879), 202–3; *Gazette des Tribunaux,* 15 August 1860; *Le Droit,* 15 August 1860; *Méd. Times Gaz.* 2 (1860): 215	Family guilty; 3,000 francs
1860	Lyon	Tardieu, "Etude" (1864): 149, *Etude* (1879), 220–1	No legal details
1866	Tribunal civil of Evreux	Drs. Fortin, Buisson, Saint, *Union Médicale,* (Nouvelle serie, 1866) 4–7	Family guilty; 1,200 francs

Date	Location	Source	Damages
1868	Court of Dijon	Tardieu, *Etude* (1879), 194–5; Dalloz, *Jurisprudence général*, vol. 2 (1869), 195; Fournier, *Nourrices*, 74	Family guilty; 5,000 francs
1874	Tribunal of the Seine	Tardieu, *Etude* (1879), 196–7; *Journal de Droit*, 5 February 1876; *Gazette des Tribunaux*, 16 April 1874; Fournier, *Nourrices*, 88	Nurse lost case, fined costs
1893	Court of Amiens	Vibert, *Précis*, 805 and 826.	Physician guilty, no details
1893	Tribunal of the Seine	Aurientes, *Nourrices*; *Bull.de la Société de Prophylaxie sanitaire et morale* (March 1906): 62	Assistance publique fined 12,000 francs
1901	Court of Lyon	Harsin, "Syphilis, Wives and Physicians," 80; "Responsabilité des parents," *Annales de l'hygiène publique* 47 (1903), (1901): 467–9	Family guilty; no legal details
	Tribunal of the Seine	Harsin, "Syphilis, Wives and Physicians," 88. Account of Dr Dubois in *Annales de l'hygiène publique* 49 (1903): 567–8	Assistance publique guilty
1906	Tribunal of the Seine	Vibert, *Précis*, 827	Family and physician guilty; fined 8,000 francs

Decision of the Court of Dijon,
14 May 1868

The landmark decision of the Court of Dijon of 14 May 1868 stated
that a doctor who has been called to visit an infant who knowingly
does not inform the infant's wet nurse that her nursling is suffering
from a contagious virus can, in the eventuality that this virus is transmitted to the nurse, be declared responsible for the harm caused to
her by his reticence.

Printed below are excerpts from the court's decision, taken from
Ambroise Tardieu , *Etude médico-légale sur les maladies provoquées
ou communiquées comprenant l'histoire médico-légale de la syphilis
et de ses divers modes de transmission* (Paris: J.B. Baillière et fils,
1879), 191–4. The translation is my own.

The Court,
The enquiry ordered by the [law] suit of 25 January shows that
the infant, whom the married couple Poncet had given to the
woman Protat as wet nurse, had shown a few days after its birth
unmistakable indications of a hereditary or congenital syphilis; that on 20 February 1863, Doctor B..., [was] called by the
Poncet family to visit the infant then twenty-five days old, [was]
aware of the existence of that syphilis and ordered the remedies
required for the infant and the wet nurse but did not inform the
nurse of the nature of the infant's illness or of the danger that
nursing could cause her; that on the 26 of February she consulted another physician, the doctor G..., who also recognized
the presence of hereditary syphilis in the infant and observed that
the Protat woman had on her left breast a flat mucous outbreak
whose shape and colour indicated that she had been infected,

[by] the same malady from which the infant suffered; that nevertheless Doctor G... had not considered it his duty to warn the
Protat woman of the nature of the illness, because, he said, the
harm was already done and it would be enough to prescribe
treatment for her; that the child appeared to have been completely cured and that during the period of nursing up to the time
of weaning the nurse Protat did not seem to have shown any new
symptoms of syphilis; but then, in the month of April 1864, the
doctor B... realized that [this nurse] was suffering from constitutional syphilis; [and] this he himself declared in a letter addressed
to M. D..., officer of health, [stating] that the malady had been
communicated to the nurse by her nursling. M. D..., called to
treat the nurse at the end of May 1864, verified in his turn very
serious symptoms, first, extreme salivation or pytalism, then par-
alysis on one side of her body, and finally complete loss of her
mind which lasted until the death of the Protat woman.

More than a year passed between the observation of early
syphilitic symptoms by Doctor G... and the time when symptoms
of constitutional syphilis had appeared.An interval of this length,
would appear to be abnormal, [and could] have raised [ques-
tions] as to [how the] contagion [had been] transmitted [to the
Protat woman.] [However] in April 1864 Doctor B... had not
attributed it to the nursing of the Poncet infant. In such a matter
it would not be [considered] the role of members of the tribunal
to disagree with or contradict the opinion of the skilled professional [homme d'art] who had observed the course of the illness;
[Nevertheless] one can concede, following the declaration of
Doctor B... himself, that the Protat woman had contracted from
her nursling the infection of the disease that had for her such terrible consequences.

Aside from professional questions depending exclusively on
the uncertainties and controversies of a scientific nature, the doctor is, like any citizen, responsible for harm caused by his lack
of judgment, his carelessness or his evident incompetence, in a
word, due to his personal fault. The doctor who knowingly keeps
from a wet nurse the dangers to which she is exposed by nursing an infant suffering from congenital syphilis can be declared
responsible for harm caused by his reticence; – that he cannot
claim that he was called upon to care for the infant only and
need not be concerned with the danger to which the nurse could

be exposed. Such a theory, which contradicts moral laws, cannot be invoked against a wet nurse whose situation by its nature
necessarily requires her confidence in the doctor chosen by the
family of the infant.

Considering, moreover, that responsibility can be assigned
only in so far as the harm is an incontestable matter of fact on
the part of the one from whom reparation is demanded [and]
that according to the declaration of doctor G... the nurse Protat
exhibited on 20 February 1863 apparent symptoms of syphilis, it
is undeniable that the contagion of the illness [must have] taken
place prior to 20 February, the date of the first visit to the infant
by Doctor B...; – [therefore] it is not certain that at that date of
20 February she would have been able to avoid contagion, even
if, warned of the danger by the doctor, she had immediately
ceased nursing. Consequently it has not been proven that the
unfortunate reticence of Doctor B... had been the cause of harm
to her; that in this set of circumstances, the demand for damages presented by Protat, as caregiver for young children, against
Doctor B... cannot be accommodated.
Confirmed, etc.,
(14 May 1868 – Court of Dijon, 1 Chamber. MM. Grasset,
pr.– Bernard, av.gén.– Gouget et Jolly av.)

General Legislative and Statutory Terms

Arrêt. Executive decision, in a general or individual sense, signed by one or more officials or administrative authorities (prefectoral or municipal).

Arrêts de principe. Generally accepted decisions, i.e., certain decisions that exercise influence on decisions handed down in similar cases – usually those of the Cour de cassation, or appeals court, and usually involving a similar outcome. See *Precedent*, below.

Civil law. A body of principal decrees, enactments passed by legally constituted authorities or agents of the state to regulate rights duties and liabilities between the state and its citizens or between each other and between members of foreign state. See above Sethna, *Jurisprudence*, 108.

Cour de cassation. Court of appeal.

Coutume (custom). Rule of law (often unwritten) and a condition of legal right in so far as it does not contradict a written constitutive law.

Dommages-intérêts. Damages, in the sense of suing for injury or harm.

Droit. A right in the sense of entitlement or obligation. It refers to the normative order, as distinct from the rule of law (*loi*), which considers in a precise way certain forms of behaviour or acts. *Droit* implies certain rules but only in relation to their acceptance by the moral conscience. It takes into account the circumstances in which individuals find themselves. The tie between *droit* and morality is close, but it can depend on time and place. See Jean Darbelly, *La Règle juridique. Son fondement moral et sociale* (St Maurice Editions de l'oeuvre St Augustin, 1945), 22–33.

Interdiction de la publicité. Any publicity of a commercial nature, whether directly or in the name of a cure and treatment of a venereal malady, is forbidden except in publications exclusively designed for the medical profession. The doctor must avoid, both in writing and speech, making any *attente* (insinuation or claim) related to the honour of the profession, all publicity, and everything that is incompatible with individual and professional dignity. He must refrain from furnishing any information susceptible to such ends; nor should he divulge in public a procedure insufficiently proven of which the blamelessness has not been demonstrated. *Dictionnaire de Droit*, 2 vols. (Paris: Libraire Dalloz, 1966), vol. 2, C. santé publique civ. Article 1 356, 5 October 1953. See article 25, p. 141. *Jurisprudence.* The set of court decisions made either by all jurisdictions or by a particular administrative branch of the legal system. In France jurisprudence is usually referred to as *"philosophie du droit."* It deals with fundamental philosophical, historical, and sociological principles and an analysis of the legal concepts on which the rules of law are based. See M.J. Sethna, *Jurisprudence* (Lakhani: Girgaon-Bouley, 1959), 1–8.

La loi. General and permanent written rule, voted by Parlement, that constitutes the principal legal forms of the civil-penal system.

Penal law. Deals with criminal responsibility.

Precedent. In France precedent does not carry the same weight of authority as in the common law tradition of Britain, though it does have persuasive authority. See *Arrêts de principe*, above.

Receuils de Jurisprudence. Collections of jurisprudence. These are private editions. Not all decisions are published. Each editor makes his own selection, although certain decisions can be found in several collections. The principal publications are Victor Alexis Désiré Dalloz, *Jurisprudence générale du royaume, Répertoire méthodique et alphabétique de législation et de jurisprudence en nature de droit public* (Paris: Bureau de la Jurisprudence générale); *Gazette du Palais*; *Gazette des tribunaux*; and *Semaine juridique*.

Receuils officials. Official collections of jurisprudence. Decisions of the high courts are listed in these collections: *Bulletin des arrêts de la Cour de cassation; Recueil du Conseil d'Etat*; and certain specialized jurisdictions such as *Recueil des décisions du Conseil constitutionnel*.

Abbreviations Used in Notes

Bull.Ac.Méd.	*Bulletin de l' Académie de médecine*
Bull.Hist.Med.	*Bulletin of the History of Medicine*
CBMH/BCHM	*Canadian Bulletin of Medical History/* *Bulletin canadien d'histoire de la médecine*
Edinb. Med. *and Surg. Journal*	*Edinburgh Medical and Surgical Journal*
J.Hist.Med. *and Allied Sci.*	*Journal of the History of Medicine and* *Allied Sciences*
Journal de Méd., Chirurg. *et Pharm. de Bruxelles*	*Journal de Médecine, Chirurgie et Pharmacie* *de Bruxelles.*

Notes

INTRODUCTION

1 Ambroise Tardieu, "Etude médico-légale sur les maladies accidentellement ou involontaireme produites par imprudence, négligence
ou transmission contagieuse comprenant L'histoire Médico-légale
de la Syphilis," *Annales de l'hygiène publique et de médecine légale*,
2d series, vol. 21 (April-June 1864), especially 129–31, and *Etude
médico-légale sur les maladies provoquées ou communiquées comprenant l'histoire médico-légale de la syphilis et de ses divers modes de
transmission* (Paris: J.B. Baillière et fils, 1879). See article 2, "Syphilis
transmise par allaitment" (Syphilis transmitted by nursing), 153–274,
especially 183–4. There is a third publication with the same title and
author that follows in later issues of *Annales* and refers to cases sixteen to twenty-seven but does not give them in the same detail as in
the references cited above, so I have for the most part depended on the
publications of 1861–64 and 1879.

2 Alfred Fournier is generally credited with asserting in 1875 the syphilitic origin of tabes, but much of the groundwork had been prepared by
Philippe Ricord. See his *Traité pratique des maladies vénériennes ou recherches critiques et expérimentales sur l'inoculation appliqué à l'étude
de ces maladies* (Paris: De Just Bouvier and E. Le Bouvier, 1838), 644.

3 Sean M. Quinlan, "Heredity and Moral Hygiene in the French
Enlightenment," *Bull.Hist.Med.* 80 (2006):649–76. In 1748 Dijon's
Academy of Science solicited manuscripts addressing the question,
"How are hereditary maladies transmitted?" One hundred years later
the contagion issue was again the subject of major debate among
members of the Academy of Medicine of Paris.

4 Cited in Tardieu, *Etude médico-légale*, 183.

5 Ibid., 184.

6 Claude Quétel, *History of Syphilis*, translated by Judith Braddock and Brian Pike Baltimore: Johns Hopkins University Press, 1990), 150.

7 Tardieu, "Étude Médico-Légale" (1864), 190.

8 Jean A.N., Marquis de Condorcet, *Sketch for a Historical Picture of the Progress of the Human Mind* (Esquisse d'un tableau historique du progrès de l'esprit) [1795] (London: Wm. Clowes and Sons, 1955), 200.

9 J.P.M. Lenoir, Conseiller d'état, Lieutenant-général de Police, *Détail des quelques établissements de la ville de Paris demandé par sa Majesté Impériale, La Reine de Hongrie à M.Lenoir* (Paris: Imprimerie royale, 1780). He pointed out that "the majority of foundlings bring at birth the germs of an illness that often poisons them and is given to their nurses" (62).

10 Dora B. Weiner, *The Citizen-Patient in Revolutionary and Imperial Paris* (Baltimore and London: Johns Hopkins University Press, 1993), 70.

11 Rachel Fuchs, *Abandoned Children: Foundlings and Child Welfare in Nineteenth-Century France* (Albany: State University of New York Press, 1984), 26.

12 Ibid., 10.

13 Edward J. Shorter, "Sexual Change in Illegitimacy: The European Experience," in *Modern European Social History*, edited by Robert J. Bezucha (Lexington, MA: D.C. Heath, 1972), 231–69. The author saw the relative sexual freedom that the city offered to unmarried young women as a factor in the increasing numbers of illegitimate infants. See also Shorter's *Written in the Flesh: A History of Desire* (Toronto: University of Toronto Press, 2005) 111, 12. This interpretation of illegitimacy as a "sexual revolution" has been disputed by feminist historians of the period. See Joan W. Scott and Louise A. Tilly, "Women's Work and the Family in Nineteenth-Century Europe," *Comparative Studies in Society and History* 17 (1975): 36–64. See also Jacques Soubeyroux, *Pauperisme et rapports sociaux à Madrid aux xviiième siècle*, 2 vols. (Lille: Université de Lille 3, 1978). The author points out that of infants abandoned in Madrid in a three-month period in 1804, almost eighty-five percent were identified by name (vol. 2, 580). See also Joan Sherwood, *Poverty in Eighteenth-Century Spain: The Women and Children of the Inclusa* (Toronto: University of Toronto Press, 1988). A study of the foundling hospital in Madrid found that

in years of economic crisis at the end of the eighteenth century the numbers of legitimate infants might actually outnumber illegitimate newborns. 95–124.

14 Jill Harsin, *Policing Prostitution in Nineteenth-Century Paris* (Princeton, NJ: Princeton University Press, 1985). See also Alain Corbin, *Les filles de noce: Misère sexuelle et prostitution (19ᵉ et 20ᵉ siècles)* (Paris: Aubier Montagne, 1978).

15 Rachel Fuchs, *Poor and Pregnant in Paris: Strategies for Survival in the Nineteenth Century* (New Brunswick, NJ, Rutgers University Press, 1992), 36.

16 Vincent J. Knapp, "Major Medical Explanations for High Infant Mortality in Nineteenth–century Europe," *CBMH/BCHM* 15 (1998): 317–36, 322.

17 From an interview with Auguste F.F. Von Kotzebue (originally published in *Meine Flucht nam Paris* [Leipzig: Kummer, 1791], 267–72) in Alexandre Tuetey, ed., *L'Assistance publique à Paris pendant la Révolution. Documents Inédits recuellis et publiés par Alexandre Tuetey*, 4 vols., translated by M. Chuquet (Paris: Imprimerie nationale, 1911), vol. 1, pp. li, lii. The interview was given in 1790, shortly after the closing of Vaugirard. It refers to the increasing numbers of abandoned infants with venereal disease being admitted to Enfants-trouvés in the second half of the eighteenth century.

18 Although envisioned originally as a separate entity, Vaugirard came formally under the aegis of Enfants-trouvés at an early stage.

19 Edward Seidler, "An Historical Survey of Children's Hospitals," in *The Hospital in History*, edited by Lindsay Granshaw and Roy Porter (London: Routledge Kegan Paul, 1989), 186. See also Margaret Pelling, "Child Health as a Social Value in Early Modern England," *Society for the Social History of Medicine* (London, 1988): 135–64. See G. Armstrong, *Account of Diseases Most Incident in Children* (London: T. Cadell, 1771). In 1769 Armstrong, a physician, founded a Dispensary for the Infant Poor that operated three to four days a week at Red Lion Square. This was an outpatient clinic. A stronger claim could be made for the Middlesex Hospital of London, opened in 1745. It was founded to deal with smallpox and to carry out vaccinations. See Michel Foucault, Blandine Barret Kriegel, Anne Thalamy, Francois Beguin, Bruno Fortier, eds., *Les machines à guérir: Aux origines de l'hôpital moderne* (Paris: Dossiers et Documents d'Architecture, Imprimé à l'Institut de l'Environnement, 1976), 21.

20 Quétel, *History of Syphilis*, 83–93.

21 Weiner, *The Citizen-Patient*, 186.
22 Alex Dracobly, "Ethics and Experimentation on Human Subjects in Mid-Nineteenth-Century France: The Story of the 1859 Syphilis Experiments," *Bull.Hist. Med.* 77 (2003): 332–66. For a discussion of the issue of contagion and secondary symptoms see pp. 335–43. Although the author does not refer explicitly to wet nurses, they figured prominently in the stand on contagion taken by the noted syphilologist Philippe Ricord.
23 Ibid., 351–2. See also Report of Gibert on "Contagion des accidents secondaires de la syphilis," *Bull. Ac. Méd.* 24 (1858–59): 936.
24 Joseph Pierre Martinez Rollet, "Commission set up to Demonstrate the Transmission of Syphilis from Nursling to Nurse, 31 May 1861," *Gazette hebdomodaire de médecine et de chirurgie*, 13 September 1861, 588–94. See also *De la transmission de la syphilis entre nourrisons et nourrices au point de vue de médecine légale* (Paris: Victor Masson et fils, 1861).
25 Rollet, "Commission," 590–94.
26 Etienne Lancereaux, *Treatise on Syphilis Historical and Practical*(London: New Sydenham Society, 1868–9), vol. 2, "Legal Medicine," 352–62. See also Charles Vibert, *Précis de Médecine Légale* (Paris: J.B.Baillière et fils, 1917).
27 Tardieu, "Etude médico-légale"(1864).
28 George Weisz, *Medical Mandarins: The French Academy of Medicine in the Nineteenth and Early Twentieth Century*, (New York: Oxford University Press, 1995). See also Weisz's "Transformations de l'Elite Médicale en France," translated by Monique de Saint Martin, *Actes de la Recherche en Sciences Sociales* 74 (1988): 33–46, and "The Emergence of Medical Specialization in the Nineteenth Century," *Bull.Hist.Med.* 77 (2003): 536–75; Pierre Guillaume, *Le Rôle Social du Médecin depuis deux siècles* (Paris: Association pour l'étude de l'histoire de sécurité sociale, 1996), 67–74; Ann LaBerge, *Mission and Method: The Early Nineteenth-Century Public Health Movement* (Cambridge: Cambridge University Press, 1992) See also LaBerge "Public Health in France and the French Public Health Movement, 1815–1848," PhD thesis, University of Tennessee, 1974 (Ann Arbor, MI, University Microfilms, 1974).
29 Ambroise Tardieu, Extract of discourse, "Des Devoirs publics du Médecin" (The Public Duties of the Doctor) given at opening session of classes of the Faculty of Medicine, Paris, 16 November 1863, 92,

quoted in *Dictionnaire des sciences médicales*, vol. 27, s.v. "Médecine légale," p.379.

30 Jan Goldstein, *Console and Classify – The French Psychiatric Profession in the Nineteenth Century* (Cambridge and New York: Cambridge University Press, 1987), 24–8. As Goldstein notes, this goes back to Vicq d'Azir and his "Nouveau plan de constitution pour la médecine en France" at the end of the Old Regime.

31 A.J.B. Parent-Duchâtelet, *De la Prostitution en la ville de Paris*, 2 vols. (Paris, 1836).

32 Alex Dracobly, "Disciplining the Doctor: Medical Morality and Professionalism in Nineteenth-Century France," 2 vols., PhD thesis, University of Chicago (Ann Arbor, MI, UMI Dissertation Services, 1998), vol. 1, 177–8.

CHAPTER ONE

1 Quétel, *History of Syphilis* (see Introduction, note 6) 24–5 and 65.

2 Michel Cullerier, *Notes historiques sur les hôpitaux établis pour traiter la maladie vénérienne* (Paris: N.p., Year 11), 27.

3 Camille Bloch et Alexandre Tuetey," Procès-verbaux et Rapports du Comité de Mendicité de la Constituante, 1790–91," *Collection de Documents Inédits sur l'histoire économique de la Révolution Française publiés par les soins du Ministre de l'Instruction Publique* (Paris: Imprimerie nationale, 1811), 611.

4 Cited in Marthe Marie Thérèse Delamare-Riche, *Les vénériennes à Bicêtre, Un chapitre de l'histoire de l'hospice de Bicêtre, 1656–1792* (Paris: Librairie Louis Arnette, 1942), 48.

5 *Traitement public et gratuit des enfans attaqués de la maladie vénérienne par Ordre de M. le L.G. de Police*, permis d'imprimeur, 3 May 1770 (Paris: De Saratine, chez Gueffier, 1770).

6 Leonard J. Goldwater, *Mercury: A History of Quicksilver* (Baltimore: York Press, 1972), 216–18.

7 Quétel, *History of Syphilis*, 60–3.

8 Ibid. For the roles of Alfred Fournier and Philippe Ricord in the identification of third-stage syphilis, see 134–5, and Introduction, note 2.

9 François Rabelais, *Account of the Inestimable Life of the Great Gargantua and of the Heroic Deeds, Sayings and Marvelous Voyages of His Son the Good Pantagruel*, Book 1, quoted in Goldwater, *Mercury*, 222. The powdering keg refers to a barrel for salting pork,

large enough to hold a person, who was then fumigated with mercury
at a high temperature to sweat out the illness. Shakespeare made several references to this process. See illustration in Quétel, *History of
Syphilis*, 83.

10 Quétel, *History of Syphilis*, 59–63 and 83–93.

11 Walter Sneader, *Drug Discovery: The Evolution of Modern Medicines*
(Toronto: John Wiley and Sons, 1985), 69.

12 I am grateful to Robert Jackson, MD, FRPC, for bringing these experiments to my attention. See A. Jarisch, *Die Hautkrankheiten* (Vienna:
Alfred Holder, 1900).

13 Quétel, *History of Syphilis*, 83. This was to induce a febrile reaction
which would cause sweating in order to extirpate the venereal virus.

14 Owsei Temkin, "Therapeutic Trends and Treatment of Syphilis
before 1900," *Bull.Hist.Med.* 29 (1955): 311. See also Winfried
Schleiner, "Moral Attitudes toward Syphilis and Its Prevention in the
Renaissance," *Bull.Hist.Med.* 68, no. 3 (Fall 1994): 389–410.

15 Ibid., 314.

16 Quétel, *History of Syphilis*, 112.

17 Paul Diday, *A Treatise on Syphilis in Newborn Children and Infants
at the Breast* [1854], translated by G. Whitley, MD (London: The New
Sydenham Society, 1859), 365.

18 Paul Diday, "Histoire naturelle et thérapeutique de la Syphilis,"
Annales Hebdomadaire de Médecine et Chirurgie 8, no.21 (1861): 35.

19 H.M.J. Desruelles, *Memoir on the Treatment of Venereal Diseases
without Mercury employed at the Military Hospital of Val-De Grâce*,
translated by G.J. Guthrie, Deputy Inspector of Hospitals, Lecturer on
Surgery (Philadelphia: Carey and Lea, 1830), vii. There is some reason
to be sceptical about Desruelles's statistics. The patients in his sample
were being treated in facilities controlled by physiologists but the
treatments were all referred to as "experiments."

20 Ibid., 84.

21 Alfred Fournier, *Traitement de la Syphilis* (Paris: Rueff, 1893), 587.

22 Michel Fontanier, "Le traitement de syphilis par le mercure selon
les auteurs parisiens de la deüxième moitié du XVIIIième siècle."
Doctoral thesis, Faculty of Medicine of Creteil, University of Paris,
1982, 44.

23 A.B. Marfan and H. Lemaire, *Précis d'Hygiène et des Maladies du
Nourrisson* (Paris: Baillière et fils, 1930), 355.

24 Cited in Goldwater, *Mercury*, 224. In the 1950s an infant teething
powder was removed from the market because it was found to be

a cause of the so-called "pink disease," for which the mercury pow-
ders were, in fact, being prescribed. See also J.E. Moore, *The Modern
Treatment of Syphilis,* 2^d ed. (Springfield, IL, Baltimore, MD: C.C.
Thomas, 1941).

25 Jan Goldstein, *Console and Classify: The French Psychiatric Profession
in the Nineteenth Century* (Cambridge: Cambridge University Press,
1987), 59.

26 Philippe Ricord, *Lettres sur la Syphilis addressées à M.le rédacteur en
chef de l'Union Médicale, suivies des discours à l'Académie Impériale
de Médecine* (Paris: J.B. Baillière et fils, 1863), 180.

27 James McIntosh and Paul Fildes, "The Theory and Practice of
the Treatment of Syphilis with Ehrlich's New Specific '606,'"
Lancet 2 (1910): 1,684. For an outline of the research involved in
finding spirochete and its treatment see Quétel, *History of Syphilis,*
139–43.

28 Ludwig Fleck, *Genesis and Development of a Scientific Fact* [1930],
edited by Robert K. Merton and Thaddeus Trinn, translated by Fred
Bradley (Chicago: University of Chicago Press, 1979).

29 Temkin, "Therapeutic Trends," 316.

30 John Burns, *The Principles of Midwifery Including the Diseases of
Women and Children* (London: Longman, Hurst, Rees, Orme and
Brown, 1814), 503–7.

31 P.A.O. Mahon, *Recherches importantes sur l'existence, la nature et la
communication des Maladies Syphilitiques dans les femmes enceintes,
dans les enfans nouveau-nés et dans les nourrices* (Paris: Chez Buisson,
n.d.), 63.

32 René Joseph Hyacinthe Bertin, *Traité de la maladie vénérienne chez les
enfants nouveau-nés, les femmes enceintes et les nourrices* (Paris: Chez
Gabon, 1810), xiv.

33 J.F. Hernandez, *Essai analytique sur la non-identité des virus gonor-
roique et syphilitique* (Paris: J.J. Paschoud, 1812). See also Quétel,
History of Syphilis, 111.

34 Mahon, *Recherches importantes,* 97.

35 John Hunter, *A Treatise on Venereal Disease* (London: 1786), 298. My
emphasis.

36 Nils Rosen von Rosenstein, *The Diseases of Children and Their
Remedy,* translated by Andrew Sparmann, MD (London: T. Cadell,
1776), 320–1.

37 William Buchan, *Observations Concerning Prevention and Cure of
Venereal Disease Intended to Guard the Ignorant and Unwary against*

the Harmful Effects of That Insidious Malady (London: T. Chapman, 1796), 155.

CHAPTER TWO

1 Dora B. Weiner, *The Citizen-Patient* (see Introduction, note 10), 36–7 and 82–3.

2 Jean Charles Pierre Lenoir, *Hospice des pauvres enfants nouveau-nés atteints du mal vénérien situé à Vaugirard* (Paris: Imprimerie Philippe-Denys Pierres, imprimeur ordinaire du Roi et de la Police, 1781).

3 Doublet, Introduction to Jean Colombier's *Médecine Pratique; Observations sur la maladie vénérienne et le millet dont les nouveau-nés font attaqués, avec reflexions sur la nature et le traitement de ces maladies par M. Colombier, Journal de la Médecine, Chirurgie et Pharmacie* (January 1783): 199. Colombier's article was originally published in *Mémoire de la Société Royale* (August 1781), vol. 5, n.p.

4 Albert Dupoux, *Sur les pas de M. Vincent: Trois cent ans de l'histoire parisienne de l'enfance abandonnée* (Paris: Revue de L'Assistance publique à Paris, 1958), 55–7 and 120. See also L. Lombeau, *Histoire des Communes annexés à Paris en 1859 publiée sous les auspices du Conseil général, Vaugirard* (Paris: Ernest Leroux, 1912); Philippe Delarivièrre, "L'Hôpital de Vaugirard des origines à nos jours," *Histoire des Sciences médicales* 12, no.2 (1978): 153–61; Paul Delaunay, "La Médecine à Vaugirard," *La France Médicale: Revue de l'Histoire de Médecine* (1913): 219–20; P. Vallery Radot, *Deux siècles de l'histoire hospitalière* (Paris: Dupont, 1967), 172–3; M. Thiery, "Guide des amateurs et des étrangers voyageurs à Paris" (Paris, 1787); Fernand Boussault, *L'Assistance aux enfants abandonnés à Paris du XVIè au XVIIIè siècles* (Paris: Rodstein, 1937).

5 Pierre J. George Cabanis, *Du degré de certitude de la Médecine* (Paris: Imprimerie Crêpelet, 1803), 187.

6 Jeanne Kisacky, "Restructuring Isolation: Hospital Architecture, Medicine, and Disease Prevention," *Bull. Hist. Med.* 79 *(2005)*: 1–49. The author discusses the theme in the context of the New York hospital in the period 1771–1930 (pp. 22 and 48).

7 Ignacio Maria Ruiz de Luzuriaga, "Estadística política-médica o estado comparativos de los Xenodochios, Dereophotorios y Horfánotriofos, o seas Casas de Amparo u Hospicios de Maternidad, Inclusas y Casas de Huérfanos o Desamparados de España," 5 vols. (1817–19), manuscript

in the Archives of the Academy of Medicine in Madrid, Spain, vol. 2, 358.

8 F. Doublet, *Observations faites dans le Département des Hôpitaux civils, extrait de Journal de Médecine, janvier, 1785* (Paris, 1785, available from the Archives de l'Assistance publique in Paris, A704, Règlements, headings 2–6, pp. 117–33. These regulations outline in detail the government and administration of Vaugirard, presumably set out originally by Colombier and described in more general terms by Lenoir, *Hospice*.

9 Jacques Tenon, *Memoirs on Paris Hospitals* [1788], edited by Dora B. Weiner (Science History Publications, Watson Publishing International, 1966), 49.

10 For an account of the dispute see Louis S. Greenbaum, "Nurses and Doctors in Conflict: Piety and Medicine in the Paris Hôtel-Dieu on the Eve of the French Revolution," *Clio Medica* 13 (1979): 247–69.

11 Ibid., 247.

12 Toby Gelfand, *Professionalizing Modern Medicine: Paris Surgeons and Medical Science and Institutions in the 18th Century* (Westport, CT: Greenwood Press, 1980), 123.

13 Lenoir, *Hospice* (see note 2, above), 5. Doublet's account in *Observations*(heading 5, article 15, 119) was given in precisely Colombier's words: "Any woman in the last months of pregnancy is obliged to follow general rules of the hospital in taking the sacraments."

14 Louis S. Greenbaum, "Jacques Necker and the Reform of the Paris Hospitals on the Eve of the French Revolution," *Clio Medica* 19 (1984): 225.

15 "Report to the to the Poverty Committee," in Alexandre Tuetey, ed., *L'Assistance publique à Paris pendant la Révolution Française*, 4 vols. (Paris: Imprimerie nationale, 1895), vol.1, *Hospices et Hôpitals 1789–91*, 338.

16 Apparently these funds were assigned under the direction of Lenoir.

17 Pierre Gallot-Lavallée, *Un Hygiéniste du xviiième siècle, Jean Colombier, Rapporteur de Conseil de Santé des Hôpitaux militaires, Inspecteur général des Hôpitaux et Prisons du Royaume, (1736–1789)* (Paris: Jouve, 1913), 57–62. This account is taken verbatim from a report written by Colombier himself.

18 Ibid., 61.

19 Ibid., 60.

20 Doublet's report to the Comité de Mendicité in Tuetey,ed.,
   L'Assistance publique, vol. 1, 340. See also Bloch et Tuetey,
   *Collections Inédits sur l'histoire économique de la Révolution
   Francaise publiés par les soins du Ministre de l'Instruction Publique*
   (Paris, 1911); and the account available in Archives nationales (Paris),
   F/15/1861,

21 Cabanis, *Du Degré*, 189.

22 Recette des Revenu et Dépense, Hospice de Vaugirard, 1781–86,
   Archives nationales (Paris), F/15/1861.

      In 1726, the livre was worth twenty sols, and the sol worth twelve
   deniers. The sol, a copper coin, was later called sou (one hundred sous
   were usually equivalent to a five-franc piece according to Cassel's
   Dictionary of 1951). The livre was equivalent to one and one-half
   pounds of silver, though it fluctuated wildly. In 1795 the livre was replaced by the franc, which at that point was worth one livre and six
   deniers. The references to currency are for the period before 1790.

23 Doublet, *Observations*, cited in Gelfand, *Professionalizing Modern
   Medicine*, 138.

24 See Michel Foucault, *Birth of the Clinic: An Archaeology of Medical
   Perception*, translated from the French by A.M. Sheridan Smith (New
   York: Pantheon Books, 1973), ix- xix. Foucault argued that the doctor
   in France at the end of the eighteenth century brought to the bedside
   of the patient a new "medical gaze" of scientific objectivity. In other
   words, the birth of modern medicine came about when the experience
   of disease became "clinical" on the basis of empirical evidence (observation, experiment etc.) rather than depending upon systems and
   philosophical theory. For an in-depth critique of the Foucault thesis see
   Othmar Keel, *L'Avènement de la Médecine clinique en Europe, 1750–
   1815* (Montreal: Les Presses de l'Université de Montréal, 2001). Keel
   points out that the "medicalization" associated with clinical practice
   as described by Foucault was in fact operative in the last half of the
   eighteenth century in a number of European countries and not original
   in France.

25 Greenbaum, "Nurses and Doctors in Conflict," 119–20.

26 Gallot–Lavallée, *Un Hygiéniste*, 59.

27 J. Colombier, "Observations faites dans le département des hôpitaux
   civils: Institution de l'hospice des Enfants trouvés atteints de la maladie
   vénérienne faite à Paris en 1780," read at Royal Society of Medicine,
   Paris, August 1780. Cited in P.A.O. Mahon, *Histoire de la médecine clinique* (Paris: Chez Gallois, 1804), 586. See also F. Doublet, *Mémoire sur*

les symptômes et le traitement de la maladie vénérienne dans les enfans nouveau-nés; lu a l'assemblée particulière de la Faculté de Médicine, dite prima mensis, le 15 octobre 1781 (Paris: Méquignon, 1781).

28 Greenbaum, "Jacques Necker," 221.

29 Gallot-Lavallée, *Un Hygiéniste*, 60.

30 Doublet, "Mémoire sur les symptômes."

31 Weiner, *Citizen-Patient* (see Introduction, note 10), 11.

32 T. Gelfand, "A Clinical Ideal: Paris, 1789," *Bull.Hist.Med.* 51 (1977): 397–411, 397.

33 Weiner, *Citizen-Patient*, 26.

34 Quinlan, "Heredity and Moral Hygiene in the French Enlightenment"(see Introduction, note 3), 649–76, 670nn78 and 81.

35 Bertin,*Traité de la maladie vénérienne* (see chapter 1, note 32), xlvi.

CHAPTER THREE

1 Seidler, "An Historical Survey" (see Introduction, note 19), 186. See also Margaret Pelling, "Child Health as a Social Value in Early Modern England," *The Society for the Social History of Medicine* (1988): 135–64, 137; and G. Armstrong, *Account of Diseases Most Incident to Children* (London: T.Cadell, 1771). See Introduction, note 19, on Armstrong's Dispensary for the Infant Poor.

2 Lancereaux, *A Treatise on Syphilis* (see Introduction, note 26), 136.

3 F. Doublet, *Observations faites dans le Département des Hôpitaux civils* (see chapter 2, note 9).

4 P.A.O. Mahon, posthumous writings collected and edited by Louis Lamauve, *Histoire de la Médecine Clinique depuis ses origines jusqu' à nos jours [including] Recherches importantes sur l'existence, la nature et la communication des maladies syphilitiques dans les femmes enceintes, dans les enfans_nouveau-nés et dans les nourrices* (Paris et Rouen: Chez Buisson, 1804), 377–81.

5 Jacques Eugène Richard, "L'Expérience, l'observation et l'expérimentation dans la littérature médicale française du XVIIIe siècle," doctoral thesis, University of Nantes (1999), 558.

6 Ibid., 119, citing Jean le Rond d'Alembert, "Experimental Philosophy, » *Encyclopedia Diderot et d'Alembert*, 32 vols., 1751–77, vol. 6 (1756).

7 Thomas Sydenham (1624–1689), sometimes referred to as the English Hippocrates, was considered controversial in his day. His writing and teaching criticized medical practice of the time, which was based on

theorizing in terms of abstract philosophies of medicine. The doctor, he believed, should rely on close observation of the patient's symptoms and record carefully the individual's response to the treatment being used.

8 Doublet, cited in Richard, 119.

9 Ibid., 120

10 Mathew Ramsey in *French Medical Culture in the Nineteenth Century*, edited by Ann La Berge and Mordechai Feingold (Amsterdam, Atlanta, GA: Editions Rodopi, 1994). This medication seems to differ from Belloste's mercurial pills, a remedy investigated by the Academy of Medicine in 1810 and again in 1830, which was a blending of mercury and purgatives and discredited as an unimportant modification of a well-known formula.

11 Doublet, *Observations*, 193.

12 Ibid, 188.

13 Ibid, 155.

14 Ibid., 226.

15 Ibid., 203.

16 Ibid., 208–13.

17 Ibid., 208

18 Marfan and Lemaire, *Précis d'Hygiène et des Maladies du Nourrisson* (see chapter 1, note 23), 355n19.

19 Mark E. Silverman, T.Jock Murray, Charles S.Bryan, eds., *The Quotable Osler* (Philadelphia: ACP, 2003), 145.

20 Antonio Nuñez Ribeiro Sanchez, *Observations sur les maladies vénériennes*, translated by M.Andry (Paris: Theophile Barrois le jeune, 1785), 38.

21 Nils Rosen von Rosenstein, *The Diseases of Children* (see chapter 1, note 36), 327.

22 Buchan, *Observations* (see chapter 1, note 37), 150.

23 Antonio Nuñez Ribeiro Sanchez, *Observations*, 165.

24 Doublet, *Observations*, 156–86.

25 Ibid., 179.

26 Ibid., 187.

27 Ibid., 245.

28 Ibid., 174–6

29 J. Colombier, "Observations faites dans le départment des hôpitaux civils." (see chapter 2, note 27).

30 F. Doublet, *Mémoire sur les symptômes et le traitement de la maladie vénérienne dans les infans nouveau-nés* (see chapter 2, note 27), 228.

31 Doublet, *Observations*, 246.

32 Registres sur les enfants qui entreront à l'hospice de Santé de
 Vaugirard, no.4, cote 6, 10 August 1780 to 23 June 1783.

33 Doublet, *Observations*, 283–4.

34 Ibid., 228.

35 Ibid., 235.

36 Ibid., 237, quoting Joseph Raulin, *De la Conservacion des enfan[t]s*,
 2 vols. (Paris, 1768).

37 Richard A. Calderone, ed., *Candida and Candidiasis* (Washington DC:
 ASM Press, 2002), 4. It referred to the whitish outbreaks that charac-
 terize the oral lesions of aphthae and came from Latin phrase *toga
 candidus*, the special white robe worn by candidates for the Roman
 Senate.

38 Doublet, *Observations*, 238–9.

39 Ibid., 240.

40 Ibid., 240–1.

41 Similarly, in 1797 Jean Abraham Auvity of the foundling hospice
 in Paris noted "emanations of natural warmth from mother to
 child during feeding contribute greatly to his strength" and ordered
 that babies should be picked up and held while being artificially
 fed. See Weiner, *The Citizen-Patient* (see Introduction, note 10),
 198.

42 Ibid., 247.

43 F. Boussault, *L'Assistance aux enfants abandonnés L'Assistance aux enfants abandonnés à Paris du XVIè au XVIIIè siècles* (Paris: Rodstein,
 1937), table 2, p.76.

44 Doublet, *Observations*, 256–8.

45 Ibid., 272–3.

46 E. Mouault, "Du marcoul de la guérison des humeurs froides," *Gazette
 des hôpitaux* (Paris, 1854), xxvii, 497–9. See also Pierre Lalouette,
 Traité des scrofules, vulgairement appelés écrouelles ou humeurs froides,
 2 vols. (Paris: Didot le jeune, Gaguery, 1780–82).

47 M. de la Rochefoucauld-Liancourt, *Rapport fait au nom du Comité
 de mendicité, des visites faites dans divers hôpitaux, hospices et
 maisons de charité de Paris*, edited by C.Bloch and A. Tuetey (Paris:
 Imprimerie nationale, 1911), 27–30, 27. For a detailed discussion
 of the treatment of orphans as depicted by the poverty commission
 see a report for the hospital commissioner of Paris in 1790 on ailments of boys at the orphanage of La Pitié, "Observations relatives
 à la partie des maladies de La Pitié," by the surgeon of that hospital,

Anne Brun, between the years 1770 and 1802. The infirmary closed with the opening of the new children's hospital. Cited in Weiner, *The Citizen-Patient*, 74.

48 Sherwood, *Poverty in Eighteenth Century Spain* (see Introduction, note 13), 110–16.

49 Alexandre Tuetey, ed., *L'Assistance Publique* (see chapter 2, note 16), 336.

50 Ibid., 338–42.

CHAPTER FOUR

1 Ignacio Maria Ruiz de Luzuriaga, "Estadística política-médica" (see chapter 2, note 7), vol.3, 378.

2 Foucault, *Birth of the Clinic* (see chapter 2, note 24). See also Ivan Illich, *Limits to Medicine* (London: Marion Boyars, 1976). For critique of the Foucault thesis see Othmar Keel (see chapter 2, note 24). He points out that the "medicalization" associated with the term "clinical practice" referred to by Foucault was in fact operative throughout the last half of the eighteenth century in a number of European countries, and not only, or even originally, in France.

3 Jack D. Ellis, *The Physician-Legislators of France: Medicine and Politics in the Early Third Republic* (Cambridge: Cambridge University Press, 1990), 68–71.

4 See Barbara Ehrenreich and Deirdre English, *For Her Own Good: 150 Years of Experts' Advice to Women* (Garden City, NY: Anchor Books, 1979); Catherine Gallagher and Thomas Laqueur, eds., *The Making of the Modern Body: Sexuality and Society in the Nineteenth Century* (Berkeley: University of California Press, 1987); John S. Haller and Robin M. Haller, *The Physician and Sexuality in Victorian America* (New York: W.W. Norton, 1974); and Yvonne Knibiehler and Catherine Fouquet, *La Femme et les médecins: Analyse historique* (Paris: Hachette, 1983). See also Valerie Fildes, *Wet Nursing, A History from Antiquity to the Present* (Oxford: Basil Blackwell, 1988), 101–26.

5 Jean Jacques Rousseau, *Emile or Treatise on Education* [1762], translated by Wm. H. Payre (New York: Appleton, 1906), 11.

6 Peter Baldwin, *Contagion and the State in Europe, 1830–1930* (Cambridge: Cambridge University Press, 1999), 434. The author discusses the legislation of wet nursing in Austria, Denmark, Sweden, Germany, and France. See pp. 434–6.

7 Fildes, *Wet Nursing*, 229. See also Nancy Senior, "Aspects of Infant Feeding in Eighteenth-Century France," *Eighteenth-Century Studies* 16, no.4 (Summer 1983): 367–88.

8 Thomas Cone, *History of American Pediatrics* (Boston: Little, Brown and Company, 1979), 132–3. The author includes a table illustrating the chemical qualities in the milk of blondes and brunettes from a German study of 1838 by J.F. Simon, *Mother's Milk and Its Chemical and Physiological Properties* (n.p.).

9 Doublet, *Observations* (see chapter 2, note 9), 137–8. Doublet's emphasis.

10 See Jane Abray, "Feminism in the French Revolution," *American Historical Review* 80, no. 1 (February 1975): 45–63; Harriet B. Applewhite and Darlene G. Levy, *Women and Politics in the Age of Democratic Revolution* (Ann Arbor: University of Michigan Press, 1990); Natalie Zemon Davis, *Society and Culture in Early Modern France: Eight Essays* (Stanford: Stanford University Press, 1975); and Olwen Hufton, *The Prospect before Her: A History of Women in Western Europe, 1500–1800* (New-York: Alfred A. Knopf, 1996). See also Hufton, *The Poor in Eighteenth-Century France, 1750–1789* (Oxford: Oxford University Press 1974), and "Women in Revolution," *Past and Present* 90 (1971): 5; Linda E. Merians, ed., *The Secret Malady, Venereal Disease in Eighteenth Century Britain and France* (Lexington, KY: University Press of Kentucky, 1996), 34–50; and Fuchs, *Abandoned Children* (see Introduction, note 11).

11 Registres entrées des femmes grosses et nourrices qui entreront dans la Hospice de Santé de Vaugirard, Archives Administration générale de l'Assistance publique à Paris. Classement 1971, vols. 6.1, 6.2, 6.3. Vol. 6.1: 10 August 1780 to 25 April 1784 (approximately forty-five months), 117 pages with two names per page, for a total of 234 nurses, 140 pages including the index. Vol. 6.2: 4 May 1784 to 28 September 1787 (approximately thirty-one months), 134 pages, two names per page, for a total of 268 nurses, 147 pages including the index. Vol. 6.3: 1 October 1787 to 30 November 1790 (thirty-eight months), 135 pages, two names per page, for a total of 270 nurses, 147 pages including the index.

12 Doublet, *Observations*.

13 Luzuriaga, "Estadística política-médica," vol. 3, 394.

14 Doublet, *Observations*, 137.

15 Bertin, *Traité de la Maladie Vénérienne* (see chapter 2, note 35), 23. See also Weiner, *The Citizen-Patient* (see chapter 2, note 1), 186.

16 Doublet, *Observations*, 138.

17 Vol.6.8, Livre de Mortalité de nourrices, no. 16, 9/5/83, folio 53.

18 Doublet, *Observations*, 149.

19 Boussault, *L'Assistance* (see chapter 3, note 43), 77.

20 Alexandre Tuetey, *L'Assistance Publique* (see Introduction, note 17), 334–50.

21 Ibid., 348. This account was explicitly attributed to Doublet. See also Doublet's account in "Mémoire concernant l'hospice de Vaugirard, questions et responses relatives à cette établissement," Archives Nationale Francaise 15 (superscript), 1861, Archives du Ministre de l'Interieur Year 2.

22 Ibid., 340.

23 Doublet, *Observations*, 145.

24 Ibid., 141.

25 F. Doublet, "Mémoire sur la fièvre à laquelle on donne le nom fièvre puerperae ou observations faites à l'hospice de Santé de Vaugirard sur les maladies produites par les metastases et les dépôts laiteux dans la cavité abdominale, lu dans un des assemblées de la faculté dite prima mensis, le 16 dec. 1782 et inséré dans le *Journal de Médecine* du mois nov. de même année."

26 Doublet, *Observations*, 143.

27 Ibid., 145.

28 Ibid., 147.

29 Ibid., 149.

30 A. Tuetey, *L'Assistance publique*, 336.

31 Doublet, *Observations*, 149.

32 Jacques Tenon, *Memoirs on Paris Hospitals* [1788, *Mémoires sur les hôpitaux de Paris*], edited by Dora B. Weiner (Canton, MA: Watson Publishing International, 1996), 215–18.

33 Weiner, *The Citizen-Patient* (see Introduction, note 10), 122–3, 193–4.

34 Boussault, *L'Assistance aux enfants abandonées*, 75.

35 Doublet, *Observations*, 140.

36 Ibid., 171.

37 Ibid., 173.

38 Doublet, "Mémoire sur les symptômes et traitement de la maladie vénérienne dans les enfans nouveaux-né lu à l'assemblée particulière de la Faculté de Médecine dite *prima mensis* 15 Oct. 1781" (Paris: Chez Méquignon, 1781), 19–22.

39 Doublet, *Observations*, 195.

40 Ibid., 193.

41 Ibid., 197–9.

42 See table 4.4, "Reasons for Wet Nurses Leaving Vaugirard."

43 Alexander Gordon, "A Treatise on the Epidemic Puerperal Fever," in Fleetwood Churchill, *Essays on the Puerperal Fever and Other Diseases Peculiar to Women* (London: The New Sydenham Society, 1849), 415–500. Less famous than Semmelweiss, Gordon recognized that the disease was an epidemic in 1789–92 among the patients of particular midwives but also among his own patients – he was the only professed *accoucheur* in the town of Aberdeen. Though he could not pinpoint the cause, he admitted that he considered himself responsible for some of the incidents. The publication of this insight "raised against him such strong prejudices in the public mind as to materially damage his professional prospects in Aberdeen" (445n2).

44 Christine Hallett, "The Attempt to Understand Puerperal Fever in the Eighteenth and Early Nineteenth Centuries. The influence of Inflammation Theory," *Medical History* 49 (2005): 1–28, p.1. The author's focus is on literature published in Britain between 1760 and 1860 including French and European works translated into English, which excludes Doublet. There is no reference to the retropulsion theory.

45 Irvine Loudon, *The Tragedy of Childbed Fever* (Oxford: Oxford University Press, 2000), 18. We now know that what was seen was a coating of streptococcal pus covering the intestines and omentum. The theory of milk metastasis was only disproved in 1801 by the experiments of Xavier Bichat.

46 J. Sherwood, "The Milk Factor: The Ideology of breastfeeding and post-partum Illnesses, 1750–1850," *CBMH/BCHM* 1 (1993): 5–23.

47 Valerie Fildes, *Breasts, Bottles and Babies* (Edinburgh: University of Edinburgh Press, 1984). The author includes an illustration from a medical text of the early sixteenth century showing the "lacteal duct" connecting the uterus to the breast (plate 6.3, p.180. The da Vinci drawing is available at the Web site *http://www.search.com/reference/ sexual intercourse*. I am grateful to Jacalyn Duffin for calling my attention to this illustration.

48 Antoine Petit, *Traité des maladies des femmes enceintes, des femmes en couche et des nouveau-nés précédé du mécanisme des accouchemens rédigé sur les leçons d'Antoine Petit, médecin de Paris, Demonstrateur et Professeur au Jardin des Plantes et membre des plusiers académies* (Paris: Baudoin, Year 7, 1799), 390.

49 E. Ashworth Underwood, *Boerhaave's Men at Leyden and Afterwards* (Edinburgh: Edinburgh University Press, 1977). See also Colin Russell, *Science and Social Change* (Toronto: Macmillan, 1983), 92.

50 Julien Offray de La Mettrie, *L'Homme Machine* (Leyden: Elie Luzac, fils, 1748).

51 Doublet, "Nouvelles Recherches sur la fièvre puerperale," *Mémoires de le Société royale de médecine* (1786), vol. 3, 309.

52 Doublet, *Observations*, 182.

53 Doublet, "Nouvelles Recherches," 188.

54 Ibid., 250.

55 Ibid., vol.3, 181–309, 242.

56 Ibid., 241–301.

57 J. Doublet de Boisthibault, "Notice Historique sur la vie et les ouvrages de François Doublet, docteur-régent de l'ancienne Faculté de Médecine de Paris, sous-inspecteur générale des hôpitaux civils du Royaume, Prof.de la Faculté et associé ordinaire de Société Royale de Médecine," in *Notices Biographique et Bibliographiques* (Caen: F. Poisson, 1822), 13–21. For a discussion of the inflammation theory, see Hallet, "The Attempt to Understand Puerperal Fever," 6–16.

58 Ibid., 17.

59 Doublet, *Observations*, 228–9.

60 Ibid., 227.

61 Irvine Loudon, ed., *Childbed Fever: A Documentary History* (New York and London: Garland Publishing, 1995), xxxvii.

62 Hallett, "The Attempt to Understand Puerperal Fever," 6n28 refers to William Fordyce, *A New Inquiry into the Causes, Symptoms and Cure of Putrid and Inflammatory Fevers*, 4th ed. (London: T. Cadell, J. Murray and W. Davenhill, 1777), 48–53.

63 Jean Astruc, *Treatise on the Diseases of Women*, vol. 3, translated from the French for J. Nourse (London, 1777); see François Mauriceau, *The Diseases of Women with Child and in Childbed as also the Best Means of Helping Them in Natural and Unnatural Labours*, 8th ed., translated by Hugh Chamberlin, MD (London: R. Ware, T. and T. Longman, C. Hitch and L. Hawes, J. Clarke and J. and J. Rivington, J. Ward, R. Baldwin and T. Field, 1755.)

64 My research suggests that, at least throughout the eighteenth century, the retropulsion explanation held considerable prominence among doctors in Spain as well as France. See Jaime Bonells, *Perjuicios que*

*acarrean al género humano y al estado las Madres que rehusan criar
á sus hijos, y medios para contener el abuso de ponerlos en Ama*
(Madrid: Miguel Escribano, 1786).

65 Churchill, *Essays on the Puerperal Fever* and Loudon, *Childbed Fever.*

66 Astruc, *Diseases of Women*, 235.

67 Ibid., 236 and 245.

68 Ibid., 239.

69 Ibid., 245.

70 Ibid., 239–47.

71 Mauriceau, *The Diseases of Women with Child and in Childbed*, 286.

72 Ibid., 293.

73 Ibid., 278.

74 Ibid., 289.

75 For instance, Thomas Denman, one of the most famous British experts on puerperal fever, wrote in 1773 that he considered it groundless. Loudon, *The Tragedy of Childbed Fever*, 19.

76 John Leake, "Observations on the Childbed Fever" London, 1772, in Churchill, *Essays on Puerperal Fever*, 140.

77 Churchill, *Essays on the Puerperal Fever*, 3; Loudon, *The Tragedy of Childbed Fever*, 19.

78 Registres de mortalité de Nourrices, vols. 6.8, 6.9, and 6.10.

79 See Tuetey, *L'Assistance Publique*, 342.

80 François Alexandre Frédéric, Duc de la Rochefoucauld-Liancourt, *Rapport fait au nom du Comité de Mendicité, des visites faites dans divers hôpitaux, hospices et maisons de charité de Paris* (Paris: Imprimerie nationale, 1790), 27–30, 29.

81 Bertin, *Traité de la maladie vénérienne*, 23.

CHAPTER FIVE

1 Weiner, *The Citizen-Patient* (see Introduction, note 10), 186.

2 Diday, *A Treatise on Syphilis* (see chapter 1, note 17), 227.

3 Ibid., 243. The statement was made during a discussion of a project called "syphilization," which raised hopes for immunizing women to syphilis in a manner similar to smallpox vaccination.

4 Ibid., 227–9.

5 Ibid., 243–4.

6 George Sussman, *Selling Mothers Milk. The Wet-Nursing Business in France, 1715–1914* (Chicago: University of Illinois Press, 1982). See also Fuchs, *Abandoned Children* (see Introduction, note 11).

7 Georges Diot, "A Propos de la Réglementation des nourrices mercenaires," doctoral thesis, Faculty of Medicine, Paris, 1903, 44.

8 Ibid., 45.

9 Sussman, *Selling Mothers' Milk*, 32, 50, and 115.

10 Diot, "Réglementation," 82.

11 Fournier, *The Treatment and the Prophylaxis of Syphilis* (see chapter 1, note 21), 27, 29–30. This second edition was translated, revised, and enlarged by C.F. Marshall, MD FRCS (London, New York: Rebman, 1906). It is a close adaptation of a series of lectures also published as *Nourrices et nourrissons syphilitiques* (Paris: V.A. Delahaye, 1878).

12 Fildes, *Abandoned Children*, 136.

13 Fernand Aurientes, "Nourrices, nourrisons et syphilis," doctoral thesis, Faculty of Medicine, Paris, 1905, 67. Also published as "Etude médico-légale sur la Jurisprudence actuelle à propos de la transmission des maladies vénériennes," in *Prophylaxie Médicale* 3, no. 475 (Paris: A. Michelon, 1906), 27–90.

14 Ibid., 67. Aurientes cites the *Bulletin de la Société de prophylaxie sanitaire et morale* (March 1906).

15 Ibid., 164–6.

16 Dracobly, "Ethics and Experimentation" (see Introduction, note 22), 337–8.

17 Lancereaux, *A Treatise on Syphilis* (see Introduction, note 26), vol. 2, 345.

18 Sherwood, "Syphilization: Human Experimentation in the Search for a Syphilis Vaccine" *J. Hist. Med. and Allied Sci.* 5, no. 3 (July 1999): 384–6. According to its originator, Joseph Alexandre Auzias-turenne (1812–18), syphilization was "the state of the organism whereby the subject is no longer susceptible to developing syphilis, the consequence of a sort of 'syphilitic saturation'" (ibid., 367). It was based on an analogy to the smallpox vaccination, though in practice it was impossible to replicate a vaccine whose source was the spirochete, which at the time had not yet been identified. Injecting pus from a primary chancre caused syphilis, unless the subject already had the disease, and a series of such injections was more likely to increase its virulence than to provide immunity. The hope was that this might prevent, or even cure syphilis. Prostitutes were subjected to experiments of a dangerous nature. A series of debates in the Academy of Medicine of Paris

took place in 1850–52 before its rejection in France as a therapeutic measure.

19 Philippe Ricord, *Letters on Syphilis, addressed to the Chief Editor of the Union Médicale with Int. by Amédee Latour* [1850–51], translated by W.P. Lattimore, MD (Philadelphia: Blanchard and Lea, 1857), Letter 20, 118–19.

20 Session in the Academy of Medicine, reported in *Union Médicale*, 16 September 1852, vol. 6, 445.

21 Ricord, *Letters on Syphilis*, letter 14, 194. See also *Gazette Médicale de Paris*, 20 April 1850.

22 In Diday, *Treatise on Syphilis*, 150.

23 From a discussion in the Academy of Medicine, *Bull. Ac. Méd.* 17 and 18 (1851–52): 509. Sessions of of 30 August and 9 September were also reported in *Union Médicale* 6 (1852): 436.

24 Auguste A. Cullerier, "Mémoire sur la contagion syphilitique entre les nourrices et les nourrissons," excerpted from the *Union Médicale de Paris* (Paris: Felix Malteste, 1854), 11–32.

25 Ibid., 12, Observation no. 1.

26 Ibid., 14, Observation no. 3.

27 Ricord, *Letters on Syphilis*, 118–19.

28 Cullerier, "*Mémoire*," 28–32.

29 Eugène Bouchut, "Mémoire sur la transmission de la syphilis des nouveau-nés aux nourrices," excerpted from the *Gazette médicale de Paris* (Paris: Felix Malteste, 1854).

30 Hunter, *Treatise on the Venereal Disease* (see chapter 1, note 35), 386–90; my emphasis.

31 Diday, *Treatise on Syphilis*, 158.

32 Ibid., 160

33 Ibid., 168–9, quoted from *Journal de Méd., Chirurg. et Pharm. de Bruxelles* (1853): 92.

34 Ibid., 161.

35 Doublet, *Observations* (see chapter 2, note 9), 228–9.

36 Ricord, *Letters on Syphilis*, 107, quoted in Diday, *Treatise on Syphilis*, 172.

37 Ibid., 172.

38 Dracobly, "Ethics and Experimentation" (see Introduction, note 22), 332–66.

39 Joseph Pierre Martinez Rollet, "Commission Set up to Demonstrate the Transmission of Syphilis from Nursling to Nurse, 31 May 1861," in *Gazette hebdomodaire de médecine et de chirurgie*, 13 September

1861, 588–94. See also Rollet, *De la transmission de la syphilis entre nourrisons et nourrices au point de vue de la médecine légale* (Paris: Victor Masson et fils, 1861).

40 Rollet, "Commission," 590–4.

41 Lancereaux, *Treatise on Syphilis*, vol. 2, "Legal Medicine," 352–62. See also Charles Vibert, *Précis de Médecine Légale* (Paris: J.B. Bailliére et fils, 1917).

42 Camille Appay, *De la transmission de la syphilis entre nourrices et nourrisons et notamment par l'allaitement avec considérations médico-légales* (Paris: A. Masson, 1875), 79–114.

43 Ibid., 115.

44 Diday, *Treatise on Syphilis*, 229.

45 Ibid., 229.

46 Ibid., 230.

47 Ibid., 231–2.

48 Quétel, *History of Syphilis* (see Introduction, note 6), 298n43, where Quétel notes an example of this kind of ambivalence, in which Diday circumvented medical confidentiality in spirit, if not quite in fact. He advised a mother who suspected that her son had syphilis to bring him the prescription of medication her son was taking, and from that he confirmed her suspicions. "All I did was make an impersonal judgment without knowing to whom it applied."

49 Diday, *Treatise on Syphilis*, 243.

50 Ibid, 243.

51 Ibid., 244.

52 Buchan, *Observations* (see chapter 1, note 37), 153–5.

53 Paul Diday, "Que y a-t-il de prouvé, qu'y a-t-il d'utile dans la syphilisation?" *Gazette Médicale de Paris* 7 (1852): 538.

54 Sherwood, "Syphilization," 384.

55 For a discussion of malpractice suits in the period, see Dracobly's "Disciplining the Doctor" (see Introduction, note 31).

56 Adolphe Trebuchet, *Jurisprudence de la médicine, de la chirurgie et de le pharmacie en France* (Paris: J.B. Baillière, 1834), 275–8.

57 Robert F. Nye, "Honor Codes and Medical Ethics in Modern France," *Bull.Hist.Med.* 69 (1995): 91–111, 94–5.

58 Dracobly, "Disciplining the Doctor." For the discussion of confidentiality see vol. 1, 262–90.

59 Alain Corbin, "La grand peur de syphilis," in *Peurs et Terreurs face à la contagion. Cholera, tuberculosis et syphilis*, edited by J.P. Bardet, Patrice Bourdelaise, Pierre Guillaume, Francois Lebrun, and Claude

Quétel (Paris: Fayard, 1988), 328–48, 334. See also Martha Hildreth, "Doctors and Families in France, 1880–1930," in *French Medical Culture in the Nineteenth Century*, edited by Ann La Berge and Mordecai Feingold, 201. Hildreth is discussing a later period, but the concerns were evident much earlier. See Quétel, *History of Syphilis* (see Introduction, note 6), 160–75.

60 M. Pelacy, "Rapport fait au conseil de salubrité de la ville de Marseille," *Annales de l'hygiène publique* (Paris, 1841), 15. The article quotes Fournier, cited in Quétel, *History of Syphilis,* 166.

61 Alfred Fournier, *Nourrices et nourrisons syphilitiques* (Paris: A. Delahaye, 1878), cited in Aurientes, "Nourrices, nourrisons et syphilis," 72.

62 Aurientes " Etude médico-légale," 27.

63 *Dictionnaire de Droit*, 2d ed., 2 vols. (Paris: Libraire Dalloz, 1966), vol. 1, article 25, 141.

64 Nye, "Honor Codes," 97.

65 Ibid., 107.

66 Victor Alexis Désiré Dalloz, *Jurisprudence générale des royaume ou Répertoire méthodique et alphabétique de législation et de jurisprudence en nature de droit publique* ... (Paris: Bureau de la Jurisprudence générale 1846–79), 44 vols. The collection merged with that of J.B. Sirey, *Les codes annotés de Sirey contenant toute la jurisprudence des arrêts et la doctrine des auteurs*, in 1965 under the title *Recueil Dalloz-Sirey.*

67 Corbin, "La grand peur de syphilis," 333.

68 Joy Harsin, "Syphilis, Wives and Physicians: Medical Ethics and the Family in Late Nineteenth-Century France," *French Historical Studies* 16, no.1 (Spring 1989): 72–95; see 80n31 and 88n68.

69 Eva Steiner, *French Legal Method* (Oxford, New York: Oxford University Press, 2002), 100; my emphasis. See also *Droit Français, Guide des Sources Juridiques imprimées (Législation-Jurisprudence-Doctrine)* (Bibliothèque Cujas de Droit et de Science Economiques, Edition 2007). It states that collections of jurisprudence publish *les décisions, arrêts et jugements* of the various jurisdictions (of the judicial and administrative order) and of the supreme courts. Under the heading Title 2 – *Receuils de Jurisprudence* (Jurisprudence collections), concerning the principal characteristics of decisions of jurisprudence, it also states, "All decisions are not published. Each editor makes his own selection" (p. 24).

70 Ibid., 103.

71 Tardieu, "Etude médico-légale" (see Introduction, note 1), *Annales de l'hygiène publique* (January- April 1854): 148–9. My emphasis.

72 Ibid., 99.

73 Dalloz, *Jurisprudence générale.*

74 Diday, *Treatise on Syphilis* (see chapter 1, note 17), 160–80.

75 Ibid. Diday refers to *Journal de Méd. de Chirur., et de Pharm. de Bruxelles* (1853): 92 and 611; *Gaz.med.Lombarda* (May 1849); *Dublin Quarterly Journal* (1846): 337 and 345; *London and Edinburgh Monthly Journal* (1844): 440 and 515; *Edinb. Med.and Surg. Journal* (1851): 366.

76 David J. Kertzer, *Amalia's Tale: An Impoverished Peasant Woman, an Ambitious Attorney , and a Fight for Justice* (Boston: Houghton Mifflin, 2008) describes a case in Italy at the end of nineteenth century where a nurse sued the foundling hospital in Bologna.

77 Fildes, *Wet Nursing: A History* (see chapter 4, note 4), 239nn99 and 100 for cases of the Tribunal of the Seine, 1858 and 1860.

78 Michel Cullerier, "Observations sur la contagion syphitilique dans les rapports des nourrices," *Journal Général de Médicine*, vol. 55, p.32.

79 Diday, *Treatise on Syphilis*, 157.

80 A. Cullerier, "Mémoire," 11–32.

81 Diday, *Treatise on Syphilis*, 174.

82 Ibid., 189, 190.

83 Ibid., Procès verbal de Nantes, 184. Diday's citation does not give the outcome.

84 See Tardieu, "Etude médico-légale" (1864) and *Etude médico-légale* (1879) (for both, see Introduction, note 1). See chapter 5 of the 1879 publication, "Syphilis transmise par l'allaitement," 160–233, which contains many of the same cases that appear in the *Annales*. A decision of 15–16 August 1856 compelled the family to pay their nurse 5,000 francs in damages, and another decision in August 1860 found the parents guilty and sentenced them to pay 3,000 francs to the nurse. In another case, a doctor who was charged with negligence, carelessness, or ignorance of things he should necessarily know was deemed not responsible because the facts of science meant his professional *conscience* (awareness of guilt) was not compromised. Also quoted is the rejection of an appeal against a decision favouring Assistance publique (Appeal Court of Paris, fourth chamber, 19 April 1877).

85 *Gazette des Tribunaux* gives an account (No. 1875) of a case of a nurse, 18 August 1831, p.984.

86 Tardieu, *Etude médico-légale* (1879) (see Introduction, note 1).

87 Report documented by the doctors Tardieu, Adelon, and Dévergie, in Tardieu, *Etude médico-légale"* (1879), 189–91.

88 Ibid., 183. My emphasis.

89 Ricord, cited in Tardieu, "Etude médico-légale" (1864), 129–31.

90 Cited in Tardieu, *Etude médico-légale* (1879), 184.

91 Tardieu, "Etude médico-légale" (1864), 24–33. See also *Gazette des Tribunaux*, 1856.

92 Ibid., *Etude médico-légale* (1879), 199–203.

93 Ibid., 166–73.

94 Ibid., 203–11.

95 Ibid., "Etude médico-légale" (1864), 145.

96 Ibid., 195–7. See also *Journal de Droit,* excerpt in *Gazette des Tribunaux,* 5 February 1876.

97 Bouchut, "Mémoire sur la transmission de la syphilis," 4.

98 Tardieu, *Etude médico-légale* (1879), 99, 198.

99 Dalloz, *Jurisprudence générale.*

100 Fournier, *The Treatment and Prophylaxis of Syphilis,* 56. My emphasis.

101 See discussion of "coutume" in appendix 3, below.

102 Messrs. Boys de Loury et de Barthelemy, "Report on a Case of Transmission of Syphilis from Infant to Nurse," *Annales de l'hygiène publique et de médecine légale* 31, 2d series *(*1869): 423–43.

103 Nye, "Honor Codes." The author quotes Emile Garçon, a principal commentator on jurisprudence, who claimed that the "secret" had less to do with relations between doctor and patient than with those between doctors and their peers, whose chief concern was the general reputation of the profession" (107).

104 Trebuchet, *Jurisprudence de la Médecine.*

105 Auguste Lutaud, *Manuel de Médecine légale et de Jurisprudence médicale* (Paris: Librairie Lauwereyns, 1877), 609. My emphasis.

106 Charles Vibert, *Précis de médecine légale* (Paris: J.B. Ballière et fils, 1917), 806.

107 Code Santé publique, art. L290, mod. Ord. 25 November 1960 prèc. disposition pénale, section 6. See Victor Alexis Désiré Dalloz, *Nouveau Répertoire de Droit,* 2d ed., 4 vols., edited by Emmanuel Vergé and Roger de Ségogne (Paris: Jurisprudence Générale Dalloz, 1963), vol. 3, 452; my emphasis. The ordinance of 1960 concludes with a reference that probably has more to do with venereal disease in general than with congenital syphilis in particular. It refers to the

obligation of the doctor to report to the director of public health any diagnosis of venereal disease. "Finally, it must be made clear that according to the terms of this legislation (25 November 1960), any doctor who has neglected to supply to a patient the warnings set out in article 256 of the Code of public health is liable to a fine of 60 NF-400 NF. The same penalty was applicable to a doctor who omitted to make declarations set out in section 2, chapter 1, title 2, book 3 of the Code of public health." This stated that the doctor must advise hospitalization, either naming the patient if treatment is rejected or if he believes there is a risk of contagion to others; in other circumstances the patient's privacy was to be respected. See R. Diedelièvre and E. Fournier, *Médecine Légale*, 2 vols. (Paris: J.B. Balliére et fils, 1963), vol. 2, 780.

108 Vibert, *Précis de médecine légale*, 827, refers to a case in 1906 in which a wet nurse was awarded damages of 8,000 francs.

109 Victor Alexis Désiré Dalloz, *Répertoire pratique de legislation de doctrine et de jurisprudence*, vol. 8, p.396, and appendix 3, section 3, nos. 8 and 9.

110 Fournier, *Nourrices et nourissons syphilitiques*, 27n1.

CHAPTER SIX

1 Bouchut, "Mémoire sur la transmission de la syphilis des nouveaux-nés aux nourrices" (see chapter five, note 29, and appendix 1). The author refers to articles by M. Bouchacourt in the *Revue Médicale* and John Egan in the *Journal de Dublin*. See also M. Lagneau fils, *Annales de l'hygiène publique et de médecine légale* 4, 2d series (July-October 1855): 297–317.

2 Fournier, *Nourrices et nourissons syphilitiques* (also excerpt in Union Médicale, 3ᵈ series, 1877), and *Treatment and Prophylaxis of Syphilis* (see chapter 5, note 11 for both).

3 Ibid., *Nourrices*, 43, and *Treatment and Prophylaxis*, 58; my emphasis.

4 Ibid., *Nourrices*, 43; my emphasis.

5 Dracobly, "Disciplining the Doctor" (see Introduction, note 31), 262n1, quoting G. Tourdes, "Secret médical," in *Dictionnaire encyclopédique des sciences médicales*, vol. 8, 3d series (Paris: Asselin and G. Masson, 1880), and 263n4, quoting Pasteur Vallery-Radot, *La médicine à l'échelle humaine* (Paris: Fayard, 1959).

6 Diday, *Le Péril Vénérien dans les familles* (Paris: Asselin, 1881), 391.

7 Ibid., 398.

8 Ibid., 402.

9 Ibid., 406.

10 Ibid., 412.

11 The standard work of the period on medical ethics by William Percival was unknown in France. See Dracobly, "Disciplining the Doctor," vol. 1, 94.

12 Diday, *Le Péril Vénérien*, 420; my emphasis.

13 Dracobly concluded that it was not until 1830 that a doctor in France was sued for malpractice. One expert on legal medicine, François-Emmanuel Fodéré, argued that such suits were relatively few, not because written laws did not deal with malpractice but because of a lack of public awareness of the law; see "Disciplining the Doctor," vol. 1, 174n44. It is likely, however, that there were cases that had not been published in the usual sources. See Steiner, *French Legal Medicine* (chapter 5, note 69), 100.

14 Fournier, *Nourrices*, 27–40, discusses the matter of principle involved in the 1868 judgment. This responsibility was only incurred in so far as the harm on which the nurse's complaint was based was necessarily the result of the doctor's reticence. If it could be shown that the illness was already present and had nothing to do with the doctor's observations, and if there was no certainty that the nurse, even if warned, could have avoided contagion, the doctor could be discharged.

15 Ibid., 30.

16 Ibid., 7.

17 Quoted in ibid., 11–12. See also *Treatment and Prophylaxis of Syphilis,* 47–8.

18 Ibid., *Nourrices*, 27.

19 Ibid., *Treatment*, 95, quoting M. Icard from "*Mémoires et comptes-rendues de la Société des Sciences Médicales de Lyon*, vol.8, 1868.

20 Ibid., 44.

21 Ibid., 9.

22 Ibid., 43. See also Fournier, *Treatment*, 57, 58.

23 Fournier, *Treatment and Prophylaxis*, 61.

24 Ibid., 62, my emphasis.

25 Fournier, *Nourrices,* 53.

26 Fournier, *Treatment and Prophylaxis*, 80; Fournier's emphasis.

27 Goldstein, *Console and Classify* (see Introduction, note 30), 162–3.

28 Tardieu, *Etude médico-légale* (1879) (see Introduction, note 1). For Tardieu's discussion of the role of the expert see ibid., 237–55.

29 Goldstein, *Console and Classify*, 166–9.
30 Tardieu, *Etude médico-légale* (1879), 241.
31 Ibid., 238–9. Tardieu goes into the issue of parental examination and points out that on this point he is in disagreement with the usual opinion of many doctors who have written on the subject. In support of his argument he quotes the decision of 22 December 1844 of the Tribunal of Tulle based on the report of Dr Bardinet of the Secondary School of Medicine in Limoges.
32 Aurientes, "Nourrices, nourrisons et syphilis" (chapter 5, note 13), 74.
33 Quoted in ibid., 27.
34 According to the judgment of the civil tribunal of the Seine of 9 November 1893; see ibid., 53. See also appendix 3, below.
35 Tardieu, *Etude médico-légale* (1879), 255.
36 Olwen Hufton, *The Poor in Eighteenth-Century France, 1750–1789*. See also "Women in Revolution," *Past and Present* 90 (1971): 5.
37 Fildes, *Wet Nursing* (see chapter 4, note 4), 149–53.
38 Ibid., 155.
39 Gay L. Gullickson, *Unruly Women of Paris. Images of the Commune* (Ithaca and London: Cornell University Press, 1996), 89–116. The author points out that only five women were put on trial as *petroleuses*, and that there was no evidence presented that they had actually set fires (p. 208). See also Edith Thomas, *The Women Incendiaries*, translated from the French (*Les Pétroleuses* [Paris: Editions Gallimard, 1966]) by James and Starr Atkinson (New York: George Braziller, 1966). For a discussion of the numbers or actual existence of "les pétroleuses" see chapter 12, pp. 165–88.
40 Dalloz, *Recueil général*, Table 1861–70, "Médecine," 139; and J.B Sirey, *Les codes annotés* (see appendix 1, below, for both).
41 David J. Rothman, "The Fielding H. Garrison Lecture, Serving Clio and the Client: The Historian as Expert Witness," *Bull.Hist.Med.* 77 (2003): 25–44.
42 Maria Cheng (Associated Press), "Syphilis Returns to China after a 20-Year Absence," *Whig-Standard* (Kingston, ON), 16 January 2007, 22.
43 43 Cited in ibid.
44 Katharine Harding, "Rise in Alberta Syphilis Cases Shows a Down Side of Boom," *Globe and Mail* (Toronto), 10 March 2007. See also "Infectious Diseases News Brief," publication of Public Health Agency of Canada (Ottawa, 2007), 1, at Infectious Diseases Web site, http://. phac-aspc.gc.ca 7 February 2008, taken from *CMA Journal* 177, no. 1

(3 July 2007). In all three examples a rise in cases of syphilis (including congenital syphilis) and other sexually transmitted diseases is related to dramatic changes in the economy.

45 M.H. Lachman, MD, "What Is the Role of Medicine in the Arctic?" Presentation at Queen's University, 29 January 2007. Based on his practice in Nunavut, Lachman observed that a large proportion of births were premature. This could be attributed to mercury in the traditional diet, although the increased reliance on junk food in the territory is also a factor. Canada claims to be making the first attempt by any country in the world effectively to ban mercury as an ingredient in paints, enamels, varnishes and shellacs used for furniture, children's toys, pencils, artists' brushes, and a variety of household surfaces. *Whig-Standard* (Kingston, ON), 11 May 2005, 12.

46 "Milk Maids: More US Moms Have Begun Outsourcing Breast-Feeding," *Time* (30 April 2007): 41.

Index

12; occupations, 97; origin,
89–93; patients, 108; prevalence
in France, 114; puerperal fever, 103, 106–8; rural nurses,
85–6, 199, 122; registers, 78, 88,
193n11; symptoms of syphilis,
99; training at Vaugirard, 78, 83;
unsatisfactory nurses, 80– 85,
87, 91, 100; vindication, 143–5,
151; wages at Vaugirard, 29, 82

ipec

glycerine

spirit of nitre

syrup of squills

laudenum

P 84   strata ?